HOLIDAYS:
HOLY OR HOLLOW?

Melda Eberle

WESTBOW®
PRESS
A DIVISION OF THOMAS NELSON
& ZONDERVAN

WestBow Press books may be ordered through booksellers or by contacting:

WestBow Press
A Division of Thomas Nelson & Zondervan
1663 Liberty Drive
Bloomington, IN 47403
www.westbowpress.com
1 (866) 928-1240

ISBN: 978-1-4908-8499-8 (sc)
ISBN: 978-1-4908-8590-2 (hc)
ISBN: 978-1-4908-8500-1 (e)

Library of Congress Control Number: 2015909745

Print information available on the last page.

WestBow Press rev. date: 06/26/2015

CONTENTS

ACKNOWLEDGMENTS

This manuscript has overcome its share of hurdles, but by the grace of God, it is now revised and re-presented.

I acknowledge my devoted husband, Jack, who has always been my prime encourager and positive moral support. Following closely in the cheering section are our five offspring: Eva, Matthew, Sarah, Rebecca (deceased), and Deborah. Each of their accomplishments has been an inspiration and a blessing.

May this book be used for the glory of God and for the edification of His people!

PREFACE

God's Word, the Bible, is currently not open for discussion in public schools. Increasingly, it is also being eliminated from public life. During my years as an educator and specifically as a correctional educator, I became disquieted that so many of my students had no conception of what many of the holidays were really about. In the limited time I had with them in the classroom, I attempted to fill in the gaps of their knowledge. To answer some of their questions, I had to do some research, which piqued my curiosity and led to in-depth research. This book is the result of much time spent agonizing over some hard-to-find answers.

INTRODUCTION

Origins of Feasts, Holidays, and Festivals

People have celebrated festivals and holidays since ancient times throughout the world. Holidays, or holy days, as they were originally called in English, though not necessarily biblical, were religious in nature and served to remind people of solemn vows, rituals, or jubilation surrounding a historic delivery from an enemy. Indeed, as long as any celebration is held in the name of a religion or a god, it is technically a festival or holy day whether sophisticated or plain, somber or sensual.

Many holidays indicated the progression of natural events such as the moon's phases or the sun's orbit. For example, of the many Roman festivals, Saturnalia in mid-December celebrated the winter solstice. Feasts and festivals sometimes glorified planting and harvesting seasons. In line with these were fertility rites such as the Lupercalia in February. These elaborate festivities commemorating many gods and goddesses are well documented in Scandinavian as well as Greek and other Mediterranean countries' mythologies. In the Western Hemisphere, we have learned about Mesoamerican deities and their feasts not from Mayan Codices but through archaeological digs and linguists decoding inscriptions found in mounds, tombs, and pyramids.

The world's religious holidays included a major Hindu holiday, Navaratri, which did and still does honor the goddess Durga for her victory over Mahisa, the buffalo-headed demon. Hatshepsut, the female pharaoh of Egypt, celebrated the Feast of the Valley, an annual festival of death and renewal. Many other pagan festivals were connected with gift offerings of the dead or in some way placating evil spirits. Undoubtedly, Huacca del Sol, Temple of the Sun, of the ancient Tucume in Peru, witnessed its share of religious "holy days" during which humans were sacrificed. Readers of the Old Testament may be well acquainted with Babylonian festivals honoring Baal and Ashtoreth. Anyone not remembering the fate of Belshazzar's great feast needs only to reread Daniel 5.

In the Bible, the first canonical reference to feasts is in Genesis 19:3, which records Lot entertaining visiting angels. The second mention is Abraham's feast at Isaac's weaning. If one accepts the book of Job as chronologically the Bible's oldest, Job 1:4 is the first reference to feasting. Job's sons held feasts, each hosting his own birthday party. Recorded deeds of faithful heroes and evil villains in the scriptures show how each rejoiced over victories with merrymaking.

Many references are found with the words *feast to the Lord*, *feast of the Lord*, or *feast for the Lord*. God clearly revealed to His people when such feasts were to be given and the purpose of each; He left nothing to chance, and there was no assumption the people could participate or not according to whim.

Most of us who have accepted Jesus as the Messiah or as our Head agree that the Hebrew feasts are not to be celebrated today, but what feasts or holidays should we celebrate? Are we expected to replace Hebrew holy days with so-called Christian ones as many have tried to do? If so, which days are to be replaced, and how do we know? At what point did well-intentioned holy days turn into commercially oriented holidays?

In contrast to the clear instructions of the Hebrew Scriptures, Jesus Christ and the twelve apostles, who were sent to the Hebrews, didn't institute any festivals. Nor did Paul, the apostle sent to the Gentiles, command any such feasts. How then can we account for the fact that Christians have long celebrated the memory of Christ's resurrection and numerous other religious events? If they were not instituted by the Greek and Aramaic Scriptures, the New Testament, the only alternative and logical explanation is that they have been developed by people over the centuries.

Thousands of books rest in libraries' archives describing "gods many, and lords many" (1 Corinthians 8:5). We know that "when ye knew not God, ye did service unto them which by nature are no gods" (Galatians 4:8). Many books feature secular and religious festivals and anniversaries around the globe for just about every day of the year. It's not my purpose here to investigate all religions' holidays; that would be tracing humanity's history. This study will deal with some of the widely celebrated holidays in the United States from a biblical viewpoint. More specifically, we will see from a "rightly dividing the word of truth" viewpoint (2 Timothy 2:15), just where we, the Bible believers of the body of Christ, fit into the holiday scheme.

Also, this book will not tell believers they should or shouldn't participate in various traditional or secular facets of these days. I want to mention where specific holidays originated and let readers be guided by the Scriptures regarding what God wants them to do.

What began as holy days, religious in character and dedicated to gods or to the supreme God, have become blurred with secular holidays that revere respected people or historical occasions. Some customs, carried over into modern-day celebrations, resist efforts to be sorted into the secular or sacred, pagan or Christian, and sometimes remain obscured in tradition. In short, we have the oxymoron of secular holy days, holidays.

Consequently, in this account, the words *feast*, *festival*, and *holiday* will generally be used synonymously. Not everyone will agree with the conclusions I have reached, but I hope everyone will read this book with an open heart and mind and open Scriptures in hand.

LEGAL HOLIDAYS IN THE UNITED STATES

By definition and tradition, modern holidays are noted for feasting and resting from work. Some include ceremonies featuring speeches and flag displays; others include religious rituals and worship.

Because of the Christian beliefs of the founders of our nation, Sunday has by tradition been considered a day for worship. Though Muslims worship on Friday and Jews on Saturday, Sunday is the only religious holiday that is also our only common-law holiday. This stems from the fact that in AD 321, during the reign of Constantine, civil legislation decreed Sunday a day of rest and served as the weekly commemoration of Christ's resurrection. Had our nation been founded for the purpose of religious diversity, we would have had Friday, Saturday, and Sunday as common-law holidays! I will not enter into the controversy here about the correct day for worship; I consider ourselves blessed to have had Sunday—in spite of its name, Day of the Sun—for worship since the founding of our great nation.

Although certain federal agencies such as post offices and banks are closed on specific legal holidays, the United States has no national holidays because Congress has no constitutional power to declare them. For example, Independence Day is celebrated nationwide, but Congress and the president can designate legal holidays only for federally owned territories and the District of Columbia. Therefore, each state must enact legislation to observe the day as a holiday.

Have you ever wondered why Washington's Birthday is now on the third Monday in February when it used to be the twenty-second of that month, or why Memorial Day is on the last Monday in May instead of the thirtieth of that month? In 1968, a federal law, effective in 1971, changed the dates of many holidays to give federal employees three-day weekends. Those changes originally included Columbus Day, which now falls on the second Monday in October, and Veterans Day, which was to have fallen on the fourth Monday in October.

Most states enacted complementary legislation to bring themselves in line but for one exception: possibly due to the outcry of those involved, namely veterans, many states chose to retain November 11, the original Armistice Day, as Veterans Day. In 1978, the federal government also reverted to the traditional date.

To complicate matters, if a federal holiday occurs on a Saturday, it may be moved to Friday; if it falls on a Sunday, it may be moved to Monday. There are normally ten of these federal holidays per year with an eleventh (January 20) after every presidential election.

Along with these eleven legal national holidays, we have approximately thirty nonlegal holidays such as Valentine's Day, Father's Day, National Day of Prayer, Easter, and Halloween, to name a few. This study will comment on the eleven official and eight unofficial holidays.

CHAPTER 1

A Brief Review of Organized Religions

Before we discuss specific holidays, let's digress for a moment and try to understand why confusion reigns in certain aspects of holiday celebrations and even our worship today. A good place to begin is in the book of beginnings, Genesis, which, besides introducing our Creator to us, also introduces the antithesis of all things godly—Babylon.

Babylonia and Assyria, two kingdoms prominent throughout the Old Testament, existed in what are now Iraq, Iran, Turkey, and Syria. These ancient countries took their names from their capital cities, Babylon and Ashur. Nimrod, great-grandson of Noah, founded Babel; Ashur, second son of Shem, or grandson of Noah, founded Ashur.

Recall that Noah pronounced a curse on Canaan, Ham's son, for Ham's sin against Noah (see Genesis 9:22). This curse developed into severe family hatred against Noah, his God, and anything touching Noah's righteousness. Ham's son Cush, undoubtedly in sympathy with his brother, Canaan, intentionally encouraged this hatred, for he named his son Nimrod.

Nimrod's name came from the Semitic verb *marad,* which meant "rebellion" or "we will rebel." Whether this was his actual name or just a derisive term given him, as some believe, Nimrod embodied the spirit of rebellion against God. Inclusive in Nimrod's descriptive name is the idea that he not only hunted animals but also trapped men by his clever stratagems, by fraud or force, and killed them or put them

1

into subjection. "Mighty hunter before the Lord" (Genesis 10:9) is not a complimentary title. "Before the Lord" may mean "in the face of Jehovah." Today, the disdainful expression "in your face" means to brazenly tout one's immoral lifestyle or loathsome habits without regard to how others feel about it. So here we have Nimrod actually or figuratively shaking his fist in God's face!

Nimrod taunted God and fumed in his all-consuming hostility against Him. Not content to vent his vehemence alone against God, he founded several cities and led their inhabitants to unite in rebellion. Among the cities were Erech, Accad, Calneh, and Babel. Ashur founded Nineveh, Rehoboth, Calah, and Resen, which later developed into Assyria; these also united with Nimrod against the Lord. In Micah 5:6, Assyria was called the land of Nimrod rather than the land of Ashur, as might be expected.

God didn't direct the unification of these cities; quite the opposite, in fact. Secular history credits Nimrod with being the first to take up arms against other cities and territories, so his leadership in this unholy alliance eventually led to a catastrophic event.

Before the flood, the earth consisted of one landmass. Approximately one hundred years after the flood, during the time of Peleg, God divided the earth (Genesis 10:32). There is sincere debate as to whether He cracked its crust like an eggshell into what are now about twenty pieces (tectonic plates) or whether He simply divided the people themselves without any upheaval. Whichever way He chose, under His divine direction, Noah had allocated specific parts of earth to his three sons and sixteen grandsons. Some of his descendants obeyed as Noah commanded and set forth to populate their portion. The rebellious ones liked the status quo and wished to stay where they lived. Perhaps they were afraid of unknown wild beasts even though God had said, "The dread of you shall be upon every beast" (Genesis 9:2). Perhaps they desired the safety inherent in numbers; perhaps they just couldn't see moving away from Mom and Dad, or maybe it was just the spirit of rebellion in them. Whatever their reasons, they wanted to stay where they were and disobeyed God; they made a pact with each other that they wouldn't move.

These people also constructed at least one ziggurat in each city, and some cities had more than one. Dedicated to each city's patron god or goddess, each tall structure had a temple at its top, where it has long been assumed the people worshipped the sun and the hosts of heaven and anxiously sought supernatural wisdom from the constellations.

Some ziggurats had ramps while others had stairways that may have been for use by the gods to make connection to earth or for their priests to get closer to them. So far, thirty-four of these towers have been located in twenty-seven cities. John H. Walton, in his online article "Is there archaeological evidence of the Tower of Babel?"[1] translates into English the names of twenty-two ziggurats. One temple's name in particular evokes a clear picture of their intent: "Temple of the Stairway to Pure Heaven" (155–75).

To prove how determined and unstoppable they were, these perverse, forward people began building an even higher ziggurat. It likely contained a more sophisticated astrological system, thus ensuring that their worship of the sun (Baal), consultation of the heavenly bodies, and communication with their gods would continue. In turn, for their devotion, the people would be protected from dispersion by the chief gods, who appeared to be in charge of the world and appeared to be more powerful than Jehovah. Nevertheless, appearances were deceiving!

For the Great Building Inspector, the Discerner of Hearts, almighty God, condescended to have a look at this structure. He condemned it not because of structural defects but because of the defects in the hearts of its builders. In our small minds, we wonder how a 20-, 50-, or even 101-story building, such as the world's tallest building in Taipei, could be threatening to the Almighty, but we know He said, "Nothing will be restrained from them which they have imagined to do" (Genesis 11:6). Indeed, the height of the building may have been a minor consideration in God's immense universe. Instead, an advanced technological misapplication of scientific or mathematical knowledge that allowed them to probe into the heavens may have been a major deciding factor.

God made us with astounding potential; we can invent marvelous things, write beautiful literature and music, and more important, glorify Him. Because God made us with such potential, He knew that what we could conceive and believe we could achieve. But what this particular group of people conceived and believed, He couldn't permit them to achieve. Their goals didn't advance righteousness and worship of Jehovah but licentiousness, immorality, degradation, and odious idol worship. "The heart of man is deceitful above all things, and desperately wicked: who can know it?" (Jeremiah 17:9).

God demonstrated that He knew the mind of humanity extremely well and scattered the people into many babbling groups and diverse ethnicities. Various Bible scholars differ as to the exact date of this dispersion. James Ussher, in his *Annals of the World,* gives the date as 2242 BC, but E. W. Bullinger, in *The Companion Bible,* gives it as 1946 BC. We can say that it was roughly around 2000 BC.

It is noteworthy that Nimrod is mentioned only four times in Scripture and God chose not to name his wife at all. We know from secular history that Nimrod had numberless generations of descendants, but perhaps God saw him as so contemptible as to be unworthy of any further mention in His sacred Scriptures. However, Satan ensured Nimrod's place in secular history, for later, we see Nimrod identified in literature and mythology across the world where his thwarted, brazen followers immigrated.

None of these scattered groups asked for forgiveness even though they undoubtedly retained some knowledge of Jehovah and His promise of a divine Redeemer. It would appear that they knew more than they wished to know or more than they wished to acknowledge. These dispersed ones could have returned to Him. Their heterodox leaders in each tongue, land, and nation had His witness in the stars, later called by the Jews the *mazzaroth.*[2] This picture of the gospel in the stars should have been taught to the masses. Instead, the spiritual leaders put their own spin on the meanings of the constellations, compounding the weight of guilt placed upon themselves. How can we say this with certainty?

> For the invisible things of Him from the creation of the
> world are clearly seen, being understood by the things

that are made, even His eternal power and Godhead; so
that they are without excuse (Romans 1:20).

Adam's perfect astronomical knowledge transmitted to Noah
became corrupted for astrological purposes because of Nimrod's
insurgency. Reprehensible versions of the Trinity, the account of the
biblical flood, and God's plan of salvation via the virgin birth appear in
ancient mythologies. No, ignorance was not the excuse. Hearts hardened
by arrogance and presumption impeded any return to Jehovah. As a
result, God, in His omniscient timing, called Abram from a city of
idolaters and astrologers, saying, "And ye shall be holy unto Me: for I
the Lord am holy, and have severed you from other people that ye should
be Mine" (Leviticus 20:26).

It is probable that at the time of God's call to Abram, Nimrod
would still have been living, terrorizing his portion of the earth, and
intimidating his followers into subjection and worship of himself.
Two theories exist concerning Nimrod's demise. One is that the Lord
destroyed him in a mighty wind that took down the Tower of Babel;
another is that he was cast into a dungeon and later put to death.
Although it piques our curiosity, we have to be content with the fact
that if God had thought it was important for us to know, He would
have told us.

What started as a few individuals rebelling, organizing, and
opposing God approximately four thousand years ago developed into
many nations consisting of millions, most still rebelling.

You may be thinking, *That stuff happened thousands of years ago.
What does this have to do with me and holidays?* Just this: many of our
customs and traditions practiced today have their roots in Babylon.
Offshoots of these practices are alive and flourish in many nations.
After all these years, innocent children encouraged by unsuspecting
parents continue to practice some of the traces of traditions that began
in antiquity and were transported around the world.

It's a topsy-turvy muddle. The pagans' claim that Christians stole
their holidays is true to some extent. And now, Christians claim the
pagans are secularizing or replacing *their* holidays. If there is a remote

chance that the Lord is being praised or that the name of Christ is in the holiday, they are.

So who celebrated what first? Let's sort through the flotsam and jetsam of the holidays. What can be discarded, and what can be kept? Also, if a fire-worshipping pagan celebrated by doing something horrific on a specific day, does that mean we can't use that day to celebrate Christ? Sincere believers seek answers to such questions.

CHAPTER 2

Organized Religion from the Fourth Century

During the Acts period and for the first few centuries, no general organization of churches existed. No city served as the authoritative center from which all other churches took their orders. All churches were generally known as Catholic churches; *catholic* simply meant "universal." In the fourth century, Constantine converted to the Christian faith and established himself as the pontifex maximus. The Roman Catholic Church with its multiplicity of rituals resulted.

From the fourth through the sixteenth century, sincere Roman Catholic pontiffs (we'll give them the benefit of the doubt since only God knows hearts) sought by any means to bring pagans into their fold. Through many compromises, various pagan holidays became Christianized; that is, instead of being totally pagan, they became either wholly or partly Christian.

Martin Luther, during the sixteenth century (in what historians identify as the Reformation) didn't intend to begin new churches with different rituals. His objectives concerned righting injustices, eliminating corruption, and correcting wrong doctrine in the existing Church. Nevertheless, many branches of Protestantism developed, each with its own ceremonial liturgies, rites, and catechisms, some of which were only slightly different from Catholicism's. Consequently, even in evangelical, Bible-believing, or fundamental churches, vestiges of the mixture are found.

Note that there will be three basic ways of referring to what is commonly known among Christendom as *church*. When capitalized, the word indicates either the Western Roman Catholic organization, one of the Eastern Orthodox organizations (Greek, Serbian, Russian, Bulgarian, etc.), or the Anglican Church. When lowercased, it will refer to any local group of believers. Otherwise, the church may be referred to as the body of Christ.

We know that all Scripture was *not* written specifically to us, but all Scripture is for our edification. As we ponder holidays, let us keep in mind these Scriptures.

- John 4:23–24: "But the hour cometh, and now is, when the true worshippers shall worship the Father in spirit and in truth; for the Father seeketh such to worship Him. God is a Spirit: and they that worship Him must worship Him in spirit and in truth."
- Matthew 15:9: "But in vain they do worship Me, teaching for doctrines the commandments of men."
- Psalm 46:10: "Be still, and know that I am God: I will be exalted among the heathen, I will be exalted in the earth."
- Isaiah 1:14: "Your new moons and your appointed feasts My soul hateth: they are a trouble unto me; I am weary to bear them."
- 1 Thessalonians 5:22: "Abstain from all appearance of evil."

CHAPTER 3

New Year's Day

New Year's Day—Past

For the last 400 years, January 1 has been the beginning of the new year for many, but ancient civilizations celebrated it at different times. The following examples are only a few.

The Babylonians began their year on the first of Nisan, roughly corresponding to our March/April. Celebrations began with the first visible crescent of the new moon and continued for eleven days. Legend says that annually, the Babylonians humiliated their king by stripping off his clothing and sending him away. For eleven days, the people could do whatever they wished without fear, celebrating with as much debauchery and depravity as they liked.

Concurrently, for the first five days, ceremonies of purification were held to their gods for the sins they were committing. At the end of eleven days, the king returned dressed in his royal clothes. He then committed blasphemy by usurping God's role and "forgiving" sins. ("Who can forgive sins but God alone?" Luke 5:21.) The party was over; people had to return to work and to behave themselves. Some did feel guilty for all the sins they committed over the eleven days and made resolutions to start anew, and of course their king/god used this chance to further deify himself, get in the good graces of a sinful people by absolving sins, and further entrenching his tyrannical power.

Another version of the Babylonian new year states that on the tenth day of their eleven-day celebration, Marduk, Nabu, and other gods gathered at Akitu House. There, Marduk held a ceremonial battle in which he overcame the forces of evil and all the gods returned to the temple at Esagila in anticipation of their new year.

The ancient Egyptians started their new year at the autumnal equinox, September 21, around the time the Nile flooded. Without this flood, the people couldn't grow crops, so this signaled a time of celebration. For a month, statues of the god Amon and his wife and son rode in a boat on the Nile, and the people feasted, danced, and sang. At the end of the celebration, the gods returned to the temple.

The different Greek societies such as the Ionians, Dorians, and Boeotians celebrated New Year's at different times. Some feasted on the summer solstice, others on the winter solstice, and some at the autumnal equinox. Later, the Greeks unified and their new year began at the winter solstice, December 21. Whenever the feast or celebration occurred, it was always dedicated to one or more deities, those thought to meet their specific needs.

The Greeks played games, held athletic competitions, danced, and held a procession to an altar in a temple. A priest or priestess led the procession as the worshippers brought food, wine, and animals to sacrifice. They sacrificed meat and sprinkled oil and wine on it so that a sweet aroma went up to the god. Finally, the celebrants ate the roasted sacrificial meat and the other foods. Part of the food ritual included eating cakes with a coin baked in them in honor of Kronos. The receiver of the piece of cake with the coin had good luck the next year.

Around 600 BC, the Greeks also introduced the tradition of using a baby to represent the new year. This baby represented the rebirth of Dionysus, god of wine, and the spirit of fertility.

The Romans thought March 1 should begin the year. On that day, they displayed nude or nearly nude female dancers in the public squares, played games, and indulged in all things sensual. Early believers frowned upon these activities and preached sermons on New Year's Day against prevailing debaucheries. In AD 567, the Council of Tours made the day a fast day and forbad any New Year's celebrations.

Centuries later, when the Gregorian calendar took effect and decreed January the first month of the year, non-Christian Romans offered sacrifices to Janus to ensure a prosperous year.

During medieval times, much of what is now continental Europe regarded March 25, the vernal equinox, as the beginning of the year. Known as Lady Day, it honored the Virgin Goddess who mated on that day with the young Solar God. Some accounts refer to her as the Great Mother Goddess, who transforms from being virgin to being mother on that day. The full story is not worthy of our consideration at this point. Probably in a sincere attempt to clean up this celebration, the Catholic Church initiated a new one, Annunciation Day. Supposedly on that day, Mary received the announcement that she would bear the Savior. (Hence, in Eastern Orthodoxy, Mary is referred to as *Theotokos*, "Mother of God." The Council of Ephesus AD 431 took issue with that term and agreed that the term meant "The bringer forth of God," but the other term prevailed.)

Today on March 25, for much of the world, rather than focusing on a pagan deity, the day focuses on Mary. Practicing pagans continue to honor Lady Day for the Virgin Goddess while the Roman Catholic Church honors Lady Day in honor of the Virgin Mary. The annunciation and conception naturally point to nine months later, December 25, examined in the "Biblical Account of the Birth of Jesus Christ" chapter.

In ancient Gaul, the new year began on October 31, the date now associated with Halloween or the Samhain, a fire festival, known as the Feast of the Dead. It celebrated one of the many pagan druidic religious holidays. The *Schaff-Herzog Encyclopedia of Religious Knowledge*, vol. IV, paints a grim picture. Druid chiefs, their philosopher-magician, and spiritual leaders

> officiated at human and other sacrifices and at all religious rites. The human sacrifices were offered sometimes in holocausts, the victims being prisoners of war, criminals, or even voluntary sufferers, and they were burned after being enclosed in huge wicker images.

This account given by Julius Caesar after the Roman conquest equated the chief gods of the druids as being the Roman gods Apollo, Mars, Jupiter, and Minerva. To trace this offshoot back to the root, Alexander equated the Roman god Mars, the god of war, to Nimrod, the original rebel warrior.[3] Modern practitioners of druidism maintain that Julius Caesar was prejudiced against the Celtic Gaelic people and that incidents like the above never happened. If not, why did Rome outlaw human sacrifices? Even without human sacrifices, there was still an abundance of evil as wicked people worshipped many gods and indulged in sinful practices. (This is covered in more detail in the "Halloween" chapter.)

In Scotland, after the Romans banned human sacrifice, other traditions took their place. Ceremonies on this day, known as Alban Eiler, "light of the earth," involved torchlight processions and people dressing up in cattle hides or igniting animal hides wrapped around sticks to produce smoke, thereby fending off evil spirits. The name *Hogmanay* came to be associated with this New Year's celebration. No one knows for sure where the word came from. Suggestions include the Scandinavian *hoggo-nott*, the Flemish *hoog min dag*, the Anglo-Saxon *oge maide*, and the French *home est ne*.

These Hogmanay celebrations were banned in Scotland because of the influence of John Knox, former Catholic priest turned reformer. They were banned from the late seventeenth century until the 1950s, when they were once again revived.

Anglo-Saxon England originally began celebrating the new year on December 21, Mother's Night, in honor of many earth mothers. Customary feasting and gift giving honored all the goddesses of the Anglo-Saxon pantheon. Twelve days of Yule featured mistletoe and ivy for decoration and for warmth, the Yule log made of oak to honor the thunder god, Thunor.

Sometime in the fourth century AD, December 25 changed from the first day of Yule to Christ's Mass, the customary birthday of Christ. Since January 1 occurs eight days later, the circumcision of Jesus as recorded in Luke 2:21 was assumed (perhaps assigned) to have been then. Thus, we have the Feast of the Circumcision of Our Lord, a holy day of obligation when Catholics must attend Mass.

Soon after this change, priests started giving New Year's sermons and wishing their congregations well on January 1.[4] When the Reformation began, Bible-believing reformers discouraged but did not forbid New Year's celebrations in Anglo-Saxon England.

In contrast, despite the world around them indulging in sinful preoccupations, the Puritans refused to participate in New Year's celebrations on January 1. Not only did they not celebrate, they would not even say the name of the month because it honored the pagan god, Janus. Instead, they said, "first month."

In the Western Hemisphere, the early Mesoamericans (Indians of Mexico, ancient Toltecs, Aztecs, Mayas, Incas, and others) had many gods and goddesses who appeared in various guises, sometimes changing into one another, and in some respects were similar to Roman deities. Authorities differ as to whether the Aztecs began their solar year on February 2 or March 1.

> The first of the 18 months in the solar year coincided with February in the European calendar. It was a time of fervent prayer for the spring rains needed to prepare the thirsty fields for planting. And so it was dedicated to the gods and goddesses of rain and terrestrial water and also to Quetzalcoatl in one of his guises as the god of the wind, who pushes the rain-laden clouds before him. Because the rain deities lived in the mountains, children were carried to their summits, where they assumed the identities of the mountain deities and were sacrificed in their names to hasten the onset of rain.[5]

The date itself is perhaps not as important as realizing that out of the eighteen-month calendar, seven of those months featured human sacrifices as part of the celebration festivities.

Pagan Sabbats

Notice the seeming coincidence of "religious" dates falling on the planetary yearly cycle. Practitioners of paganism have a simple system of dividing the year represented by an eight-spoke wheel to specify eight sabbats. The four quarter-days represented by the solstices and the equinoxes are their lesser sabbats: June 20, midsummer solstice; December 21, midwinter solstice; March 20, vernal equinox; and September 22, autumnal equinox. The greater sabbats, the cross-quarter days, are October 31, Samhain; February 2, Imbolc; May 1, Beltane; and August 1, Lughnasadh.

Professed pagans inform that *sabbat* was originally Babylonian and used to designate the quarter-days of their lunar cycle. Pagans claim the Hebrews borrowed the word to designate a day of rest. Undoubtedly, they are right about their sabbats being older than our holidays and not being man-made, but they appear to not recognize God as having had any right to appropriate a Sabbath for His people.

One Sun, One Moon, Many Calendars

Our modern Western civilization is influenced every day by the Romans of antiquity who renamed the months of the year in honor of rulers and Roman gods and goddesses. To become thoroughly befuddled, one has only to read a couple of encyclopedia articles on calendar reforms, but to keep this as uncomplicated as possible, I will discuss the basics of the calendars of Julius Caesar and Pope Gregory XIII. The Islamic, Jewish, and Oriental calendars receive less attention.

Julius Caesar conquered Egypt in 48 BC by our current calendar system, or 709 AUC (*ab urbe condita*, "from the founding of the city" of Rome). The Roman calendar had only ten months at that time and proved inadequate for their needs. Caesar consulted an Egyptian astronomer regarding calendar reform. This consultation led to the adoption of the Julian calendar consisting of a solar year of twelve months of 365 days with an extra day every fourth year. Two additional months were added between November and December to bring the calendar in line with the equinoxes.

The Roman bureaucracy of the day apparently became confused and had a leap year every three years, which understandably threw everything out of balance. Also, in order not to have Augustus Caesar feel inferior to Julius, the extra February day was taken from February and added to August so July and August would both have thirty-one days.

All this tampering with the calendar produced inevitable inaccuracies that caused the calendar to become increasingly off kilter regarding solstices and seasons. Augustus Caesar further skewed it by suspending leap years for a few years. Historians cannot say for certain just when the Julian Calendar became stabilized, but it was used throughout the Roman Empire, and, of course, by Christian churches influenced by Rome.

In AD 532, Dionysius Exiguus began the accounting of time from the date of Jesus' birth. No one has access to the materials he used in his calculations, but his calculations missed the mark by a few years.

In 1582, Pope Gregory XIII used much of Dionysius Exiguus's research, the influence of the Vatican librarian, and a mathematician-astronomer, Fr. Christopher Clavius, to come up with what is now known as the Gregorian calendar. This changed January from the eleventh month of the year to the first. New Year's Day had already been celebrated by Roman Catholic countries on January 1, but this made it official.

Three big changes occurred with the Gregorian calendar.

1. The Gregorian calendar omitted ten days; October 4, 1582, was followed by October 15, 1582.
2. The rule for leap year changed so that a year divisible by four is a leap year except if it is divisible by 100 but not by 400. Thus, the year 2000 was a leap year, but the year 2100 will not be a leap year, for it is not divisible by 400.

3. New rules were adopted for determining Easter dates because by the disordered Julian calendar, Easter often came near the summer solstice instead of the vernal equinox.

Protestant countries in Reformation Europe resisted changing to the new calendar but gradually followed suit and changed from the Julian to the Gregorian. Germany led in 1700, followed by Great Britain and the America colonies in 1752 and Sweden in 1753. To complicate matters, for a couple hundred years, both the Julian and Gregorian calendars were used. Anyone doing historical research finds this a nightmarish complication.

As noted above, the calculations are off by a few years. According to biblical astronomers, Christ's birth probably took place between the years 5 BC and 1 BC. This is a bit confusing because we have the oxymoron of Jesus being born at least four years "before" Christ. Nevertheless, this is the system in use, and we will continue to use it. Much of the non-Christian world also adopted this dating system for uniformity in trade relations and for administrative purposes but kept their own religious calendars.

The Gregorian calendar is also known as the Christian calendar because the birth of Christ is used as the central date. Years preceding the birth of Christ are designated BC (before Christ), after His birth as AD (Latin *anno domini*, "in the year of our Lord"). Indeed, history should be centered on *His* story since the center of the purpose of the ages is the Lord Jesus Christ: "Unto him be glory in the church by Christ Jesus throughout all **ages**, world without end. Amen" (Ephesians 3:21). (Author's emphasis)

Regrettably, many refuse to acknowledge Jesus Christ as Messiah or Savior or even to acknowledge that the Son of God came to earth to die for the sins of humanity. They prefer to designate the years as AM (Latin *anno mundi*, "the year of the world") and BCE (before the common era) or CE (common era).

No matter how it's written, whether BC or BCE, what's being pinpointed? The incarnation and birth of Christ of course! Do we agree with David, "The fool hath said in his heart, there is no God" (Psalm 14:1)?

Islamic Calendar

The Gregorian calendar is a solar calendar, but the Islamic or Hijrah calendar consists of twelve lunar months totaling 354 11/30 days. The Muslim new year begins at the vernal equinox at the first sighting of the new moon.

Oriental New Year

The Oriental new year generally begins the day of the second new moon after the winter solstice. On the Gregorian calendar, that would occur between January 21 and February 21. Festivities last for fifteen days. New Year's is a major holiday in China, Korea, Vietnam, and any cultures influenced by Confucian and Buddhist traditions.

Jewish New Year

The Jewish religious new year begins on the first day of Tishri (Ethanim) corresponding to the period between our September 6 and October 5 and is known as Rosh Hashanah or the Feast of Trumpets. Rosh Hashanah begins with ten days of penitence and ends on Yom Kippur; thus, the High Holy Days of the Jewish year. The days of penitence are a memorial to the creation of Adam and Eve and their sin and repentance even though no biblical evidence shows Adam and Eve ever truly repented. On the Hebrew calendar, the year AD 2015 is designated 5775, the estimated date from the creation of Adam.

The Jewish new year is mentioned specifically to stress this point: other than in Scripture, the earliest record of a New Year's celebration is from around 3,000 BC in Mesopotamia, land of the ancient city of Ur, from which Abraham received God's call. It is intriguing to envision the contrast of Abraham and his descendants celebrating the solemn Feasts of Trumpets in Palestine while his relatives were worshipping the Sumerian moon god, Nanna.

New Year's Day at Present

Traditions Unique to Specific Countries

Looking at practices from ancient and medieval times, we see each culture had many things unique, and yet much was the same in the celebration of the gods. Time has not changed some things. Here are a few current ways of welcoming in the new year. Do they sound scriptural, antiscriptural, or secular?

Not on January 1

Israel: many countries following the Gregorian calendar for business list New Year's Day as a public holiday with the exception of modern Israel. Because the day is considered a Christian holiday, antithetical to the Jewish religion, there is no celebration on January 1.

China: the Chinese set off firecrackers to scare away evil spirits and seal windows to keep them out. The year is also welcomed with dragon and lion dances.

Korea: Koreans place rakes or sieves on door and walls to protect them from evil spirits. An ancestor memorial is held on the first day of celebration. People visit the beaches to make wishes, and they play traditional games.

Thailand: the custom is to wash all statues of Buddha to ensure the rains will come. To bring even more good luck, they release fish from their bowls and birds from their cages. Traditionally, families visit grandparents to ask them to assure good fortune.

Vietnam: the god who lives in each home travels to heaven every year to report on the behavior in the home. (No one has yet reported on what message he leaves.)

Cambodia: families visit Buddhist monasteries and ask monks to pray for their ancestors as well as wash Buddha statues to ensure rain during the coming year.

On January 1

Netherlands and other European countries: fireworks bring in the new year, and Christmas trees are burned.

Scotland: remote parts of the country continue Hogmanay as practiced centuries ago as an integral part of New Year's festivities. Glasgow, Edinburgh, Aberdeen, and Dundee advertise in tourist promotional material all-night Hogmanay parties including large fireballs reminiscent of the druidic past. The evening ends with singing "Auld Lang Syne."

Austria: Vienna begins the year with a concert.

Denmark: they break dishes. The more friends they have, the more dishes get broken!

Brazil: priestesses of the macumba voodoo cult wear white blouses and blue skirts in honor of a ceremony dedicated to Yemanja, the goddess of water. Brazilians go to the beach, jump waves, and throw flowers in the sea for its goddess. If she takes the flowers out to sea, it will be a good year ensuring fulfillment of their wishes. Generally speaking, the day is now a nonreligious one with fireworks displays catering to tourists.

Colombia: Mr. Old Year, a big, stuffed, male doll representing the old year, is filled with objects that caused bad memories or sad times in the past year and is burned at midnight. This custom may have begun as a substitute for a human sacrifice, a remnant from the old Inca religion in which Viracocha, the chief god, ruled and ritual human sacrifices were common.

Greece: the custom continues for coins to be baked in cakes. The father of the house cuts the cake; now, Christ is honored with the first piece, the next is for the house, and the remaining pieces go to all present. The one who finds the coin has good luck in the coming year.

The Greeks also have the custom of choosing a small child to be the first to enter a house on New Year's Day. A small child is considered innocent and will bring good luck to the house.

British Columbia: people don swimsuits and do the traditional polar bear swim.

Bahamas: Mesoamerican culture is depicted in song and dance, including a depiction of a human sacrifice being made to the Aztec gods. Traditional colors worn by Maya and Aztec feature feathered headdresses of high priests and chieftains.

United States: folks in our country get a head start by beginning celebrations on New Year's Eve with masquerade balls and festive parties. The countdown to midnight is viewed from Times Square in New York City, where thousands gather and millions watch on television as a lighted ball drops down a pole. As the clock strikes twelve, people hug, kiss, shout, and wish each other a happy new year. Numerous cities and towns across the nation have similar countdowns.

Not everyone, though, is looking at Times Square or any other public spectacle. Scattered throughout the land, many Bible believers gather in their congregations, fellowship halls, or homes to usher in the new year with watch night services, services anticipating the *parousia*, presence, of Christ or fellowship featuring good food, hymns of praise, and the study of God's Word.

The Day Itself

Whether the day is considered sacred or secular by celebrants, families get together to eat and relax as well as watch the bowl games.

Across the nation, small cities and towns have unique celebrations. Lewisburg, West Virginia, for example, sponsors the Shanghai Parade. Where the name came from, no one knows. For many years, the New Year's baby leading the parade was actually a grown man wearing only a diaper and a sash!

New Year's Superstitions

Superstitions result from ignorance or fear of the unknown. Some of our current ones had their origins during the Middle Ages, when paganism prevailed and one had to pacify evil spirits. Today, they might be passed to the next generation just for fun or to educate the young about the old days and old ways. These are just a few of dozens.

- A baby born on New Year's brings wealth and great luck to all the family.
- Don't have empty pockets or empty cupboards on New Year's or you'll have poverty the rest of the year.
- Scare away the evil spirits by making as much noise as possible at midnight.
- Avoid crying or breaking anything. It sets the tone for the whole year.
- Open the door at the stroke of midnight to allow the old year to pass on and the new year to come in.
- Kiss at midnight or you'll have a year without affection.
- Wear new clothes to make sure you'll receive more new clothes during the year.
- To make sure your wallet is never empty, put a wrapped piece of cabbage next to your money.
- Originating in Scotland is the superstition of "first footing." To ensure good luck, the first foot in the household must be a dark-haired male. Some speculate this comes from the old Viking days when a blond-haired man entering the door meant big trouble.
- Malaysian immigrants mix sacred water with incense to expel the grasshopper demon.

Food Superstitions

Because our country has been a melting pot of diverse ethnic groups, food traditions have also been informally bequeathed through the generations. Those of Dutch extraction believe eating donuts symbolizes good luck. Italians serve lentils (*lenticchie*). Those of Asian extraction may have a rice dish such as the Korean rice cake soup. Descendants of the Scots serve honey and lemon chicken or steak pie. Southerners in the United States of whatever extraction might serve collard greens and black-eyed peas along with hog jowls or ham and cornbread. Besides just good eating, most foods are accompanied by at least one superstition, the meaning of which may be long lost.

Paul's View of Superstition

Paul encountered his share of superstition. When he addressed the philosophers at Mar's Hill, he said, "Ye men of Athens, I perceive that in all things ye are too superstitious" (Acts 17:22). *Superstitious* meant the same in his day as it does in ours: be wary of all the gods and the trouble they can cause. At that time, Paul hadn't begun to preach the great truth of the body found in Ephesians, but he did offer a chance for them to cure their ignorance: "And the times of this ignorance God winked at; but now commandeth all men everywhere to repent" (Acts 17:30). Some mocked him, but others wanted to hear more; however, they too were without excuse.

Traditions Bad and Good

Family traditions are an integral part of what makes us family. Specific foods cooked specific ways year after year and gathering at family or friends' houses on special days give us a sense of stability and a feeling we belong. According to God's Word, traditions can be good or bad. Again, our apostle to the Gentiles, Paul, gave an example of both.

1. "And profited in the Jews' religion above many my equals in mine own nation, being more exceedingly zealous of the traditions of my fathers" (Galatians 1:14). Paul followed strict regulations of Jewish oral tradition. He would have taken quite seriously the tradition that forbad such Sabbath work as weaving two threads, tying a knot, erasing two letters, or writing two letters of the alphabet. Before Paul's conversion, traditions meant more than anything else to him. He would kill for them or die for them himself.

2. "Therefore brethren stand fast and hold the traditions which ye have been taught whether by word or our epistle" (2 Thessalonians 2:15). At that point, Paul changed in regard to traditions. He no longer followed oral tradition blindly but stated explicitly that if traditions were according to Scriptures, by all means Christians should keep them.

New Year's Celebrations

Is it wrong to bring in the new year with celebrations? There are drunken parties and there are God-fearing ones. Anytime members of the body get together, it should be one of joy and celebration. Anyone participating in a Bible study or a Bible conference at any time of year will testify to the love and joy that abounds among the saints of God. "We know that we have passed from death unto life because we love the brethren" (1 John 3:14).

We can have a good time of fellowship in His name any day; we don't need to be as the besotted godless, the brainwashed, modern, lawless barbarian, the well-mannered but unsaved, or those professing paganism today. It is revealing that both words *drunken* and *glutton* appear together in Deuteronomy 21:20 and Proverbs 23:21. We can guard the appetite, have a sober, satisfying meal, and give God the glory.

Surely the believer has more to celebrate every day including New Year's than the unsaved!

New Year's Resolutions

Should we make resolutions? Should we vow to pray more, eat less, get physically fit, and to keep all the other worthy intentions that have eluded us the previous year? Should drug addicts or alcoholics promise new lives for themselves and their families? The idea of resolutions brings Paul to mind again: "For that which I do, I allow not; for what I would, that do I not; but what I hate, that I do" (Romans 7:15). In other words, we can have good intentions but might not manage to keep them because "the spirit is willing, but the flesh is weak" (Matthew 26:41).

We must first make sure that we are not confusing resolution with salvation. We must see our need of the Savior and acknowledge Him.

- "For all have sinned and come short of the glory of God" (Romans 3:23).
- "But to him that worketh not but believeth on Him that justifieth the ungodly, his faith is counted for righteousness" (Romans 4:5).
- "In Whom we have redemption through His blood, the forgiveness of sins, according to the riches of His grace" (Ephesians 1:7).
- "But now, in Christ Jesus, ye who were sometimes far off, are made nigh by the blood of Christ; for He is our peace" (Ephesians 2:13).
- "That the God of our Lord Jesus Christ, the Father of glory, may give unto you the spirit of wisdom and revelation in the [ac]knowledge[ment] of Him" (Ephesians 1:17).

Jonathan Edwards, the eighteenth-century Presbyterian minister who influenced our young nation toward righteousness and independence, wrote seventy New Year's resolutions between 1722 and

1723. It is an impressive list of "I wills." It's daunting, to say the least, but the resolutions display a humble attitude. However, they may have leaned a bit far toward a works-oriented religion. We all must be careful of the "I wills."

A word-for-word interlinear of Colossians 2:18 reads, "Let no one defraud you of the prize of doing will, humility, and worship of the angels."[6] "Doing will" literally means "to have a religion of the will," "a religion based on our own decisions" in contrast to Colossians 2:19, "holding the Head, from Whom all the body by joints and bands having nourishment ministered, and knit together, increaseth with the increase of God."

If we are saved, is it wrong to make resolutions? Possibly our only one should be to study God's Word, for in it are the answers to our daily problems. Regular meditation in the Scriptures puts into perspective those things we need to make right. If we are overweight or recovering from alcoholic or other addiction, Proverbs 23:21 warns us, "For the drunkard and the glutton shall come to poverty." In fact, for daily wisdom in general, we can't go wrong following the advice in Proverbs. The book of Romans warns of God's judgments concerning specific sins and the shameful results. Ephesians instructs the pattern for family organization. In His Word, we learn the negative effects of *not* following what God has *positively* spoken.

What about starting the new year with a positive or self-help book to improve our self-images? Self-image seems to have been the buzzword among educators and psychologists for several years now. We are told a good self-image is the answer to many of our society's needs. If only people felt better about themselves, things would change for the better; people would not lie, cheat, steal, and so on, or so we are led to believe. Obviously, there is a grain of truth to this; correctional educators will tell you that many criminals lack self-esteem. They will also tell you about the many arrogant, self-confident criminals who think they made only one mistake: getting caught. No, a good self-image is not the answer to the sin problem.

Self-help books have made an impact on many lives. By all means, read positive books, listen to motivational tapes, and follow their advice as long as that advice conforms to God's Word.

The "I wills" cannot get us very far. In the final analysis, God's Word is the ultimate for teaching positive thinking and living. Yes, it certainly presents us with the negative nature of fallen man, but can anyone believe that he or she was created in God's image and have a *poor* self-image? Perhaps we should begin every new year reading Ephesians 4:24–32. We would truly be magnanimous personalities if we all forgave others as Christ forgave us. Also, there would be no need for illegal drugs or alcohol to forget our troubles as many in the world feel the need to do.

- Ephesians 4:22–23: "That ye put off concerning the former conversation the old man, which is corrupt according to the deceitful lusts: And be renewed in the spirit of your mind." This is not a self-made resolution but a command from God to us, who are members of the body.
- Ephesians 1:3: "Blessed be the God and Father of our Lord Jesus Christ, Who hath blessed us with all spiritual blessings in heavenly places [*en tois epouranios,* "the above heavens"] in Christ." One simply cannot get higher than in heavenly places with Christ.

CHAPTER 4

Martin Luther King Day

In our previous chapter, we discussed the background of holidays and the Christian intention for New Year's Day. Whether that intention would coincide with God's criteria for a holy day is another subject, but New Year's Day is an example of a holiday once pagan and then declared and decreed Christian but that now has primarily turned secular. Our next holiday for discussion began as a secular day to honor the man whose name is synonymous with the modern civil rights movement in the United States.

The Man Compared to the Myth

As with many men in history, it is sometimes difficult to separate fact from fiction. In the case of Martin Luther King Jr., the facts are glaring, but the media prefer to suppress the truth in favor of the idolized image.

King was born in Atlanta on January 15, 1929, to Michael King and Alberta Williams King. His father pastored the Ebenezer Baptist Church, a black congregation that had been founded by Martin Luther King Jr.'s maternal grandfather, A. D. Williams. His mother taught school. He had an older sister, Christina, and a younger brother, Alfred Daniel.

He exhibited a degree of intelligence; he was admitted to Morehouse College in Atlanta at age fifteen without having finished high school. In 1948, King graduated from Morehouse and entered Crozer Theological Seminary in Chester, Pennsylvania, from which he graduated valedictorian of his class in 1951. In 1955, he graduated from Boston University with a PhD in theology.

King met Coretta Scott in Boston and married her in 1953. They had four children: Martin Luther King III; Dexter Scott, Yolanda Denise, and Bernice Albertine.

These facts are in any up-to-date encyclopedia. The generally unpublished and unheralded facts tell us a story far different about the man whom schoolchildren have been taught to idolize. The man doesn't conform to the image in the myth, nor is our perception of him the reality. Many regard King as a great Christian leader. It is necessary to shed some light on this from a scriptural perspective.

Discrimination

It is a sad fact that during his lifetime, King met with much discrimination in stores, buses, and trains of the South and sometimes in the North. One can sincerely empathize with his family or with any other members of the black race who may have been unjustly treated during the years of slavery, Reconstruction, or through the era of the civil rights movement. Surely, many times God has frowned upon His sons and daughters who with their lips professed to love Him when in reality they couldn't sit beside another of a different color, who also professed to love Him. "Beloved, if God so loved us, we ought also to love one another" (1 John 4:11).

Family Background

Perhaps to understand King, we need to get a thumbnail sketch of his father, affectionately known as Daddy King. The elder King ruled his house sternly with no disobedience tolerated. Theologically, he preached a conservative message that included personal deliverance from sin. Due to the circumstance of the times, he also preached a social gospel that demanded racial justice. However, he believed the Bible and had no desire to question its authority.

In 1935, King Sr. renamed himself Martin Luther King and informed his congregation that this is what they would address him as, and that his son would be known as Martin Luther King Jr. Researchers tell us that the names were never officially changed on either birth certificate.

Antibiblical Rebellion

Martin L. King Jr., especially in his youthful days, expressed contempt for white and black Baptists; that is, he expressed contempt for those who believed in a literal interpretation of the Bible, and this included members of other conservative denominations.

This attitude carried over into his adult life as he sat under professors who reinforced his own youthful, biblical ignorance and rebellion. He scorned the bodily resurrection of Jesus and followed liberal theologians who bound Christianity, Judaism, Buddhism, and Islam together as ways of finding God. He chose to ignore Christ's claim, "I am the Way the Truth and the Life. No man cometh unto the Father but by me" (John 14:6), and "Neither is their salvation in any other: for there is none other name under heaven given among men, whereby we must be saved" (Acts 4:12). He believed that Jesus was less than the second person of the Trinity, and in fact, he probably didn't believe in the Trinity, nor did he believe in the doctrine of Original Sin.

In his doctoral dissertation (which was attacked as largely plagiarized), "A Comparison of the Conceptions of God in the Thinking of Paul Tillich and Henry Nelson Wieman," he adopted a bit more of a conservative viewpoint in regard to the doctrine of Original Sin but didn't return absolutely to it.

Perhaps it was his father's early teaching, or perhaps his conscience caught up with him in regard to his own adulterous relationships, but he evidenced more of a slight inclination toward a return to the conservative viewpoint before his death.

Although he scorned the literal message of sin and redemption, he adopted the old-fashioned, Baptist-preacher style, used some of the terminology, and manipulated it eloquently for his own purposes.

Is God's Law Relevant?

Throughout all ages, God has had specific ways of dealing with his people with the aim of bringing them salvation and blessing. The Law was given to Moses with this in mind. Until the bodily resurrection of Christ, "the law was our schoolmaster to bring us unto Christ that we might be justified by faith" (Galatians 3:24).

> We are now found under a new economy, that of grace. Under the dispensation of grace, however, *the moral law will be kept as certainly as if our salvation depended upon it.* The dispensation of grace only sets the law aside as a means of salvation; when the law enunciates moral truth, this remains as true under grace as before. (C. H. Welch, 1948)[7]

Paul explained this carefully in Romans 13:8–10.

> Owe no man anything, but to love one another: for he that loveth another hath fulfilled the law. For this, **Thou shalt not commit adultery, Thou shalt not kill, Thou shalt not steal, Thou shalt not bear false witness, Thou shalt not covet;** and if there be any other commandment, it is briefly comprehended in this saying, namely, **Thou shalt love thy neighbour as**

thyself. Love worketh no ill to his neighbour: therefore love is the fulfilling of the law.

Plagiarism

If someone doesn't think the Ten Commandments are inspired or literal, it's easy to defy or ignore them. Someone considered a great Christian leader should not. The eighth commandment, "Thou shalt not steal" (Exodus 20:15) applies to every aspect of our lives, including the literary. *The Martin Luther King, Jr., Plagiarism Story* by Theodore Pappas details the plagiarism that began while King was an undergraduate student at Morehouse and continued at Crozer and on through to his doctoral dissertation at Boston University.

This literary theft has been attributed by some to merely sloppy work on the part of King, such as not putting in quotation marks or not citing references he may have quoted. Others attribute the misrepresentations as the fault of overworked professors who permitted laxity in written work. Yet others see this as the blatant promotional efforts of liberal white professors and the beginning of the controlled media era.

Clayborne Carson and his associates at the Martin Luther King, Jr. Center for Nonviolent Social Change have edited the first five volumes of King's papers and documents. They anticipate releasing a new volume every other year.

These documents are a compilation of speeches, sermons, and schoolwork. They follow King's theological and intellectual development through the years. The Center for Nonviolent Social Change has documented in great detail King's flagrant plagiarism, mentioning specifically from whom he plagiarized. This must be quite embarrassing to them, but at least this aspect is now admitted, whereas for many years, King's plagiarism was denied. This attempt at truthfulness should be respected.

Boston University admitted that King's dissertation had been plagiarized. Suggestions to revoke his doctorate met opposition by the university. Their point of view was that revocation "would serve no useful purpose" according to the *New York Times* of October 11, 1991.

The sad fact remains that King had not learned the proper methods of research or chose to ignore them. Equally distressing, had he gone to a conservative or Bible-believing college or university or a university that held to conventional dissertation standards, neither of the above would have been allowed to occur.

Social Involvement

As pastor of the Dexter Avenue Baptist Church in Montgomery, Alabama, King was in a position to influence his people in nonviolent resistance to combat the social problems associated with segregation. The Montgomery Improvement Association, founded by the black community, chose King to lead them in the 1955 boycott of the segregated city buses. For a year, black people in Montgomery found other ways to get to work. Not only the transit system but also shops and restaurant suffered a decrease in business. More important, the yearlong effort undoubtedly led to the 1956 Supreme Court decision that forced desegregation of the buses.

However, that boycott would not have occurred had it not been for the courage of Rosa Parks, who refused to give up her seat on the bus to a white man. Perhaps it would be more fitting to celebrate December 1 as Rosa Parks Day, even though, sadly, Rosa Parks was a participant in the Highlander Folk School in Monteagle, Tennessee, a known Communist training ground.

Funding by the Communist Party

Desperation may tempt the unscrupulous to use any means to justify reaching their goals. For financial backing, King turned to the Communist Party, which funded many of his activities. The Communist Party exists for the sole purpose of undermining the sovereignty of the

United States and other sovereign nations not under Communist rule. It is not a political party in the same sense as are the Democratic, Republican, or Constitution parties.

In 1957, King attended and taught at the Highlander Folk School in Monteagle, Tennessee. While there, he was photographed with Carl and Anne Braden as well as other well-known Communists. The Highlander Folk School later forcibly closed because of its Marxist, subversive activities and was taken over by the Southern Christian Leadership Conference, which in turn elected King as its president. It has been conjectured by some in authority that only the name changed.

Another well-known member of the National Committee of the Communist Party, Hunter Pitts O'Dell, was hired by the SCLC staff in 1960. When the public learned of O'Dell's Communist Party affiliation, King fired him, but he quickly and quietly rehired him and promoted him to a higher post in the SCLC as director of the New York office. Stanley Levinson, yet another Communist Party member, financed King's activities for twelve years and was highly praised by King's widow in her memoirs.

David Garrow, in his 1981 biography of King, *The FBI and Martin Luther King, Jr.*, wrote that privately King described himself as a Marxist.

During the Vietnam War, it was not the United States that earned King's praise but Vietnam. Communist publications gleefully quoted his description of the United States as the world's "greatest purveyor of violence." Yet King's "nonviolent marches" usually left black neighborhoods in shambles with much destroyed property among those who could least afford it.

Sacrosanct or Sanctimonious Sinner?

President John Kennedy and Attorney General Robert Kennedy were aware of King's subversive activities. To determine the extent of King's involvement with known Communists, Attorney General Kennedy ordered FBI surveillance and telephone wiretaps. Many of these wiretaps captured King on record with known Communists and with various women in sexual encounters. Generally speaking, a person's sex life should be his or her own business. However, one who professes to be a Christian clergyman should be aware that his private life could also be under scrutiny, surveillance tapes or not. Yes, women sought him as well as he sought them, but that didn't change the seventh commandment, "Thou shalt not commit adultery" (Exodus 20:14). To the serious believer, God says,

> But fornication, and all uncleanness, or covetousness, let it not be once named among you as becometh saints; neither filthiness, nor foolish talking, nor jesting, which are not convenient; but rather giving of thanks. (Ephesians 5:3–4)

Historian David Garrow summarizes a forty-eight-hour FBI surveillance tape of King as being filled with obscene jokes, sacrilegious jokes, and insulting sexual remarks about Jacqueline Kennedy and the recently assassinated President Kennedy.

A January 31, 1977 court order by Judge John Lewis Smith Jr. of the District Court for the District of Columbia ordered that all recordings, transcripts of recordings, or descriptions of recordings made under FBI surveillance be removed from FBI jurisdiction and placed in the National Archives. These will remain sealed until the year 2027.

Because of the Freedom of Information Act, some of the 17,000 pages of the FBI collection have been released. Much cannot be given to the public to protect confidential sources, sensitive information, and as-yet living persons.

Sen. Jesse Helms filed suit in federal court in October 1983 to have these tapes released before the vote was taken on the King holiday, but Judge John Lewis Smith Jr. denied access to the sealed records.

The Holiday

Unfortunately, the media created the image it wanted of the man; that image bore little resemblance to the facts. President Ronald Reagan knew the facts, but because of public perception of the image, went along with Congress. On November 2, 1983, he signed the bill creating the national holiday, observed on the third Monday of January, on or near King's January 15 birthday.

J. A. Parker of the black, conservative, Lincoln Institute in Washington, DC, also knew of King's personal weaknesses and Marxist persuasion. He stated in October 1988, "The King holiday is an insult to all Americans—black or white."

Revere or Repudiate?

Judging by the evidence, was King a patriotic Christian who should be emulated? Does an adulterer-plagiarist deserve to be revered by innocent schoolchildren? Do teachers in the United States want the children of the nation to emulate him by copying their schoolwork from classmates?

Many believe King's accomplishments outweigh his reprehensible indiscretions. And who could possibly take issue with King's "I Have a Dream" speech, especially these lines: "I have a dream that my four little children will one day live in a nation where they will not be judged by the color of their skin but by the content of their character"?

Character? Yes indeed! There are many fine, deserving black men and women who deserve much more to be recognized for their character-filled efforts at liberty and justice for all. Let's find these heroes in our churches and civic organizations and give them our praise, admiration, and help.

George Washington and Abraham Lincoln, two of our greatest presidents, share a common Presidents' Day, at least according to public opinion. Should a proven plagiarist and sexual degenerate have his own holiday?

Some Scriptures are timeless and ring true through all dispensations of believers. "Woe unto them that call evil good, and good evil; that put darkness for light, and light for darkness; that put bitter for sweet, and sweet for bitter" (Isaiah 5:20). Woe.

CHAPTER 5

Inauguration Day

Inauguration Day is a secular celebration observed every four years after the presidential elections. The day is a federal holiday but only for federal employees in the District of Columbia and selected counties or cities in Virginia and Maryland. To relieve traffic congestion for this major ten-day event surrounding the day, selected locations might be Montgomery or Prince George's Counties in Maryland, Arlington, or Fairfax Counties in Virginia, and the cities of Fairfax and Alexandria in Virginia.

History of Inauguration Day

George Washington took his first inaugural oath April 20, 1789. For many years thereafter, Inauguration Day was held on March 4. The ratification of the Twentieth Amendment (also known as the Lame Duck Amendment) to the Constitution moved the date to January 20. This earlier day lessened the time lapse between election day and the beginning of the new presidential term.

According to the Twentieth Amendment, the president and vice president's term begin at noon on January 20. This amendment, ratified on January 23, 1933, didn't affect the 1933 inaugural because of Section V, which specifically states that Sections I and II wouldn't take effect until

October 15 following ratification. The first president to be affected by the new date, Franklin D. Roosevelt, took the oath of office on January 20, 1937.

This day of pomp and splendor befitting royalty follows a precise agenda historically beginning with worship services and ending with a grand inaugural ball.

Worship Services

Even though this holiday is nonreligious, all presidents beginning with George Washington have begun the day with worship or prayer services. This is certainly fitting since documents of our founding, including the Declaration of Independence, the Constitution, and the Bill of Rights are based on principles drawn from the Bible.

Those men chosen to govern by citizens' votes and allowed to reign by the grace of God should take heed: "For there is no power but of God: the powers that be are ordained of God" (Romans 13:1). And as was true of ancient Israel, so should we hold our rulers to a higher standard: "He that ruleth over men must be just, ruling in the fear of God" (2 Samuel 23:3).

George Washington attended worship services at St. Paul's Chapel in New York in 1789 after his swearing-in ceremony. Other presidents have generally attended services before taking their oaths. The current tradition was begun by Franklin D. Roosevelt, who, with his wife, Eleanor, attended services at St. John's Episcopal Church in Washington, DC, prior to the swearing in at three of his inaugurations: 1933, 1937, and 1941. At his fourth inauguration in 1945, President Roosevelt attended private services at the White House. All presidents after Franklin Roosevelt except one have followed this pattern of attending public services or private prayer services on Inauguration Day.

Our forty-fourth president, Barack Obama, with wife Michelle, and Vice President Joseph Biden, with his wife, Jill, attended the Washington National Cathedral for a national day of prayer the day after the inauguration.

The interfaith worship service consisted of Protestant pastors, rabbis, and Catholic bishops as well as Hindu and Muslim leaders. Dr. Sharon E. Watkins, president of the Christian Church (Disciples of Christ) became the first woman to deliver an inaugural sermon. Her sermon integrated religious passages from all faiths represented.

March to the Capitol

After the morning worship services, the Joint Congressional Committee on Inaugural Ceremonies escorts the president-elect and the outgoing president to the Capitol, where the oath is administered. They are followed by the vice president–elect, the vice president, their wives, and other family members and members of the cabinet.

Breaking with the tradition of riding in a carriage or an automobile, Thomas Jefferson and Andrew Jackson walked to their swearing in. Outgoing president James Monroe's carriage followed president-elect John Quincy Adams's carriage in 1825. President-elect William Henry Harrison proudly rode his distinctive, white horse to his ceremony in 1841. In 1845, President John Tyler and president-elect James Polk rode together. Thus was resumed and established the tradition of the outgoing and the incoming president riding together, which had begun with Van Buren and Jackson in 1837.

Over the years, small changes have altered the routine. Members of the Senate Committee on Arrangements for the Inauguration began escorting the president and president-elect at James Buchanan's 1857 inauguration.

Abraham Lincoln's second inauguration in 1865 was significantly different for two reasons. Lincoln's inaugural march proceeded without him, for he was already at the Capitol signing last-minute bills into law, and African-Americans marched in the inaugural parade for the first time.

President Andrew Johnson and President-elect Ulysses S. Grant had strong political disagreements regarding the South's treatment following the War between the States. As a result, in 1869, on Grant's inaugural day, Andrew Johnson stayed at the White House signing legislation until noon, as his term expired. He didn't join the president-elect's procession to the Capitol, nor did he attend President-elect Grant's swearing-in ceremony.

In 1877, President-elect Rutherford B. Hayes went to the White House to meet the outgoing president before going to the Capitol for the ceremonies. They rode together to the Capitol. The vice president–elect and the outgoing vice president followed, riding together in a separate carriage. This set a precedent that has been followed since with few exceptions.

The first first lady to accompany her husband in the carriage procession to the Capitol was Edith Galt Wilson in 1917. Times were changing, and women in general were experiencing a bit more freedom. Mrs. Wilson witnessed many changes in society during her lifetime, including the progression from carriage to automobile. She lived to ride in John F. Kennedy's inaugural parade in 1961 and died on December 28 that year.

Warren G. Harding was the first to ride to his inauguration in an automobile in 1921.

After Lyndon Johnson completed the term of assassinated President Kennedy, he won the next presidential election. For security reasons, he rode to the Capitol in a closed, bulletproof limousine in 1965.

Swearing In of the Vice President

The current vice president delivers his farewell speech before the new vice president takes his oath of office. To keep within the adjournment before noon requirement, in past days, the timekeeper would push the clock hands back! Since 1981, these inaugural ceremonies have been held on the west front terrace of the Capitol.

The Constitution doesn't specify what form this oath must take; it specifies only that he must swear to uphold the Constitution. Since 1884, the vice president, senators, representatives, and other officials take this oath.

I do solemnly swear (or affirm) that I will support and defend the Constitution of the United States against all enemies, foreign and domestic; that I will bear true faith and allegiance to the same; that I take this obligation freely, without any mental reservation or purpose of evasion; and that I will well and faithfully discharge the duties of the office on which I am about to enter: So help me God.

The Constitution doesn't specify who must administer the oath, and it has been done by various government officials. Following World War II, most vice presidents have asked governmental associates or friends to perform this duty. Following the swearing-in ceremony, the new vice president delivers an inaugural address.

After his speech, the new vice president calls the Senate into a special session and administers the oath of office to senators-elect. They proceed to the west front portico of the Capitol for the president's swearing-in ceremony.

Swearing In of the President

The Constitution provides clear instructions for qualifications of the president. At the time of the Constitutional Convention in 1787, it was stated that the candidate must have lived in this country for fourteen years. He must be a native-born citizen of the United States and be at least thirty-five.

According to the Constitution, Article II, Section 1, the new president must swear or affirm this oath.

I do solemnly swear (or affirm) that I will faithfully execute the office of President of the United States, and will to the best of my ability, preserve, protect and defend the Constitution of the United States.

After a slight glitch in the wording of the swearing in of President Obama on January 20, 2009, Chief Justice John Roberts re-administered the oath of office in the evening on January 21 at the White House. The second swearing-in ceremony took place due to concerns regarding the legality of the first oath with its mixed-up wording.

Locations for the swearing-in ceremonies have changed several times since Washington's first oath in 1789 in New York on a balcony overlooking Wall Street. He took his second oath in Philadelphia at Congress Hall, near Independence Hall. Congress was meeting temporarily in Philadelphia because the permanent capital was being built along the Potomac.

By March 1801, the new Capitol (one wing of it) in Washington was completed. Thomas Jefferson holds the distinction of being the first president to be inaugurated there in the Senate chamber. Chief Justice John Marshall administered his oath of office. After delivering his inaugural address, Jefferson ate at a nearby boarding house.

The Capitol's east front served as the location for the inaugurations of presidents from Martin Van Buren in 1837 to Theodore Roosevelt in 1905. William Howard Taft's 1909 ceremony moved indoors to the Senate chamber because of a blizzard.[8]

But it was back to the east front for Woodrow Wilson's 1913 inauguration. The ceremony remained there through the three inaugurations of Franklin Roosevelt. His fourth inauguration moved to the south portico of the White House.

Harry Truman's inauguration returned to the east front of the Capitol. Subsequent inaugurations remained there through Jimmy Carter's 1977 ceremony.

For Ronald Reagan's 1981 inauguration, Congress shifted locations to the west front of the Capitol. Among reasons given included improved visibility for more spectators. Extremely cold weather forced Reagan's second inaugural inside to the Capitol Rotunda. From the first George Bush in 1989 to George W. Bush in 2005, the west front tradition has continued.

Eight vice presidents have been pressed into service by the death of a president and one by a presidential resignation. Therefore, vice presidents have taken oaths of office in unhappy and tragic emergency situations in what would seem unlikely places.

Upon the death of William Henry Harrison, John Tyler left Williamsburg, Virginia, for Washington and took the oath of office at the Indian Queen Hotel on April 6, 1841. Chief Justice William Cranch of the Circuit Court of the District of Columbia administered the oath.

Following the death of Zachary Taylor, Millard Fillmore on July 10, 1850 was sworn in in the chamber of the House of Representatives. Chief Justice Cranch again administered the oath.

Following Abraham Lincoln's death on April 15, 1865, Chief Justice Salmon P. Chase administered the oath of office to Andrew Johnson at Kirkwood House in Washington.

On July 2, 1881, President Garfield was shot at a Washington, DC railroad station. He died on September 19, having served less than five months of his term. Chester A. Arthur took the oath at his home in New York on September 20. He later repeated the oath in the presence of ex-presidents Grant and Hayes in the Capitol.

Theodore Roosevelt took the oath in the home of Ansley Wilcox in Buffalo, New York, after William McKinley was assassinated in Buffalo on September 14, 1901.

Warren G. Harding died of a stroke while visiting San Francisco on August 2, 1923. Calvin Coolidge took the oath early the next morning at his family's home by kerosene lamp. His father, Colonel John Calvin Coolidge, a farmer, notary public, and justice of the peace, administered the oath. Coolidge repeated the oath at the Willard Hotel in Washington on August 21.

On the evening of April 12, 1945, Vice President Harry Truman took the presidential oath in the Cabinet Room of the White House following President Franklin Roosevelt's death.

Lyndon Johnson was sworn in on Air Force One at Love Field in Dallas, after John F. Kennedy was assassinated on November 22, 1963. Judge Sarah T. Hughes administered the oath, becoming the first woman to swear in a president.

Vice President Gerald Ford became the ninth vice president to complete an unexpired presidential term when Richard Nixon resigned on August 9, 1974. The East Room of the White House was the setting for his swearing-in ceremony.

Our elected representatives and all citizens should take these oaths seriously. For as Patrick Henry said, "The Constitution is not an instrument for the government to restrain the people, it is an instrument for the people to restrain government—lest it come to dominate our lives and interests."

Inaugural Addresses

It is most enlightening to read our presidents' inaugural addresses. If one had no other historical documents to read, it would still be possible to detect changes in the moral attitudes of our society from the beginning of our nation to today. As we read these documents, we become aware of the obvious changes in what was once and what now is considered acceptable moral behavior. Of course, differences in elocution have evolved from the formal, eloquent speeches of George Washington and John Adams to the informal, conversational styles of Bill Clinton and George W. Bush.

Each president in his inaugural address voiced concerns over the state of the nation and usually optimistically presented grand designs or themes for his coming administration. With few exceptions, most acknowledged God's working and blessings on our republic.

It is not feasible to adequately summarize each of these addresses in our limited space; instead, I will offer some noncomprehensive excerpts of a few selected addresses. These excerpts are taken from documents from the University of Oklahoma School of Law available at www.law. ou.edu/ushistory.

In the first hundred years of our history, presidents assumed that listeners understood that our nation was built on Christian principles and that God was the source of the brilliance and motivation of the founding fathers. However, through the years, certain changes in attitude lean away from recognizing a greater Providence in our daily affairs and from our Constitution and its focus on national sovereignty.

Latter presidents have assumed an "I'll do as I please" attitude of putting international interests above the wishes of their own constituency but with a prayer amounting to "God bless us anyway."

1789, George Washington marveled at the steps toward independence, noting, "Every step ... seems to have been distinguished by some token of Providential agency." He observed, "Propitious smiles of Heaven can never be expected on a nation that disregards the eternal rules of order and right which Heaven itself has ordained." Not the least of his concerns were how the people would handle the republican model of government, "the experiment entrusted to the hands of the American people." He closed his first inaugural address appealing to the

> benign Parent of the Human Race in supplication that since He has been pleased to favor the American people with opportunities for deliberating in perfect tranquility, and dispositions for deciding with unparalleled unanimity on a form of government for the security of their union and the advancement of their happiness, so His divine blessing may be equally conspicuous in the enlarged views, the temperate consultations and the wise measures on which the success of this Government must depend.

For the first fifty years of our young republic, newly elected presidents traveled over muddy or bumpy dirt roads to get to their ceremony, but by 1841, travel was becoming easier. William H. Harrison arrived in Washington by railroad, the first to ride the train to his inauguration. He delivered the longest speech of any new president—8,455 words. He expressed "a profound reverence for the Christian religion and a thorough conviction that sound morals, religious liberty, and a just sense of religious responsibility are essentially connected with all true and lasting happiness."

James K. Polk's 1845 inauguration was covered by the year-old telegraph. Samuel Morse telegraphed events to Baltimore; from there, the news sped to Europe, making it possible for readers of the *London*

News to read articles regarding the latest inauguration. Polk decried debt and wished for every state as well as the federal government to be completely debt free.

> I fervently invoke the aide of that Almighty Ruler of the Universe in whose hands are the destinies of nations and of men to guard this Heaven-favored land against the mischiefs which without His guidance might arise from an unwise public policy.

Polk's inauguration is thought to have been the first photographed. James Buchanan's election amid impassioned debates on slavery undoubtedly instilled in him the gravity of the state of the nation. His position in 1857 was,

> Congress is neither to "legislate slavery into any Territory or State nor to exclude it therefrom, but to leave the people thereof perfectly free to form and regulate their domestic institutions in their own way, subject only to the Constitution of the United States."

He too invoked

> the God of our fathers for wisdom and firmness to execute its high and responsible duties in such a manner as to restore harmony and ancient friendship among the people of the several States and to preserve our free institutions throughout many generations.

Distressed by the national confusion brought on by the secession of the South and the installation of Jefferson Davis as president of the Confederacy two weeks earlier, Abraham Lincoln's first inaugural speech in 1861 vowed the "laws of the Union be faithfully executed in all the states." In his mind, the states remained under the Constitution and could not lawfully leave the Union. "In doing this there needs to be no bloodshed or violence, and there shall be none unless it be forced upon the national authority." Unfortunately, we all know the history of the pain and heartache caused by the War between the States in which brother fought against brother and the rivers ran red with blood.

> If the Almighty Ruler of Nations with his eternal truth and justice, be on your side of the North, or on yours of the South, that truth and that justice will surely prevail by the judgment of this great tribunal of the American people.

The nation survived the horrors of that war and its equally horrifying Reconstruction that followed. From the Civil War through the Spanish American War, enterprising Americans invented the commercial typewriter (1867), the telephone (1876), the cash register (1879), and a myriad of other new items.

President McKinley's inauguration in 1897 was captured on Thomas Edison's new motion picture camera, and his speech was recorded on Edison's gramophone. McKinley's prime concerns were maintaining a safe balance in the treasury, parity between our gold and silver money, and easing life for those who had been hardest hit by the lingering four-year depression that affected farmers, miners, and factory workers. He also had a few words to say on the immigration situation of his day.

> A grave peril to the Republic would be a citizenship too ignorant to understand or too vicious to appreciate the great value and beneficence of our institutions and laws, and against all who come here to make war upon them our gates must be promptly and tightly closed.

McKinley rejoiced that the North and South no longer divided along the old lines but differed upon principles and policies. He pledged to cheerfully do everything possible to promote and increase the growing sentiment of unity and harmony.

At the end of his address, McKinley repeated the oath of office he had previously taken and added,

> This is the obligation I have reverently taken before the Lord Most High. To keep it will be my single purpose, my constant prayer, and I shall confidently rely upon the forbearance and assistance of all the people in the discharge of my solemn responsibilities.

Taxes were on Calvin Coolidge's mind in 1925. With World War I behind them, he admonished the people to avoid extravagance and to rescind wartime taxes. "The collection of any taxes which are not absolutely required, which do not beyond reasonable doubt contribute to the public welfare, is only a species of legalized larceny." He urged tax reform "unless we wish to hamper the people in their right to earn a living." Coolidge's final inaugural thoughts urged

> developing waterways and natural resources, [being] attentive to the intuitive counsel of womanhood, encouraging education, desiring the advancement of religion, supporting the cause of justice and honor among the nations.

> The higher state to which she [America] seeks the allegiance of all mankind is not of human, but of Divine origin. She cherishes no purpose save to merit the favor of Almighty God.

Coolidge's address reached the entire nation via radio broadcast, a first for any president.

Harry S. Truman had completed Franklin D. Roosevelt's term of office (1945–49) and had won the 1948 election. He took his oath on his personal Bible and a Gutenberg Bible, the gift of Missouri constituents. World War II had ended, but unrest and Communist agitation in Korea found Americans again facing an unsettled world and an uncertain future. Another war seemed almost certain, (indeed, the Korean War began in 1950).

Truman's speech expressed desire for a just and lasting peace. His hopes rested in the recently formed United Nations (1948). Four courses of action outlined his plan for peace and freedom for all people. First, he pledged unfaltering support for the UN. Second, he urged the continuation of programs for world economic recovery. Third, the North Atlantic Treaty Organization must strengthen free nations against aggression. Fourth, our scientific and industrial progress must be available to underdeveloped countries.

Truman realized that national security was at stake, but international security took a high priority in his speech. Our nation is not referred to as a republic (which it is) but as a democracy (which it is not). Many examples of the contrast between communism and democracy abound in the speech. Nevertheless, Truman petitioned God for help and support.

> Steadfast in our faith in the Almighty, we will advance toward a world where man's freedom is secure. To that end, we will devote our strength, our resources, and our firmness of resolve. With God's help, the future of mankind will be assured in a world of justice, harmony, and peace.

Truman's speech, broadcast over radio, was the first inaugural that was televised.

William Jefferson (Bill) Clinton's 1993 inaugural speech recognized the vast changes from the beginning of our republic.

> When George Washington first took the oath I have just sworn to uphold, news traveled slowly across the land by horseback and across the ocean by boat. Now the sights and sounds of this ceremony are broadcast instantaneously to billions around the world.[9]

That the economy was global was recognized as a given.

> To renew America, we must meet challenges abroad as
> well as at home. There is no longer division between
> what is foreign and what is domestic—the world
> economy, the world environment, the world AIDS
> crisis, the world arms race—they affect us all.

Deterioration was recognized whether intended or not in the above
quote and in "Let us give the capital back to the people to whom it
belongs." This certainly is in reference to high crime in the capital city
area.

> I challenge a new generation of Americans to a season
> of service—to act on your idealism by helping troubled
> children, keeping company with those in need,
> reconnecting our torn communities. There is much to
> be done—enough indeed for millions of others who are
> still young in spirit to give of themselves in service, too.

Clinton's final sentences challenge to faith, discipline, and work.
"The scripture says, 'And let us not be weary in well-doing, for in due
season, we shall reap, if we faint not.'"

George W. Bush's first inaugural address acknowledges the
American story as one "of flawed and fallible people, united across the
generations by grand and enduring ideals." He pledged to

> reform Social Security and Medicare, sparing our
> children from struggles we have the power to prevent.
> And we will reduce taxes, to recover the momentum of
> our economy and reward the effort and enterprise of
> working Americans.

> Americans are generous and strong and decent, not
> because we believe in ourselves, but because we hold

beliefs beyond ourselves. When this spirit of citizenship is missing, no government program can replace it. When this spirit is present, no wrong can stand against it.[9]

Almost without exception, the inaugural speeches acknowledged God and his bounteous blessings. Most presidents invoked God's aid to perform their duties well.

Only the Lord knows whether these words were sincere at the moment or religiously correct to satisfy a primarily Christian population. But does it matter? Public thankfulness and acknowledgement to God can't be wrong.

President Obama's inaugural speech sounded the call for individual and governmental "responsibility." Reiterations throughout called for honesty and courage while stressing legacy and heritage.[10]

Congress Hosts Inaugural Luncheons

From the mid-1800s to the early 1900s, after a new president had taken his oath of office and delivered his inaugural address, he went to the White House for a luncheon prepared by the outgoing president and first lady. After the luncheon, they viewed the inaugural parade from a special stand erected in front of the White House.

Over time, the parade became longer and lasted later. In an effort to hurry things along, organizers suggested the president go directly to the Capitol and eat there if he wished.

In 1897 and 1901, the president and his party dined as guests of the Senate Committee on Arrangements in the Capitol. In 1905, the luncheon returned to the White House in an effort to get the parade started earlier. Organizers continued trying to shorten the luncheon but to no avail. It finally occurred to organizers to shorten the parade rather than the luncheon.

In 1945, President and Mrs. Roosevelt entertained over two thousand guests in the last White House post-inaugural luncheon. Beginning in 1953, the Joint Congressional Committee on Inaugural Ceremonies began today's tradition by hosting a luncheon for President and Mrs. Dwight D. Eisenhower, Vice President and Mrs. Richard M. Nixon, Senate leaders, other guests, and of course, the Joint Congressional Committee on Inaugural Ceremonies. Today, the luncheon takes place in the Capitol in Statuary Hall.

The menu generally consists of foods traditional to the new president and vice president's home states. Speeches, gifts, and toasts to the new administration conclude the luncheon, after which the president and vice president and guests view the parade.

Inaugural Parade

When George Washington began his journey from Mount Vernon to New York on April 30, 1789 for his inauguration, military groups from many towns along his route joined as he passed by. After he arrived in New York, distinguished citizens accompanied him to Federal Hall for his swearing-in ceremony. Among those were members of Congress and other governmental officials.

Another impromptu parade accompanied Thomas Jefferson in 1801. At his second inaugural in 1805, members of Congress and naval yard personnel formed a procession at the naval yard to accompany him from the newly completed Capitol to the White House after his swearing in. The Marine Band performed military music and has done so at every presidential inauguration since.

James Madison's inauguration in 1809 had the first organized parade with a Georgetown cavalry troop escorting him to the Capitol. Each future parade became more elaborate and extravagant with more clubs, bands, and college students joining. Today, schools vie for the honor to represent their respective states in the parade.

Abraham Lincoln's 1865 parade was joined by the first African-American troops, an African-American Odd Fellows lodge, and African-American Masons.

Reviewing stands have been built for presidents from James Garfield in 1881 to the present. President McKinley's viewing stand was enclosed with glass to protect him from harsh weather.

Ronald Reagan's second inaugural parade in 1985 was cancelled due to extremely frigid temperatures.

The longest parade, lasting over four and a half hours, occurred at President Eisenhower's first inauguration. Since that time, the parade has been limited to 15,000 participants. Requests and applications to participate are now received by the Joint Task Force Armed Forces Inaugural Committee.

Inaugural Ball

A week after Washington's inauguration, on May 7, 1789, his friends held a ball in his honor. Today's tradition began with Dolly Madison in 1809. She sold four hundred tickets for a ball held at Long's Hotel in honor of President Madison.

Andrew Jackson attended two balls in his honor in 1833, and William Henry Harrison attended three in 1841.

By 1858, it was decided to have one grand ball rather than several smaller ones. In the early years, temporary wooden buildings were built for the occasion. Most proved unsatisfactory with various muddles recorded. The most disastrous snafu seems to have been President Grant's 1873 second ball. In an unheated building, guests danced in their overcoats and hats, food was cold, hot chocolate and coffee were not hot, and caged canaries froze to death.

From 1885 through 1909, inaugural balls were held at what is now the Smithsonian Arts and Industries building and the Pension Building.

In 1853, Franklin Pierce asked that the ball be cancelled as he was mourning the death of his son. But from 1885 to 1913, the inaugural ball continued as expected. In 1913, President Wilson objected to a ball, stating that it was too expensive and not in keeping with the solemn occasion of the inauguration.

President Harding hoped to set an example of thrift in his administration. He too requested no inaugural ball. The committee chairman complied but held an elaborate private party at his home instead.

In recent decades, President Truman revived the official ball in 1949. These have grown in number through the years. President Eisenhower's second inauguration in 1957 featured four, President Kennedy attended five in 1961, George H. Bush's inauguration saw a total of eleven, and President Clinton's fourteen.

George W. Bush's inaugural ball agenda listed nine balls. A new addition, the Commander in Chief Ball, was free of charge to 2,000 members of the armed services and their families who had recently returned from Iraq and Afghanistan or who would soon be deployed there. The budget for the week's festivities was $40 million, excluding security costs.

After his first inauguration, President and Michelle Obama attended ten inaugural balls on the evening of January 20, 2009. For his second-term festivities on January 21, 2013, President Obama had downsized the number of official balls from ten to two.

Inaugural Budget

It is estimated that $170 million was spent on the 2009 inauguration. Of that amount, the federal government spent $49 million. Maryland and Virginia's combined expenses exceeded $75 million. Most of that, of course, went for law enforcement, mass transit, and emergency medical services.

The historical significance of inaugurating America's first African-American president made the event unparalleled in Washington, DC, with record-breaking numbers attending. Approximately 8,000 police officers from around the United States assisted DC police. One thousand FBI agents provided additional security, and a Secret Service countersniper team operated from hidden locations. Five thousand National Guard troops also provided security, some as unarmed troops helping park police with crowd control at the National Mall. No doubt, this was the most expensive and complex inaugural in our history.

Our Higher Power

Members of the body of Christ would do well to reread Romans 13 from time to time. We in the United States are blessed that we do not live under a king or any group of men. Our supreme law is the constitution, to which all presidents profess allegiance. Conservative pastor and political commentator Chuck Baldwin observed,

> This means that in America the "higher powers" are not the men who occupy elected office, they are the tenets and principles set forth in the U.S. Constitution. Under our laws and form of government, it is the duty of every citizen, including our elected officials to obey the U.S. Constitution. Therefore, this is how Romans Chapter 13 reads to Americans:
>
> Let every soul be subject unto the [U.S. Constitution.] For there is no [Constitution] but of God: the [Constitution] that be [is] ordained of God. Whoesoever therefore resisteth the [Constitution], resisteth the ordinance of God: and they that resist shall receive to themselves damnation. For [the Constitution] is not a terror to good works, but to the evil. Wilt thou then not be afraid of the [Constitution]? do that which is good, and thou shalt have praise of the same: For [the Constitution] is the minister of God to thee for good. But if thou do that which is evil, be afraid; for [the Constitution] beareth not the sword in vain: for [the Constitution] is the minister of God, a revenger to execute wrath upon him that doeth evil. Wherefore ye must needs be subject, not only for wrath, but also for conscience sake. For this cause pay ye tribute also: for [the Constitution

is] God's minister, attending continually upon this very thing. Render therefore to all their dues; tribute to whom tribute is due; custom to whom custom; fear to whom fear; honor to whom honor.[11]

Never in world history have there been such magnificent man-made documents as the Declaration of Independence, the Constitution, and the Bill of Rights giving the common person so much personal freedom. Even though Inauguration Day is not a holy day in the scriptural sense, we should give testimony to God for the tenets and principles embedded in those historical documents.

CHAPTER 6

Valentine's Day

Valentine's Day is not an official holiday; that is, banks, post offices, and other businesses don't close for the day. But in terms of commerce, it's one of the big moneymakers of the year.

Where the Money Goes in February

Statistics from the U.S. Census Bureau inform us that in February, jewelry stores in the Unites States sell around $2.4 billion worth of merchandise.

Florists deliver approximately 110 million roses—the majority of them red—within a three-day time span around February 14. Most customers request one single red rose surrounded by baby's breath as their preferred arrangement. Beside the $350 million spent for gifts and flowers, consumers spend yet another $45 million on food and chocolate.

Valentine's Day ranks second largest in terms of seasonal card-sending, following Christmas. All ages honor those they love by sending or receiving cards. Teachers get the most valentines, followed by children, mothers, wives, and sweethearts. Altogether, around one billion cards are given every Valentine's Day.

Undoubtedly, retailers like February 14, and those who are remembered affectionately feel loved and flattered. But how did this holiday originate?

Legends Surrounding the Name

Stories are told about the origins of the day's name. Three martyrs, each named Valentine, who lived during the third through fifth centuries, are credited with the name. One legend has it that the Roman emperor, Claudius II, forbad his young soldiers to marry because he believed that single men made better warriors and also because married men were refusing to go to war, preferring instead to stay home with their wives. A priest named Valentine secretly married couples against the emperor's wishes. When Valentine's activities were discovered, the emperor ordered him put to death.

A second story tells of an early Christian named Valentine who befriended children. Because he refused to worship Roman gods, he was imprisoned. During his imprisonment, children he had befriended tossed notes through the bars to his jail cell to encourage him.

Yet another legend says that a Roman presbyter named Valentine defended the martyrs during the persecution of Claudius II. Valentine was so hated that he was arrested, beaten with clubs, and beheaded on February 14, 270.

The New Schaff-Herzog Encyclopedia names four Valentine martyrs: Valentine, Bishop of Spoleto, and Valentine, Bishop of Terni, who could be the same person; an African Valentine about whom nothing is known; and Valentine, Bishop of Raetia, whose remains were transferred to Passau in AD 768.[12]

One of these Valentines is credited with writing a note to his jailer's daughter before his execution and signing the note, "From your Valentine." But which one?

The legends of the Valentines are at least fifteen hundred years old, so it would be extremely difficult to find the exact truth about the Valentine from which our day received its name. We know a Valentine became the patron saint of lovers in the Catholic Church. As such, he became the religious supervisor of an annual Roman festival. The ecclesiastical reasoning behind Valentine's canonization have not been divulged to us, but it is evident that the motive was an attempt at extinguishing the moral corruption of a particular profane feast, the Lupercalia (pronounced loo puhr *kay* lee uh).

Lupercalia

If you recall our section on mixed-up calendars, you will remember that February 14, the day of Lupercalia in the third century, would correspond to our spring or mid-March. In many ancient civilizations, as in Rome, springtime and fertility rites were synonymous. Thus, the primary purpose of the Lupercalia festival was to ensure fertility of the people, fields, and flocks. The people invoked the blessings of at least three gods of the Roman pantheon: Faunus, god of fertility and forests; Lupercus, god of flocks; and Februata Juno, goddess of light, birth, and marriage.

The feast itself took its name from the Lupercal, a cave in the Palatine Hill, one of the seven hills on which Rome was built. The Latin word for "wolf" is *lupus*; therefore, the god Lupercus protected the flock against wolves.

Lupercalia also served as a feast of purification. Why did people of so many cultures need to have purification rites? Could it be that deep within their hearts they sensed the truth of the verse, "For all have sinned and come short of the glory of God" (Romans 3:23)?

At the Lupercalia, a corporation of priests called Luperci presided over the rites. These began with sacrificing two male goats and a dog. Next, two Luperci smeared blood from the butcher's knife on their foreheads. They used wool dipped in milk to wipe the blood away. At that point in the celebration, custom required the Luperci to laugh before the eating could begin. After the meal, whips from skins of animals were carried as two groups of men known as *creppi,* male goats, ran around the outside of the city walls. These men wore only goatskin girdles made from sacrificed animals.

Any women who wanted children would stand where they could be struck by the whips as the men ran past. This act of *februare,* being struck with purification instruments, was supposed to cure infertility as well as avert bad luck. This magic flagellation kept good influences inside the city wall and bad luck out. Romans dedicated much of the month to purification ceremonies, hence the name, February.

Another custom of the Lupercalia we might term the "lovers' lottery." Names of eligible young women of Rome went into a box. Each young man drew a young woman's name, offered her a gift, and they were sexual companions for the duration of the feast or as long thereafter as they chose to be, perhaps a year or longer.

Immoral sexual practices certainly had no place in any form of Christianity. Therefore, Pope Gelasius in AD 494 changed the celebration of the Lupercalia to the Feast of the Purification of the Virgin Mary. The populace switched from honoring three gods in the pagan pantheon to giving worship to Mary.

In AD 494, Valentine was canonized and his name given to February 14. To abolish the custom of the lovers' lottery, many priests substituted saints' names for the names of women on the notes placed in the lottery boxes. The one who drew a name from the saints' box would attempt for a year to imitate the good deeds of his selected saint. Valentine's name appeared as one to be emulated on many of the notes. The saints' lottery lasted for a couple hundred years and died out, but gradually, the Lupercalia's influence diminished while Valentine's increased.

Medieval Customs

In 1415, the French duke of Orleans was captured during the Battle of Agincourt. From the Tower of London, where he was held prisoner, he sent a love note to his wife on February 14, 1416. Consequently, he was credited with writing the first "official" valentine. His love note is on display in the British Museum along with many others he wrote.

The medieval belief that birds mated on February 14 initiated the romantic custom of sending a love note to a desired mate on that day. Due to the day also being ruled as the patron saint of lovers, lovers signed their love letters "from your valentine" or "to my valentine."

Over the years, some unique superstitions accompanied the day. The first person seen after arising on the morning of Valentine's Day was the future spouse. Shakespeare alluded to this in 1603 in *Hamlet* when Ophelia speaks.

> Tomorrow is Saint Valentine's Day,
> All in the morning betime,
> And I a maid at your window,
> To be your Valentine.[13]

By the 1700s, a new superstition arose. Women wrote names of men on scraps of paper, rolled them in clay, and dropped the balls of clay in water. The first clay ball that bobbed up would be the future mate.

The festival of Valentine's Day superseded the Lupercalia by the end of the Middle Ages. Men continued to seek the affections of women by writing them special notes invoking Valentine's name.

The eligible singles' lottery was revived but probably without the sexual overtones. It had a slightly different approach. Eligible bachelors and young women drew names from a bowl. The men wore the maidens' names on their sleeves for many days, some say for a year, and vowed to attend to their needs and protect them from ungentlemanly advances from other men. An old figure of speech derives from this source. Today, if one wears his heart on his sleeve, it means he's showing too much emotional desire for someone.

Commercial Valentines

For centuries, most valentine love notes were handwritten with sketches and drawings limited only by the writers' or artists' imagination and ability, and they were also hand delivered. Most of these were very simply designed. The exceptions were those elaborately designed by Kate Greenway in the 1800s in England.

An American, Esther A. Howland, saw one of Greenway's ornately decorated cards and decided to make her own. In 1847, Howland made some samples and took orders for them. The cards proved to be an immediate success. Their popularity increased to the point that Howland soon hired a staff of women to write verses and glue on lace, flowers, hearts, and cupids. Her venture grossed over $100,000 a year for her—a lot of money for that time. Would she be shocked if she could have foreseen Hallmark producing and selling over 1,330 cards specifically for Valentine's Day!

In 1797, printers in England produced some ready-made cards complete with verses so lovers didn't have to be quite as creative or spontaneous. They could simply send "mechanical valentines" in the mail rather than hand write and deliver them.

Handmade and mechanical valentines coexisted for a time, but mechanically producing valentines brought their prices down until just about everybody could afford to send a "penny valentine." The downside of lower prices resulted in the creation of the "vinegar valentine" or the "penny dreadful." There were also insulting, possibly obscene cards that could be sent anonymously. In the late 1800s, the Chicago post office refused to send 25,000 such cards, rejecting them as being too obscene to go through the mail.

Cupid

A representation of Cupid, another god of love in Roman mythology, is on many cards today. His original image was that of a manly, athletic young warrior. Somehow, over the years, his image devolved into an effeminate, teenaged archer and then into a chubby infant with wings who shot arrows at people. To be shot in the heart with his lead-tipped arrow meant hate, but to be shot with his gold-tipped arrow meant love.

Cupid's Ancestors

Many roads led from Babylon, but not necessarily in the way we might think. Some have stated emphatically that Cupid, known in mythology as the son of Venus and Jupiter, was the son of Nimrod and Semiramis. However, God in His wisdom didn't tell us the name of Nimrod's wife, as there is no mention of her in the Bible or in the ancient Hebrew texts. It is postulated that her name was Semiramis. Based on this supposition and on the biblical fact that Nimrod was a mighty hunter, it is easy to follow the reasoning that Cupid's arrows indicate Cupid to be a warrior in training following in the footsteps of Nimrod. It is also presumed that Semiramis was Venus.

Semiramis may indeed be identical with Venus, but since Nimrod lived around 2348 BC and Semiramis reigned around 810 BC, according to one secular scholar, it might be a logical hypothesis that Semiramis could have been the wife of a descendant of Nimrod but not of Nimrod himself.[14]

Nimrod is a biblical fact, whereas Nimrod married to Semiramis is a legend. We do know that in mythology, Cupid was the Roman god of erotic love. In Greek mythology, he was Eros; his two Latin names were Eros and Amor. In ancient literature, Cupid was depicted as fickle and perverse and as one who incited erotic passions in others. He was known for his debauchery and of course shouldn't be emulated in that classical Greek role.

What of the innocent babe pictured on today's cards? He is as far from the Cupid of old as the Lupercalia is from valentine exchanges in second grade.

Valentines, Love, and Imitations

The word *love* is ambiguous though philosophers, theologians, and psychologists have attempted to define it over the centuries. Plato, Aristotle, Thomas Aquinas, and Sigmund Freud all attempted to do so but fell short.

There are many classifications for love; it can be considered as conjugal, illicit, normal, perverted, sexual, childish, adult, romantic, familial, and so on. Unfortunately, Freud didn't distinguish between any of those, but he wrote that sexual union is the aim of all love.

Fortunately for us, the Bible speaks differently. The Bible also counters many "loves" against one another, God vs. mammon, perverse vs. pure, and idols vs. God to mention a few.

We can understand love best by transliterating four Greek words, three that God used to speak of it and one from classical Greek.

Stergo: Natural Affection

This would be as a parent toward a child or a child toward a parent. This root is not used at all in the New Testament Greek, but *astorgoi*, a derivative, is used once in 2 Timothy 3:3. Paul informed Timothy that in the last days, people would be "Without natural affection, trucebreakers, false accusers, incontinent, fierce, despisers of those that are good."

Eros: Sexual Love

This word is not used in New Testament Greek, but we get our word *erotic* from it; the basic meaning is the arousal of sexual desires. A biblical example of eros is in Ezekiel 23:11 (written in Hebrew so it's not this exact word). And of course, modern examples constantly fill our television screens.

Sexual desire of itself is not wrong, but the entertainment media portrays couples having multiple lovers and indulging in immediate gratification with new acquaintances as perfectly normal. In former times, it was not considered normal, but perhaps it is normal for the last days spoken of by Paul. Normal or not, it steals the innocence of our young people, and those who imitate what they see often end up with sexually transmitted diseases the media didn't bother to tell them they could get.

Philos: Brotherly Love

This is love of friend for friend. Examples: Philadelphia, the city of brotherly love, is the Greek root for love plus the Greek root for brother. *Philanthropy*, the root word for love plus the root for man, means a desire to help humanity. The highest representation for love that secular Greek writers used was *philos*.

It is difficult to find good examples of television programming portraying this type of love. Fortunately, newspapers sometimes describe heroic measures that one person performs to save the life of another or to perform a kind deed for another because the hero reacts spontaneously in the spirit of philanthropy when the occasion warrants it. *Philos* is the word used to describe the friendship between Jesus and Lazarus in John 11:3 and John 11:36.

Agape: Unconditional Love

Christ has unconditional love for us, and we in turn have love for our fellow human because of Him. This unique love, Bible scholars inform us, is found only in New Testament Greek writings; the word is never used in secular Greek writings at all. No wonder they missed the point! If they didn't know God's love, how could they possibly define love? These words are never used synonymously or interchangeably. God is always precise in what He says. He, unlike humans, says what He means, and He means what he says.

Where to Find Love

The Bible has been said to be God's love letter to us. Probably its most quoted verse contains the words, "For God SO LOVED the world" (John 3:16).

In 1 Corinthians 13, nicknamed the love chapter, we gain insight into love, but perhaps the most gentle admonition is this simple statement: "Beloved, let us love one another" (1 John 4:7), and later in the same chapter, the results of love are described.

There is no fear in love; but perfect love casts out fear; because fear hath torment. He that fears is not made perfect in love. We love Him because he first loved us. If a man says, I love God, and hates his brother, he is a liar: for he that loves not his brother whom he hath seen, how can he love God whom he hath not seen? And this commandment have we from him, That he who loves God love his brother also (1 John 4:18-21).

This is the noblest and highest representation of love for us to emulate.

Celebrate the Day

In spite of the fact that originally there probably was no connection between St. Valentine and exchanging love notes, Valentine gets the credit.

To be sure, cleansing the moral atmosphere of Lupercalia blotted out most of the bawdy and carnal practices that were prevalent amid all the worship of false gods. Unfortunately, Lupercalia is not dead altogether. Some classified ads in large cities and on the Internet will tell you exactly where to find a Lupercalia party on the fourteenth and what you can expect to find there.

Does this mean that Christian young people can't have a valentine party or send cards to friends in school? Can a wife not send her husband a card of love and appreciation? Also, if a day was once a pagan celebration and it was a stench in His nostrils, does God wipe the day from the calendar? If He did, how much of the calendar would we have left?

The world lay in darkness before the coming of Christ; every day on the calendar was given to worshipping false gods. We know this because of the name of the days of our week, and worshipping those gods was generally accompanied by ritualistic immorality.

Our present Valentine's Day is far removed from Lupercalia. As believers in the body of Christ, we don't venerate or perform ritual acts of devotion to any canonized deceased person. May we forget the "saint" part and go with the generic meaning of valentine, which has been with us so long and rejoice with our love in a way pleasing to God?

Each day given to us is an opportunity to make known "the manifold wisdom of God" (Ephesians 3:10). Sometimes, that witness will be in the act of avoiding even the appearance of evil associated with certain holidays. On other occasions, it might be celebrating a secular holiday in holy service to God. "This is the day which the Lord hath made. We will rejoice and be glad in it" (Psalm 118:24).

CHAPTER 7

Presidents' Day

The primary meaning of *holiday*, "holy day" as in the religious sense, doesn't apply to Washington's Birthday, but the secular meaning of a man-made special day, a day in which one is exempt from work in commemoration of an event, does.

Once upon a Time, Two Great Men Received Recognition

Many folks remember when Abraham Lincoln and George Washington had birthdays on different days and schools and businesses closed on both days in their honor. More important, schoolchildren received patriotic instruction regarding the legends, facts, and wisdom of these men.

Every year from second through sixth grade, we cut out profiles from black construction paper and competed to have the neatest cutout. Profiles of Washington facing Lincoln covered bulletin boards. Even though we did this yearly, no one complained but eagerly anticipated the routine. We looked forward once again to hearing stories revealing honesty and courage: lad George's confession to chopping down the cherry tree and honest Abe's walking a mile to return a penny to a customer.

Lincoln's birthday celebration became official when in 1892, Benjamin Harrison (president 1885–1889) declared February 12 an official holiday. Each state had liberty to choose its own holidays, however, and not every state considered Lincoln a hero. Depending in which part of the country you lived, you might have gotten the day off school or work; this holds true today as some states continue to honor Lincoln on February 12.

Washington's Birthday has occupied three dates on the calendar. Under the old Julian calendar, his date of birth was February 11, 1731. With the adoption of the Gregorian calendar in 1752, the date became February 22. In 1968, its celebrated date changed yet again.

In a previous chapter, I stated that all presidents share one holiday. That's a common thought, and in many people's minds, they do. This confusion arose with the passage of the Monday Holiday Bill, also known as the Uniform Holiday Bill of 1968. The bill intended to create three-day weekends for federal employees by moving the observance of Washington's Birthday, Memorial Day, and Veterans Day to specific Mondays and to establish Columbus Day as another federal holiday.

Washington's new birthday, now honored on the third Monday of February as Presidents' Day, will never be February 22; the twenty-first is the closest it will ever get to his actual birthday.

Executive Order 11582, issued on February 2, 1971, established Washington's birthday as the one to be celebrated, but President Nixon's public proclamation that year declared the day to be "set aside to honor all presidents, even myself." The law and the proclamation are in conflict, so there is continued confusion over the name and who receives honor. The media began calling the day Presidents' Day, and with enough repetition, the public accepted this as true. Now, the day is known as President's Day, Presidents' Day, and Presidents Day.

Perhaps to rectify the media's mistake and to give Lincoln his rightful respect, on February 6, 2001, Representatives Bartlett, Tancredo, Chambliss, Weldon, and Petri introduced H.R. 420, the "Washington-Lincoln Recognition Act of 2001." This act requested that the legal public holiday known as Washington's Birthday (U.S. Code, Title 5, Section 6103) be called by that name only and no other and that the president issue a proclamation each year recognizing Abraham Lincoln on February 12. That proposal failed to clear subcommittee; therefore, it was never voted upon, so Lincoln has no official federally recognized day. Some states have reassigned his birthday to the day after Thanksgiving, in effect giving a credible explanation for a four-day weekend without creating another paid holiday.

Until Congress or an executive order changes the United States Code, the third Monday in February remains Washington's Birthday only.

Sketches of George Washington

George Washington was born in Westmoreland County, Virginia, to Augustine and his second wife, Mary Ball Washington, by whom Augustine had six children. Augustine died when George was around twelve. Though George remembered his father treating him affectionately, he couldn't remember details of their relationship. His rearing and discipline fell on the shoulders of his half-brother, Lawrence, fourteen years older, and his mother.

By all accounts, Mary Washington was a kind but firm disciplinarian who taught her son obedience and honesty. Although the story of the cherry tree is legend, the following anecdote written by George's orphaned grandson, whom George adopted as his own, addresses George's honesty.

It seems that Mary had a favorite Arabian horse left her by her deceased husband. It was assumed and commonly spoken that the horse couldn't be broken and would always be unmanageable. The horse had reached near full growth never having let anyone ride him. George challenged his youthful companions to help him put a bridle in the horse's mouth and assured them he would conquer it before breakfast.

After they put the bridle on the horse, the youthful accomplices released the horse, immediately wishing they had not. The struggle between George and the vicious animal left them fearing for George's life as he clung to the horse, appearing like a centaur. "The gallant horse, summoning all his powers to one mighty effort, reared, and plunged with tremendous violence, burst his noble heart, and died in an instant."[15]

At breakfast, Mother Washington inquired of the lads at table how her Arabian colts were, especially the largest, her favorite sorrel. After an embarrassing silence, she repeated her question. George informed her that the sorrel had died, explaining the circumstances: "I backed him, I rode him, and in a desperate struggle for the mastery, he fell under me and died upon the spot."[16]

Mother Washington's cheeks flushed, perhaps with momentary anger, but she soon regained her composure and replied, "It is well; but while I regret the loss of my favorite, *I rejoice in my son, who always speaks the truth.*"[17]

At age sixteen, George experienced surveying, working as an assistant to official Prince William County Virginia's surveyor. Their assignment: to map and plat five million acres of land belonging to Lord Fairfax in northern Virginia and the Shenandoah Valley. On this rugged journey, he learned to coexist with fleas, lice, and other discomforts, but it sparked a lifelong interest in surveying and land ownership.

The next year, he received an appointment as surveyor of Culpepper County, a position he held for two years. Excursions further into the frontier kindled his interest in developing the West.

Washington's life changed drastically in 1752, when his half-brother, Lawrence, died of tuberculosis. A few months later, Lawrence's daughter, Sarah, died. Lawrence's will appointed George heir in the event Sarah died without issue. Thus, at age twenty, George acquired from Lawrence's widow the 2,000-acre estate, Mount Vernon, which he ultimately increased to 8,000 acres.

Along with the estate came eighteen slaves whom he fed, clothed, and housed well, hiring a doctor by the year to tend to their needs. Although he added to their number, he didn't sell any. That would have been trafficking in human life, something in which he professed not to believe. (Many years later, he specified in his will that the slaves were to be released upon the death of his wife.)

Personal Description and Habits

Washington stood six two and never exceeded 220 pounds. His adopted son described him as having large hands and feet, hazel-brown hair, and light-grayish-blue eyes. When he walked, he placed his feet as though on precise parallel lines. For forty years, after Washington's marriage in 1759 to Martha Dandridge, widow of Daniel Parke Custis, he wore her miniature portrait on a chain around his neck.

While at Mount Vernon, before and after the Revolutionary War, Washington followed methodical habits. He arose one or two hours before daybreak in winter and at daybreak in summer, either working in his library or visiting the stables until breakfast.

After breakfast, he rode through one of his five farms, averaging ten to fifteen miles per day, overseeing and visiting with his laborers. Each of these self-contained farms had its own overseers, slaves, livestock, and farm equipment.

At 2:45 p.m., he returned home, changed clothes, and ate at exactly 3:00. His favorite meal included fish; he ate few desserts, and he generally drank Madeira wine with his meal.

He spent afternoons in his library; at night, friends joined the Washington family for tea. On rare evenings when no visitors gathered, George read aloud Sunday sermons, other religious works, or current publications to his family. Only relatives were welcomed visitors on Sunday evening—with the one exception of John Trumbull, governor of Connecticut. Washington ate no supper, and at 9:00, he went to bed.

According to his biographer, Washington attended religious services every Sunday morning (referred to as Sabbath services) but not evening services. Washington was a member of the Protestant Episcopal Church; while residing in New York as president, he attended St. Paul's; while in Philadelphia, Christ Church.

A difference of opinion exists in his taste for clothes. One encyclopedia states that Washington insisted on the best and fanciest articles of clothing he ordered from London; however, his son stated that as president, "His personal appearance was always remarkable for its being old-fashioned, and exceedingly plain and neat."[18] We know that because of his size, it was difficult for him to obtain well-fitting clothes.

French and Indian War

Washington fought in the French and Indian War (1754–63), attaining rank of lieutenant colonel at age twenty-two. In April 1754, his troops were forced to surrender at Fort Necessity, Great Meadows, Pennsylvania, but Washington proved to be such a good negotiator that his troops were permitted to march back to Williamsburg with their weapons. In spite of this defeat, his reputation grew, resulting in his promotion to colonel and appointment to chief of the Virginia militia, responsible for guarding the frontier. When first assigned this post, he often sent opinionated letters to his superiors, but as he matured, he acquired skill in dealing with authority.

From Soldier to Statesman

Encouraged by influential friends, he entered politics and served in the Virginia House of Burgesses from 1759 to 1774. Spurred by the refusal of the British crown to give the colonies more home rule, he led the Non-importation Association, a group boycotting British goods. Again intensifying the call for more home rule, he later chaired the committee that adopted the Fairfax Resolution.

Washington's hope of reconciling the colonies with Britain proved futile, and in 1775, Congress unanimously approved him as commander in chief of the entire Continental forces in the beginning of what proved to be an eight-year war for independence.

Statesman to Soldier: Man of Prayer

Providence guided Washington—not the ethereal "maybe" but the Being who oversees all human endeavor, a very personal God. Some of his recorded prayer journal entries ask forgiveness of sins, beseech God to mold him in the likeness of His Son, thank Him for undeserved blessings, and ask God for favor for relatives and friends all for Jesus Christ's sake. These are not the prayers of a deist or a lukewarm, half-hearted believer but of a sincere seeker after truth.

At each meal, he always asked a blessing from a standing position; moreover, any minister present would be asked to return thanks before and after dinner.

Mr. Potts, the Quaker who owned the house where Washington dwelled at Valley Forge, once heard a strange sound coming from a thicket. He observed "the beloved chief upon his knees in prayer, his cheeks suffused with tears." Not wishing to intrude, he backed away and later told his wife, "If there is any one on this earth whom the Lord will listen to, it is George Washington."[19]

Indian Prophecy

When fighting alongside General Braddock in the French and Indian War, two horses had been shot from under Washington and four bullets had passed through his coat. General Braddock died from wounds, but Washington, protected by God, was never wounded. During the battle, the Indian commander pointed to Washington and cried, "Fire at him no more; see ye not that the Great Spirit protects that chief; he can not die in battle."[20]

Seventeen years after that battle, White Mingo, ambassador for the Six Nations, related how he had tried unsuccessfully to kill Washington. Speaking through interpreter John Nicholson, White Mingo said, "He can not die in battle. The Great Spirit protects that man, and guides his destinies—he will become the chief of nations, and a people yet unborn, will hail him as the founder of a mighty empire!"[21]

Inaugural Address, Death, Funeral

Hundreds of books have been written on Washington's able leadership during the War for Independence, his bringing the war to a successful conclusion with the surrender of Cornwallis at Yorktown in 1781, the ensuing, chaotic years before the adoption of the Constitution of the newly formed United States, and his presidency. I wish not to restate well-known details pertaining to those events but to conclude this portion by noting the first inaugural address, the public celebrations of his birthday, and his death with dignity.

First Inaugural Address

Article II, Section I of our Constitution specifies the oath each president recites.

> I do solemnly swear (or affirm) that I will faithfully execute the office of President of the United States, and will to be best of my ability, preserve, protect and defend the Constitution of the Unites States.

There is no requirement that a Bible be sworn upon as part of the ceremony. However, in April 1789, Washington insisted that a Bible be found for the occasion of his inauguration. After some confusion, New York State chancellor Robert R. Livingston produced a Masonic Bible and administered the oath of office. Washington randomly opened to Genesis 49, rested his left hand on that page, raised his right hand, took the oath, and added, "So help me God!" He then leaned over and kissed the Bible.

First Public Birthday Celebration

It had been the custom to honor the birthday of King George on June 4. Shortly after the end of the Revolutionary War, French officers and the colonial populace began honoring Washington with parades and ceremonies, ending with an evening ball, the day ranking in importance with the Fourth of July.

Washington wrote to Count de Rochambeau in 1784 that

> the flattering distinction paid to the anniversary of my birthday, is an honor for which I dare not attempt to express my gratitude. I confide in your Excellency's sensibility to interpret my feelings for this, and for the obliging manner in which you are pleased to announce it.[22]

Death of First President

After three short years of retirement from the presidency, Washington died at his beloved Mount Vernon of acute laryngitis (his doctors called it *Cynanche tonsillaris*) on December 14, 1799 at 10:00 p.m. Three doctors attended him. He knew time was short and directed Martha to bring his two wills; he instructed one to be burned. Those at his bedside said that though he had been in constant pain, he raised himself up as if to thank them, folded his arms across his chest, and passed quietly away.

At his funeral, Major General Henry Lee delivered a lengthy oration extolling the virtues of the late president. Only one partial sentence from Lee's wordy oration has been quoted over the years summarizing the national feeling toward the father of his country: "First in war, first in peace, and first in the hearts of his countrymen."[23]

In death, his tomb bears evidence of his trust in God. Over the vault door are the words. "I am the resurrection and the life; he that believeth in me, though he were dead, yet shall he live" (from John 11:25).

Resurrection

Resurrection is a weighty topic for theologians as well as beginning or advanced Bible students. There is always more food for thought than can be chewed and digested. I concur with Charles H. Welch.

> In resurrection there will be some raised to sit at the right hand of God far above all; some will walk the streets of the New Jerusalem; some will inherit the earth, and for each sphere of blessing an appropriate body will be given.[24]

God chose not to inform us how this is possible. Also, it would probably be pointless to try to determine in which resurrection George Washington thought he might be.

As members of the body of Christ, we can anticipate with Paul,

> Henceforth there is laid up for me a crown of righteousness, which the Lord, the righteous Judge, shall give me at that day; and not to me only, but unto all them also that love His appearing. (2 Timothy 4:8)

CHAPTER 8

St. Patrick's Day

Another holiday not commanded by God but observed by many is St. Patrick's Day, March 17. It is not a federal legal holiday in the United States, but it is observed in many countries with large Catholic populations. The day is not considered a holy day of obligation that requires attendance at Mass, but it is an important day for many.

Originally, only Catholics observed the day, but as time passed, the day evolved into a celebration for anyone proclaiming Irish heritage. Today, schoolteachers, merchandisers, and a myriad of others use the day to spread the concept of cultural diversity. In bygone days, we worked for assimilation of all those seeking freedom and good fortune; America was the great melting pot.

Today, merchandisers promote special sales amid graphic displays of shamrocks, tobacco pipes, leprechauns, and dollar signs. Cities with Irish-American populations sponsor parades featuring participants wearing green, symbolic of Ireland's green landscape. Participants enjoy the light-hearted atmosphere, but many haven't any notion about this Patrick they celebrate wholeheartedly or have a clue why he has a day named for him.

Birth of Sucat

The person commonly known as St. Patrick was given the British name Sucat at his birth. The name probably means "warlike." Along with his British name, he was given a Roman name, Patricius. It is impossible at this late date to determine for certain the dates during which he lived. Possible years of his birth range from AD 385 to 389; however, the date of his death is generally agreed upon as March 17, 493. Although his age is not known, most authorities agree that he lived to an advanced age.

Besides disputing Patrick's date of birth, the place is also challenged. Some claim it to be in Glamorganshire. Others claim the coast of Gaul (France), and yet others claim Kilpatrick, Scotland. We know with certainty that in his youth, he lived near the west coast of Britain, within easy range of raiders looking for slaves.

Such obscurity surrounds his life and career that one school of thought relegates him to pure fiction. I suspect this is the same group mentality that says there's no evidence that Jesus Christ ever lived. But based on past and current scholarship, it is safe to say that Patrick was indeed a bigger-than-life personality, though some of the legends surrounding him are a bit far-fetched.

According to writings attributed to Patrick himself, his parents were high-ranking Romans named Calpurnius and Conchessa. His father, Calpurnius, helped rule the Roman colonies in Britain as well as being a deacon in the Christian church. He was the son of Potitus, a priest, but the uniqueness of a married priest or deacon is not mentioned as causing distress.

From his youth, Patrick's parents taught him the Christian religion and instilled in him good moral character. At the same time, he also learned allegiance to the Roman Empire. By his own admission, he ignored the biblical instructions until times of adversity overtook him. When those times came, he did as the book of Proverbs advised and eagerly inclined his ear to knowledge and applied his heart to understanding what he had learned. Again, one of God's promises becomes evident: "Train up a child in the way he should go, and when he is old, he will not depart from it" (Proverbs 22:6).

Captured

Irish marauders under the leadership of the Irish King, Niall Noigiallach, captured many youths and took them to Ireland, where they were sold into slavery. These pillagers captured Sucat when he was sixteen, according to tradition and his own testimony. While a slave, he attended the swineherds of a chieftain, a druidic high priest named Milchu.

The place of his servitude is disputed. Some references say it was in the Slemish mountains near County Antrim; others prefer the location of Connaught near Croagh Patrick.

In any case, during his six years of slavery, he learned to speak Celtic and became familiar with the religion of the druids. While observing the druids in their pagan worship, he remembered his former training and sought the Lord.

He later wrote that the Lord had pitied him in his youth and ignorance and had guarded him when he was least aware of His presence. He observed that the Lord had allowed his British kinsmen to be captured because they had turned away from Him and had rejected His salvation. Perhaps he saw an analogy with ancient Israel. When the people of Israel sinned, God gave them over to their enemies. When Israel repented, God delivered them.

> For thus saith the Lord of hosts; As I thought to punish
> you, when your fathers provoked Me to wrath, saith
> the Lord of hosts, and I repented not. So again have
> I thought in these days to do well unto Jerusalem and
> to the house of Judah; fear ye not (Zechariah 8:14-15).

These similarities can certainly hold true for any ethnic group that has turned from God.

Escape

At some point during his captivity, Patrick had visions that encouraged him to escape from his master. The word *vision* has many denotations. When Patrick wrote of them, we assume he wasn't referring to supernatural trances but to concepts, thoughts, or discernment regarding his confined situation.

Consequently, he did escape, eluded his captors, and fled to the coast of Wicklow, some 200 miles away. There he boarded an export ship carrying Irish wolfhounds. After three adventurous days at sea, he landed on the coast of Gaul. He may have spent several years at a monastery at Leirns before finally reaching his home in Britain.

The plundering Irish had killed or captured Patrick's closest family members, but a relative welcomed him and cared for him as if he were her own. This surrogate mother entreated him to make his home there permanently, but it was not to be.

In Britain, he experienced several disturbing visions, one similar to Paul's. "And a vision appeared to Paul in the night; there stood a man of Macedonia, and prayed him saying, 'Come over unto Macedonia and help us'" (Acts 16:9). Patrick's own "Macedonian call" in his night vision pierced his heart with compassion. The caller begged Patrick to come and walk among the Irish again and to help them. This plaintive cry awakened Patrick, and with a tender heart aching for the unsaved Irish, he knew he had to return to Ireland.

Education

Once more, we have a discrepancy in the tales and traditions. Some authorities maintain that after Patrick decided to return to Ireland to win converts to Christianity, he went to St. Martin at Tours, where he studied for some years. Another view insists that Patrick's writings show an ignorance of the major Roman Catholic doctrines and that he couldn't have spent much time with the recognized Roman Catholic scholars of his day. Tradition holds that he did spend some time at Auxerre, France, studying under St. Germanus, a French bishop.

At any rate, around eighteen years elapsed while he prepared for his work among the Celtic druids. Whether he prepared on his own or under a mentor is not certain because his own writings do not give us any personal details during those years. We know that Bishop Amator ordained him deacon along with two other men who helped him later in his work in Ireland.

Patrick had expressed his desire to evangelize Ireland to the Catholic hierarchy and eagerly awaited permission, but the priests considered his education to be inferior and didn't want to send him as a missionary. Instead, they sent Palladius, who had formerly been sent to Britain in efforts to exterminate the doctrines of Pelagianism. (Pelagius and his followers denied the doctrine of Original Sin.) Palladius served in Ireland only a few months and died in 431. Hence, Pope Celestine I reconsidered Patrick's request and sent Patrick to serve in Ireland.

Ireland at Last

Patrick landed at Inverdea at the mouth of the River Vartry. As can be imagined, the druids were apprehensive about seeing him even though they were expecting him. An old druidic chant had foretold his coming not by name but by a nickname, Adze-head: "Adze-head will come/Over a furious sea; His mantle head-holed/His table in the east of his house;/All his household shall answer, 'Amen, amen!'"[25]

After they saw the round, shaven spot on his head, his tonsure, they knew this was the foretold Adze-head who would be extinguishing their pagan practices. Over a period of several months, they captured him and his companions twelve times and at least once condemned him to death. Yet the Lord sustained him through these vexations and delivered him from them all.

After numerous narrow escapes, Patrick went to his old master and paid the price for his own freedom. Again, we have conflicting accounts. One asserts that this act so influenced the master that he and his family converted to Christianity. Another version states that rather than converting to Christianity, Milchu was so shamed that he preferred to die. He built his own funeral pyre by gathering all his belongings into his house, setting fire to it, and burning himself as a sacrifice for his god.

Soon thereafter, Patrick proceeded to northern and western Ireland, where no one had ever preached Christianity. He hoped to convert the chieftains of the various tribes. He reasoned that from the leadership of the chiefs, the clan members would be encouraged to adopt the new religion. This concept is known today in government and business as the trickle-down effect. Perhaps he expected those in authority would compel their subjects to become Christian as Constantine and others had done. This would of course result in a superficial faith, but from a practical or worldly standpoint, it would be an efficient means of evangelizing many at once. This effort at winning the local kings was partially successful.

It seems that wherever he went, Patrick earned the respect of the people, and many were willing to help him with his evangelizing endeavors. One of Patrick's converts, Dichu, gave him a wooden barn to use as a worship site. From there, he extended his outreach. Eventually, his zealous activities in seeking converts caused a confrontation with King Laoghaire (pronounced *Leary*), son of King Niall Noigiallach, under whose reign Patrick had been captured many years earlier. Apparently, Patrick challenged the royal authority on the night of Easter Eve in regard to lighting the "Pascal" fire.[26] The custom at a pagan festival held during this same time forbad lighting any fire until the royal fire was lit.

During these years, druids from various parts of Europe traveled to Britain and Ireland to receive instruction in the magical and ritualistic practices of druidry. These practices included domestic animal sacrifice and occasionally human sacrifice. Their meetings were held at the central location of a *nemetonae,* "sanctuaries" or in "sacred groves," where sacred fires flamed. Patrick faced death many times when he dared challenge these practices. Sometimes, the druids would cast magic spells on him and he would retaliate with his own magic rather than with the message of Christ.

Feats of magical skill between the missionary and the druids resulted in a truce of sorts. King Laoghaire didn't wish to accept Christianity for himself, but he placed Patrick under his protection. King Laoghaire's brother, Conall, as well as many in their extended family, readily accepted the new religion.

King Laoghaire's goodwill, clearly blessed by God, opened the door for evangelism; Patrick is credited with founding more than 300 churches and baptizing more than 120,000. Even though Patrick professed little proficiency in Latin, Latin became the common religious language under his guidance.

Writings of Patrick

Confession and *Letter to the Subjects of Coroticus* are two works attributed to Patrick. Both were written in Latin and reveal his knowledge of the Vulgate translation of the Bible.

Confession is an account of his life, works, and spiritual development. In it, he described himself as ignorant and unequal to the task of evangelizing the Irish; nevertheless, he expressed thanks that God let him serve in Ireland in spite of his shortcomings. He refused to accept any praise for accomplishments but humbly passed all glory to God.

In *Letters to the Subjects of Coroticus*, Patrick urged the Christian subjects of King Coroticus to have nothing to do with their king until the king released certain captives. From a fort at Dumbarton, Coroticus had reigned over the British kingdom of Strathclyde. From there, he had ordered the massacre or capture of many Christian converts on the day of their baptism, and many new converts had been killed while yet wearing their white baptismal robes.

Patrick verbally indicted Coroticus for these heinous acts and insisted Coroticus return all stolen goods and prisoners. Of course, Patrick's requests were answered with insults. To make matters worse, some of the raiders were themselves "professing Christians" whom an outraged Patrick denounced as not being fellow believers or worthy of being called fellow Roman countrymen. In this letter, Patrick also requested excommunication for Coroticus if he didn't comply with Patrick's requests. Nowhere was the outcome recorded, but Patrick had clearly demonstrated his courage by taking a stand against an evil despot.

Legends

Many tales and legends arise from the deeds of good men. Countless legends surround Patrick, but we will confine our account to only four.

One of the legends surrounding Patrick alleges that during a plague of snakes and frogs, he forced them to drown themselves in the sea. All the snakes had gone except one; it had refused to leave. After much persuasion, the final snake crawled into a box to prove to Patrick that the box was too small. Patrick shut the box, fastened the lid, and threw it into the sea. Snakes were associated with pagan worship, and this legend may have begun as a metaphor representing his driving the pagans from Ireland.

According to another legend, Patrick spent forty days on a mountain being attacked by demons in the form of blackbirds. Patrick prayed and rang his bell to scare away the birds until finally an angel appeared and assured him that all his prayers would be answered and that the Irish would keep the Christian faith until the final judgment.

Perhaps the most unrealistic legend states that after Patrick died, darkness enveloped Ireland for twelve days. Twelve days of total darkness would have killed much plant life as well as wreaked havoc on the minds of unstable people. Contrast the twelve days to when Christ was crucified: "Now from the sixth hour there was darkness over all the land unto the ninth hour" (Matthew 27:45). It is improbable that God would allot more time of darkness as a testimony to an extraordinary man than to his beloved Son.

Of all the legends recorded, the one that has the most credibility is the legend of the shamrock. In short, in order to explain the mystery of the Trinity, Patrick picked a shamrock and used it for an object lesson. He explained that the three leaves represented the three persons of the

Trinity while the stem represented the godhead—the unity of three in one.

Death of Patrick

After Patrick's visit to Rome from 441 to 443, he spent the remainder of his life in Ireland and died in 493. The Cathedral of Down, Downpatrick, was later built on the place where he was buried.

The Roman Catholic Church has long claimed Patrick as its own for obvious reasons. In the last century, a Protestant claim has also been set forth based on his writings. In his manuscripts, Patrick didn't give credit for his call to preach to any official of the Roman Church. There is no recognition of some of the prominent doctrines of the Roman Church. For example, there is no mention of purgatory, adoration of the Virgin Mary, transubstantiation, or the authority of the pope. It would seem strange that he would be ignorant of these doctrines in view of his long association with Roman Catholic teachers. If he believed these doctrines, why did he not write about them?

To be sure, Patrick was not the first Christian in Ireland. Common Roman citizens who had unrestricted travel privileges had probably carried Christianity to Britain and Ireland. They were followed later by Palladius in his official capacity, but Patrick will always be given recognition for evangelizing the country.

Patrick was undoubtedly an impressive servant of God. Contrary to traditional belief, which painted him as rustic and unsophisticated, current scholarship suggests that he had great literary talents.[27] He certainly didn't understand right division of God's Word, and like many modern preachers, he assumed water baptism to be a part of his calling and his duty to perform. He didn't recognize the difference between the preaching of the kingdom as proclaimed by Peter in Acts 10:36 and the preaching of the church of the one body as proclaimed by Paul after Acts 28:28.

However, his autobiographical *Confessions* gave God all the glory for what he accomplished and enumerated God's countless protections on his life. We know that on the one hand, after much duress, he had escaped a harsh taskmaster and left Ireland. On the other hand, he returned willingly to that violent land to bring the message of Christ. And bring it he did. An English translation of the words from *The Breastplate* reads,

> Christ in the heart of every man who thinks of me,
> Christ in the mouth of every man who speaks to me
> Christ in every eye that sees me
> Christ in every ear that hears me.[28]

Is this not a good expression of "And whatsoever ye do in word or deed, do all in the name of the Lord Jesus, giving thanks to God and the Father by Him" (Colossians 3:17)? It's not certain that Patrick wrote this, but the fact that it may even have been written *about* him speaks of his good testimony.

It would seem that here, indeed, lived a humble man of God. If given the opportunity, he likely would object to the capitalized "Saint" in front of his name and would opt for the common "saint" as intended in the Greek Scriptures to mean holy, or one of God's chosen.

Unfortunately, the legends surrounding Patrick have become more exaggerated with the passing of the centuries. What a shame that millions celebrate St. Patrick's Day but know nothing about the man or more important, the saving grace of Christ that Patrick proclaimed! If celebrants knew more of the authentic Patrick and less of his legends, perhaps less liquor would flow on this day and more of Christ's love would flow into needy hearts.

God's Plan Must Stand

This question then arises among those who endeavor to rightly divide the Word: what is the final destination of one who does not understand or teach the mystery of the one body? What about those who sincerely believe in Christ but their preaching is a dispensation or two behind? That is, some are teaching the gospel of the kingdom while others are listening for the trumpet.

Some teach a sort of Gentile/Jewish stew, a mixture of many of God's purposes for different peoples of different times all stirred in together, like beef and vegetables blended into a tasty dish. Just as beef stew may satisfy our palates, the hodgepodge of doctrines may make us feel pious, but what do the Scriptures say?

At Acts 28:28, Israel's hopes of the rapture and walking the streets of the New Jerusalem were cut off. Paul's new hope (and ours) became to "appear with Him in glory" (Colossians 3:4). People might preach the kingdom, the rapture, or any doctrine whatsoever and have a great deal of faith in it, but as Oscar Baker stated, "No amount of faith can change the plan. It must stand as it is."

Oscar has summarized the answer to our question concerning destination. He asserted that the only hope offered today is the hope to be seated with Christ at the right hand of the Father as revealed in Colossians.

> Friends, that [to "appear with Him in glory"] is the only hope that is **offered** to you today. You will either take it by faith or you will not get it. So far as the Word reveals anything about the matter, the only alternative is the Great White Throne Judgment. You might or you might not receive eternal life there. It may be somewhat in question according to the description given. That is the last of the resurrections. All special blessings will be over by that time. You will miss the coronation in the superheavens, the rapture of the saints of Israel, the supper of the Lamb, the Millennium. If I can judge rightly from the Word, those will only have terrestrial bodies and will not be able to visit any place outside of the earth. Neither will they be allowed in the New Jerusalem which comes down out of heaven to the new earth. **It is not so much a matter of being lost as it is that one**

may suffer great loss. (Truth for Today, January 1949). (Emphasis is this author's and not Oscar's.)[29]

The Plan Still Stands

God's current offer of salvation is to Jews and Gentiles alike reconciled into one body. If we try to teach "to the Jew first," we are behind on God's timetable for us. Today, God's love and pity for aching hearts extends equally to every individual of every ethnicity.

> In Whom we have redemption through His blood, the forgiveness of sins, according to the riches of His grace, Wherein he hath abounded [overflowed in large measure] toward us in all wisdom and prudence (Ephesians 1:7-8).

This all abounding love "gave Him to be the Head over all things to the church who is His body, the fullness of Him that filleth all in all" (Ephesians 1:22–23). Why? "That in the dispensation of the fullness of times, He might gather together in one all things in Christ, both which are in heaven, and which are on earth; even in Him" (Ephesians 1:9–10).

As businesspeople or lawyers might say, "The offer's on the table." God's plan for this age stands. This offer of the one body is the one now on the table.

CHAPTER 9

Spring Celebrations: Precursors to Confusion

After even a mild winter, most people seem ready for spring. Solomon expressed the beauty of spring in the Hebrew Scriptures.

> For, lo, the winter is past, the rain is over and gone; the flowers appear on the earth; the time of the singing of birds is come, and the voice of the turtle is heard in our land (Solomon 2:11-12).

Like Solomon, most of us are delighted and feel energized as we eagerly anticipate the equinox and the first twelve hours of daylight. We know that soon we will be planting flowers and enjoying the outdoors more fully once again. Truly, human nature and desires have not changed over the millennia.

New Season, New Year?

Some Oriental calendars in use today, which have their origins in antiquity, not only proclaim the vernal equinox as the first day of spring but also as the first day of the new year. Did God create the world on the vernal equinox? Or is the Jewish new year, which corresponds closely to our autumnal equinox, more nearly correct? Will we ever know for sure, but is it even worth speculating about?

At least one man thought he had proved with certainty that God had created the world on October 23, 4004 BC. In our naïveté, we have a good laugh at such an absurd idea and pat ourselves on the back that we are in good company with a few modern wannabe scholars who assert that this ancient researcher had to be naïve or an outright fake. But was he?

The man in question, James Ussher, was born in Ireland in 1581. From age twenty, he began earnestly pursuing his love of church history. He read every history book he could find, and in his quest for truth, he became proficient in Semitic languages. He assumed—and we should agree—that the Bible is the only reliable sourcebook on anything dealing with biblical times. Scholars had generally agreed upon the date of Nebuchadnezzar's death, so Ussher took that date and working backward, anchoring all previous biblical occurrences to it. His history covered the beginning of creation to AD 73.

The republishers of Ussher's voluminous work inform us that Ussher's original calculations—obviously done without benefit of modern computers or calculators—covered a hundred written pages.[30]

Upon his death, Ussher, a well-respected and learned scholar of his era, was buried in Westminster Abbey; he was neither a charlatan nor naïve but a sincere man on a mission for truth. Unmistakably, only God Himself could confirm or deny the accuracy of Ussher's work concerning dates, but it might be worthwhile to meditate on his findings and to ask ourselves why some societies choose not to celebrate an autumnal creation but a vernal one.

Is it reasonable to assume that the chosen people were following knowledge given to them in Leviticus 23:24–25 and Numbers 29:1? God told Moses in Exodus 12:2 to begin the calendar year on the first day of Nisan, our March/April, but the traditional day of celebration of the Creation of the world was kept the first two days of Tishri (our September/October).

Each Hebrew month had a constellation assigned to it (Job 38:32), and according to rabbinical tradition, each tribe carried one of the signs of the mazzaroth (our Zodiac).[31] The current name for Nisan's sign is

Aries, the ram or lamb. The Hebrew term is transliterated *taleh,* the lamb. Our Savior was crucified on the fourteenth of Nisan in the sign of the lamb. "Behold the Lamb of God who taketh away the sin of the world" (John 1:29).

If God created the earth in the fall of the year, would Satan ensure humanity's trespass into observations in its opposite season, spring? Satan is highly skilled at blindfolding, spinning around, and pointing his chosen dupe in the opposite direction. This may be the case here, for some of the ancient spring rites were so reprehensible that they could have been spawned only by Satan.

When we begin to delve into the names, characteristics, and seasons celebrated in the past, we generally find that the celebrations revolved around gods, goddesses, and idols. These deities were worshipped in similar fashion throughout Asia and Europe. From the point of origin, worshippers carried beliefs and practices to lands around the Mediterranean and to northern Europe primarily through Phoenician and Celtic merchant ships. As these religions were transported from place to place, their characteristics evolved or sometimes became assimilated with the indigenous gods or goddesses.

> The cult of the Great Goddess was known in Anatolia, Syria, Iran and Babylonia as well as Cyprus and the lands eventually overrun by the Greeks. She was named Ishtar, Ashtoreth and Astarte and her consort was called simply "Lord," that is Baal or Bel. Sometimes the Great Goddess was addressed as "Lady," a feminine form of Baal which was Baalath, Bilit or Milit. The last of these forms passed into Greek as Mylitta. It was from Greece that the cult of the Great Goddess Earth Mother passed northwards through Europe.[32]

Due to space limitations and our focus on U.S. holidays, the next chapter will address only a few of these goddesses but no gods except in a perfunctory light. As we search, their relationship to one another and to one of our most important modern holidays will become apparent.

CHAPTER 10

Pagan Goddesses Honored on or around Passover

Cybele, Great Mother of the Gods

The first spring celebration we will deal with briefly is that of Cybele (*bel* meaning "god"). Cybele, also known as Kybele, Magna Mater (Great Mother), and Idaia Mater, possessed all knowledge. On the Roman calendar, her festival came first.

Legends say that her early places of worship were Mt. Ida (mount of knowledge) and Mt. Sipylus in the Roman province of Phrygia, a mountainous territory in what is now western Turkey. As the nature deity of all Asia Minor, her worship spread to Greece, where Greeks merged her identity with their goddess Rhea. Cybele would also be confused and often identified with the sibyls, who were fortune-teller priestesses, of which there were ten allocated to different parts of the world such as Babylonia, Egypt, Italy, and so on.

In 204 BC, a sibylene priestess predicted war would be made on Italy by an unknown enemy from abroad. However, the Italians would be victorious if the Great Mother of gods and her sacred symbol were brought in from the city of Pessinus in Galatia. This sacred symbol had to be a goddess, for it had fallen from the sky. In reality, terrified onlookers probably had witnessed a passage of light from a meteorite remnant shaped like the female torso as it fell to earth, but to secure their city, the Romans transferred Cybele to Rome and placed her in a temple on the Palatine.

Rites connected with this cult shocked even broad-minded Romans, and Roman citizens were at first forbidden to participate in them. However, by AD 394, during the reign of Eugenius, Cybele's worship had been legalized, and it had spread so that many minor shrines of the Great Mother existed in and around Rome along with the great shrine dedicated to her on the Palatine.

Cybele, a fertility goddess, ruled over primitive earth. As the Great Mother, she parented gods and men as well as lower life forms. Because of her role of mother over nature, worshippers also called her Mountain Mother. Thus, her followers worshipped her on mountaintops as well as in caves.

The main public festival of Cybele, the Megalesia, originally took place April 4–10, but it was later changed to March 15–27. The Megalesia was a time of Cybele worship and games. Worship of Attis, the vegetation and sun god, accompanied worship of Cybele. In this myth of bizarre incest, Attis had castrated himself, died as a result, and rose again; therefore, Cybele's festival primarily celebrated Attis's death, burial, and resurrection.

As is apparent in most Greek and Roman mythology, bisexual, homosexual, and heterosexual impurities were prevalent. So too in this tale of which there are several versions. Anyone desiring explicit details may refer to other texts on Roman and Greek mythology.

Corybantes, eunuch priests, known for their frenzied dancing, led the Megalesia worship. In modern parlance, we would describe these men as cross dressers. They wore long hair and dressed in feminine clothing. Cymbals, drums, and flutes accompanied orgiastic, emotional ceremonies after which the worshippers scourged and mutilated themselves probably as initiation rites into this mystery religion.

Specific rituals occurred on each day of the Megalesia. On March 15, a six-year-old bull would be sacrificed to commemorate the exposure and survival of the infant Attis on the banks of the Gallus.

On March 24, fasting, abstinence, and purification by baptism in bull's blood took place. In this ritual (*taurobolium*), a high priest in process of being deified wore a silk toga and a golden crown and took his place in a pit covered by a grating. This grating, made of wooden planks, had been bored with many holes. Over the grating, priests killed a fierce bull garlanded with flowers, and the slain bull's blood spilled through the grating, thus "baptizing" the participant.

The priest made sure to put blood under his ears and lips, in his nostrils, and even in his throat. When he emerged from this blood bath, even his beard and clothing dripped with blood. According to religious tradition, by this ritual, the priest's adoring followers would worship him as a supernatural being. The effects of purification lasted "for eternity" but no less than twenty years. After twenty years, the rites might be repeated if the blood-baptized one desired to be purified again.

On March 25, as a direct result of spring returning and Attis's supposed resurrection from the dead, gaiety and joy would return to the crowds.

On the last day of the festival, March 27, worshippers would carry Cybele's statue (upgraded over time to one made of silver) in grand procession and bathed it in a tributary of the Tiber River.

Illustrations picture Cybele in chariot pulled by lions and accompanied by Attis or in a chariot drawn by snakes, symbols of the ancient mystery religions. In time, her worship faded somewhat to make room for yet more gods and goddesses in the world's pantheon, or her identity became merged with others.

Does this blood baptism sound like a feeble imitation of the terms of the first Hebrew covenant in which Moses took half the sacrificial blood and sprinkled it on the people? "Behold the blood of the covenant which the Lord hath made with you concerning all these words" (Exodus 24:8).

Of course, by AD 394, the first covenant had been put away. Christ had been crucified, buried, and resurrected: "Neither by the blood of goats and calves, but by His own blood He entered in once into the holy place having obtained eternal redemption for us" (Hebrews 9:12). By any reckoning, they were missing the mark.

This of necessity is a shortened and cleansed version of the story. If it's difficult for you to imagine the gross wretchedness of these spiritually blind sinners and the depths to which they would go to obtain relief from sin, it is because of "the eyes of your understanding being enlightened" (Ephesians 1:18).

Let us be thankful we have been delivered from spiritual darkness. But for the grace of God, "such were some of you: but ye are washed, but ye are sanctified, but ye are justified in the name of the Lord Jesus, and by the Spirit of our God" (1 Corinthians 6:11).

As we see in our daily studies, religions can be compared, and religious leaders can be compared, but Jehovah is incomparable: "For the Lord is great, and greatly to be praised: He is to be feared above all gods" (Psalm 96:4).

Ceres

Another ancient spring festival we shall consider briefly is that of the Cerealia. Ceres, the Italian goddess of grain, received honor at this nine-day celebration that began April 19 and originally occurred every five years but later became an annual festival.

Ceres's name may come from an Indo-European word meaning "to grow." Mythologists inform us that Ceres and Demeter were synonymous and that Demeter's name means "barley." Ceres and Cybele were considered goddesses of human fertility and of motherhood in general. Cybele's cult of Magna Mater catered specifically to the patrician social class, the ruling elite, whereas Ceres served as a rival goddess for the plebian, the common class.

Ceres worship took many forms and may have begun early as 753 BC. Priests known as *flamens cerealis* celebrated the ritual known as *sacrum cereale* in which they alone could recite the name of the twelve minor gods who assisted Ceres in her work as Mother of the Corn.[33]

Priests recited names of the following gods whom Ceres supervised: Vervactor, who turned the fallow land; Reparator, who prepared land; Imporcitor, who plowed wide furrows; Insitorn who sowed seeds;

Obarator, who plowed the surface; Occator, who harrowed; Sarritor, who weeded; Subruncinator, who thinned over sown plants; Messor, who harvested; Conuector, who carted; Conditor, who stored; and Promitor, who distributed grain.[34]

One fertility rite involved sacrificing a fertile female pig (*porca praecidanea*). If a pig couldn't be obtained, a large pumpkin might be cut open and the seeds offered to Ceres instead of the pig's entrails.

A funeral sacrifice (*porca praesentanea*) performed over the corpse of a testator cleansed survivors from the stain of death and ensured return of fertility to the family of the deceased. Perhaps even more important to survivors, this funeral service was prerequisite to receiving the inheritance, so if no funeral service transpired, no tangible legacy could be bestowed on the survivors.

Great crowds flocked for a yearly festival honoring Ceres on the estates of Pliny, a Roman scholar of the first century AD.[35]

Ceres's cult received official status in 496 BC with the erection of her temple on the Aventine Hill. Prior to then, during a time when the grain supply was nearly depleted, she presided over the distribution of grain to the poor. The plebians readily formed an attachment to her, for they were the grain handlers of the day. They considered Ceres their benefactress because of specific rights she had sponsored in their interest. These rights protected the plebian class from patrician magistrates who sometimes levied unjust fines against them. Due to Ceres's intercession for the plebeians, many fines levied by the magistrates went directly to the coffers of the goddess instead of to the civil rulers.

Ceres is generally illustrated similarly to Demeter, her Greek counterpart, also worshipped as the Corn Mother or Corn Spirit. Illustrations derived from old coins portray her with a mystic basket of flowers or fruit and a garland of grain. One unearthed coin pictured her with a grain-measuring instrument on her head. Ancient literature describes her with golden or flaxen hair and blue eyes.

On the surface, this seems to be another simple, tall tale. However, it goes beyond the simple into the realm of complex initiation into the ancient mysteries whose rites couldn't be revealed. Initiates kept their eyes or mouths closed, symbolic of secrecy. These highly secretive rites couldn't be written but were passed orally through the generations. The rites did follow specific known steps, with purification being the first step and garlanding the last.

Purification could be as simple as sprinkling with water or sprinkling with pig's blood or as complex as having various purification materials attached in a circle around someone for a specific ailment. If this were the case, the initiate would always be accompanied by his "circle of purification" accoutrements, perhaps genuine medicinal herbs combined with some magic spell for extra punch. Tracing magic circles or other magical geometric designs helped keep evil out and blessings in. The Lupercalia ceremony is a good example.

The final step of initiation, the bestowal of the garland, completed the process. The initiate then had all rights and privileges of the mystery religion, including the right to initiate others.

Uninitiated followers of Ceres worshipped her in thankfulness for literal grain with which to sustain their bodies. Initiated members of her cult believed that in her capacity as the Mother of Corn or Grain she had endowed them with the bread of spiritual or eternal life.[36] From where did this idea come?

Asaph recalled the miraculous feeding of the Israelites in the wilderness.

> He had commanded the clouds from above, and opened
> the doors of heaven, And had rained down manna upon
> them to eat, and had given them of the corn of heaven
> (Psalm 78:23-25).

They ate until they were full. Paul pointed out that this wilderness manna pointed ahead to the Savior, who would nourish them with spiritual manna (1 Corinthians 10:3).

Let us not fool ourselves. Satan knew the prophecies of Scripture. What he did not know—because it had not been prophesied—was the "mystery which from the beginning of the world hath been hid in God, Who created all things by Jesus Christ" (Ephesians 3:9) and was revealed to Paul during his prison (house) confinement.

Satan previously induced rebellion against God. The distance between rebellion, the spiritual blindness of idol worship, and total disregard of all sexual restraints narrowed quickly. "Professing themselves to be wise, they became fools" (Romans 1:22).

It was no coincidence that the initiates of Ceres believed they had found the true spiritual bread. Satan instigated, manipulated, and diverted worship from the coming Savior to false messiahs, male and female. "For false Christs and false prophets shall rise, and shall shew signs and wonders, to seduce, if it were possible, even the elect" (Mark 13:22).

Nor was it by accident or whim that our omniscient Lord said of Himself, "I am the bread of life. He that cometh to me shall never hunger and he that believeth on Me shall never thirst" (John 6:35) and "I am the living bread which came down from heaven: If any man eat of this bread, he shall live for ever; and the bread that I will give is My flesh, which I will give for the life of the world" (John 6:51). Christ knew very well the figures of speech of the patricians and the plebians. He knew the hopelessness, the desperation, the sinfulness pervading society, and for that, He willingly gave His life.

How many knowingly worship Ceres today? Of course, many do because of the revival of paganism. For those of us who are believers in Christ, although we have no desire to worship Ceres, we are consigned to honoring her whether we wish to or not. Our common household word *cereal* derives from her name, and we speak it nearly every day.

One might ask, what has this to do with legal holidays in the United States other than that someone might have cereal for breakfast on Memorial Day? This unholy religious festival is another example of devotion misdirected or diverted from the spring Passover and the "Lamb without blemish and without spot: Who verily was foreordained before the foundation of the world" (1 Peter 1:19–20).

Artemis

In the autumn of AD 52, the apostle Paul went to Ephesus.[37] This city was a common meeting place for all classes of people from Asia and Europe; ships from many Mediterranean as well as northern European ports docked there. Ephesus stood a mile from the Aegean Sea near the mouth of the River Cayster and connected to major markets by good roads in the interior. The city was in essence the metropolis of Proconsular Asia.

For two and a half years thereafter, Paul proclaimed "the things concerning the kingdom of God" (Acts 19:8). He had laid his hands upon many new converts, and Jewish believers in the Messiah had spoken in tongues and prophesied. His widely extended proclamations of the Lord Jesus reached "all they which dwelt in Asia" (Acts 19:10), Greeks and Jews alike. Paul had confidence in his proclamations of the saving grace of Christ, but the results of his preaching took an unexpected turn.

The one message the inhabitants of Ephesus couldn't tolerate was Paul's incessant theme that there were no gods made by hand. He had made inroads into a specific pagan worship, and the craftsmen of various guilds were losing money. Not enough people were buying shrines to their goddess, Artemis, and the artisans were in a fighting mood.

Hand in hand with Artemis worship went the practice of magic. In fact, magic was so prevalent that "a common name for scrolls inscribed with magic spells was 'Ephesian letters.'"[38] Even some of the charlatan Jewish rabbis indulged in the use of magic for their profit.

After Paul debated with the Jews for three months in their synagogue, he rented a lecture hall from the divinity school of Tryannus (Acts 19:9). His teaching continued each day from eleven in the morning to four in the afternoon for two years. Undoubtedly, any remaining time would have been occupied with his vocation of tentmaking. Paul succeeded in convincing many of the new converts of the ungodliness of their activities, so to counteract effects of their previous mischief, many practitioners made certain spells ineffective by revealing their secret meanings; ultimately, many converted magicians held a great fire to destroy the rest (Acts 19:19). As the magic scrolls went up in smoke, so also did profits from shrine sales.

By spring AD 55, after two years of declining profits and after the dramatic public burning of the magic books, the craftsmen determined that Paul had to be stopped and worship of Artemis had to continue. After all, she was the patroness and protector of the silversmiths, their guardian and supporter. Her month-long spring celebration had to continue. The enraged artisans of the various guilds, led by Demetrius, the silversmith, brought matters to a head, and Paul's very life, humanly speaking, hung by a thread. (See complete text in Acts 19 and 20.)

Who Was Artemis?

In the Greek texts of the Acts, the goddess who caused such a ruckus was identified as Artemis, Diana being her Roman counterpart. The two shared many characteristics, and their identities are often confused. Translators of the King James Version succumbed to Roman influence and translated the name as Diana.

Like Cybele of Pessinus and Ceres of Sicily, Artemis was a vegetation and fertility goddess whose image in ebony also fell from Jupiter, that is, from the sky (Acts 19:35). Like Cybele, she was venerated as a moon goddess.

In reality, there were many different goddesses with the name Artemis in various provinces. In history and literature, their identities have become confused and their characteristics merged with one another. This sketch will concentrate upon the Ephesian Artemis.

Temple of Artemis

Her magnificent temple was one of the seven wonders of the ancient world. The original temple had burned on the day Alexander the Great was born. Contemporary travelers journeyed from afar to view the replacement temple, an architectural masterpiece that took 220 years to build. The massive, marble structure stood outside the city walls, measured 342 feet by 164 feet, and was supported by 127 columns 56 feet high—each column a gift from a king.[39]

Contained within the enormous structure behind a curtain stood the goddess herself, and behind her shrine was a storage facility comparable to a modern bank vault in which the wealthy stored their treasures. The temple also housed sculptures and paintings by the artistic masters of the day.

Image of Artemis

Artemis has been depicted in various ways, perhaps due to her many functions. Coneybeare and Howson write that her image enshrined within the temple was not nearly as magnificent as her temple.[40] It consisted of a crude block of wood roughly resembling a female form with a metal bar in each hand and mystic writings on her garment.

A more familiar concept of Artemis is that of an alabaster statue in a Naples museum that represents her as mother of all creation. As such, it depicts her with many nodes on her body conjectured to be breasts, symbolic of her role as nourishing mother to all humanity. Whether they are breasts or testes of bulls, as others have argued, their purpose affirms her role as fertility goddess, even though, paradoxically, she remained a "chaste" goddess.

In Greek mythology, there are several versions of the Artemis tale. One version states that Artemis helped deliver her twin brother, Apollo, so she by her very nurturing aspect became a patron of childbirth. Women in childbirth invoked her aid, and after safely delivering, offered clothes or locks of hair to her.

Because of her warm, protective nature and sympathies toward the vulnerable, the Amazons, warrior women of Greek mythology, came to the temple for asylum when they suffered from unjust treatment by the male Olympian patriarchy. Artemis, therefore, also became known for her fearless hunting skills through her associations with the Amazons.

Those hunting skills were questioned by Apollo, who challenged Artemis to hit a distant object swimming in the ocean. Her arrow hit its mark, but the object happened to be Orion, the only mortal she had ever loved. She turned her dead lover into stars in the constellation Orion, and she became depicted as a goddess of light associated with the crescent or new moon.[41] Coins of cities other than Ephesus depict her as carrying a torch with her head surrounded by the crescent moon. (Today's pagans view her as their "feminist" goddess.)

Preparations for Artemisia

Beginning at the vernal equinox, the people of Ephesus began preparations for the month-long May celebration of Artemisia, also called Ephesia and Ecumenica. The celebrations were not just for Ephesian residents; they were attended with enthusiasm by coastal dwellers and inland inhabitants who considered Ephesus Asia's common meeting place. Gymnastics contests, music contests, and general debauchery prevailed the entire month.

It is easy to imagine the bustling activity of that time by comparing preparations for Artemisia to modern Olympic preparations. Today, carpenters, electricians, and plumbers work overtime to meet the demands of new facilities to accommodate multitudes of tourists. One can visualize artisans of Ephesus hiring workers to help meet the demands of that most prosperous month of their year.

Paul's listeners venerated the primitive image of Artemis and her gorgeous temple and replicated their likenesses countless times. They crafted small, portable shrines of wood, gold, silver, or terra cotta for travelers to carry on journeys or for household use. Much like modern souvenir seekers, what ancient traveler would willingly leave Ephesus without a copy of the great temple and the Great Mother of all creation?

Artemis Worshippers

Artemis worship seems to have been based on a confutation and a confusion of the role of the sexes in society. Her worship was closely aligned with the worship of Dionysus, who has been referred to as male or female.

Phrygian music (minor mode) accompanied her worship, led by eunuch priests, *megabyzi*. Many of the megabyzi had been castrated as young boys and sold by their poor parents for use as household servants or in sodomidic temple rituals. Some had become high-ranking, influential citizens. They were pledged to follow strict dietary requirements and rules of chastity, which seems a bit inconsistent to our way of thinking when one considers their licentious role in the temple worship.

Like Cybele, this Ephesian goddess was also served by *hierdules*, temple prostitutes. Young girls, "sacred slaves," were brought in to serve in one of the three classes of priestesses. A large staff of such priestesses undoubtedly accommodated the many sailors frequenting the port. In addition, vast numbers of common slaves had charge of sweeping and cleaning the temple.[42]

Here, then, were the hostile ones who railed against Paul because of his high moral standards and his teachings regarding Jesus Christ, the Son of God. A population consumed by lust and greed had no desire to hear anything Paul had to say. These organized demonstrators shouted for two hours, "Great is Artemis of the Ephesians."

God intervened through the town clerk, who assured the demonstrators that Paul had not blasphemed Artemis and further, if they had a complaint, they should take it to court. By God's grace, Paul survived the Ephesian uproar. Simply put, God was not finished with His pattern. "Howbeit for this cause I obtained mercy, that in me first Jesus Christ might show forth all longsuffering, *for a pattern* to them which should hereafter believe on Him to life everlasting" (1 Timothy 1:16). Paul could not be duplicated, but he would yet mentor facsimiles in the faith, most notable of whom were Timothy, "my own son in the faith" (1 Timothy 1:2) and Titus, "mine own son after the common faith" (Titus 1:4).

As a devout Jew, Paul observed the Passover in the form of the communion, at least until after God revealed the message of Colossians. Certainly he experienced heaviness of heart at the misappropriation of God's holy month, Nisan, into this most unholy of holidays.

CHAPTER 11

Pagan Goddesses and Customs Honored in the British Isles

"And we know that we are of God and the whole world lieth in wickedness" (1 John 5:19). The more one delves into ancient and medieval history, the more one begins to understand, if only slightly, to what Christ might have been referring in that passage.

In spite of the fact that the United States has a Christian majority, every week, we unintentionally honor ancient Norse and Roman gods. Tuesday, *tiwesdaeg*, honors Tiw, the old Norse god of war; Wednesday, *wodnesdaeg*, belongs to Woden, the chief god of war; Thursday, *thursdaeg*, honors Thunor (Thor), god of the thunderstorm; Friday, *frigadaeg*, honors fertility goddess Frig; Saturday, *saeterndaeg*, honors the Roman god Saturn; Sunday, *sunnandaeg*, honors the sun, Monday, *monandaeg*, honors the moon.

These objects countless times received homage by human sacrifice, but in our apathy—mostly in our ignorance—we are continuing to name them in our everyday affairs. One might ask, "Do we have any other option?" At this point, we don't seem to have any unless we wish to label our documents with numbers, that is, instead of saying Sunday, we say the first day, Monday, the second day, etc.

Traditional Judaism does this, naming only one day, the Sabbath. Most agree that it is hard to buck a custom so deeply entrenched, but won't it be a wonderfully blessed time for those who will dwell in the millennial kingdom of Christ? What will be the names of the days? Certainly not pagan gods or goddesses, for everything there will be Christ-centered!

We who are descendants of Europeans have a legacy of despicable violence enacted in the name of worship. This is not to say that Europeans were more despicable than any other group of people, for wickedness and depravity have occurred and are occurring at this time all over earth. However, because we are tracing our holiday lineage, we will confine the study to Europeans and their forebears.

Indeed, when God dispersed the rebellious Bel worshippers from Babylon, they carried their odious practices to the far reaches of the globe. From the black smoke pits of Russia to the islands of the South Pacific, from the various tribes scattered throughout the Americas to the tribes of Africa, evidence of human sacrifice has been found either in literature or by discoveries of anthropologists and archeologists. These sacrifices often occurred during vernal equinox rites as well as in other seasonal celebrations.

Celts

A Celtic trade network stretched from Ireland, down the west coast of Britain, and across to the Mediterranean. Where trade went, there also traveled Celtic religion. On return voyages, knowledge of Roman and Grecian deities traveled with the cargoes.

Not only by sea, but also by land, the British Isles received religious practices from tribes migrating northward from Greece through Spain, Gaul, and the Germanic lands bordering the North Sea. With this intermingling knowledge of gods and goddesses, is it any wonder there were so many comparable versions of the pagan deities?

The Celts affirmed literally thousands of gods and goddesses.

The names of over four thousand Celtic gods have been recorded, but it is likely that most of them were local variants of prominent gods such as Mabon, Lleu, Taran, and Nudd. It has been argued that the Celts lacked an organized pantheon, but there are suggestions that they possessed a notion of a single divine spirit, and that, despite the cruelty of some of their rituals, their moral comprehension was well developed.[43]

Since this is from a secular writer, one wonders what he meant by "moral comprehension"!

Druids did teach the existence of one God, but they gave him the name Be'al, source of all life or of all beings. Their Be'al seems to have much in common with the Phoenician Baal.

Druidism

Much of our information concerning early Celt religion comes from the writing of Julius Caesar and other Roman authors along with supplemental archaeological evidence. These manuscripts inform that male and sometimes female druidic priests were the intellectuals of the Celtic communities. Considered the upper class, they were highly respected teachers of children and the community and keepers of the religious rituals. They performed animal and human sacrifices. They also foretold the future by the way blood flowed from the dying and by the convulsions of the limbs of the victims, a practice undoubtedly originating in Babylon.[44]

Caesar considered them a learned but secretive group who enjoyed special privileges in that they enjoyed unrestricted travel, and they were exempt from paying taxes and fighting in wars. Even though they were literate, the druids wrote nothing for instruction; thus, all knowledge passed orally. Consequently, some students of druidism took twenty years to learn the divination, healing, poetry, magic, and religious rites connected with their vocation.

Ancient Druid Beliefs: Animism, Shape Shifting, Totemism

Belief in animism pervaded the culture. Basically, animism attributes conscious life to inanimate objects (rocks) or phenomena of nature (thunder) and equates animals with humans. All were thought of as social, emotional, or psychological beings. The stare of a stag, the squeal of a pig, or the flooding of a creek was explained in psychological or emotional terms.

To get a small grasp of animism, we must adjust our thinking from the comfort of our modern lives to the agrarian simplicity of a people who lived in thatched huts, often with animals inside for winter warmth. What to us is irrational was to them true and obvious. To eyes blinded by sin, animate and inanimate nature in rural landscapes worked together to shape every hope and daydream or to account for every demonic nightmare.

Animism and shape shifters (those who could change from one identity to another) went hand in hand. Shape shifting from human to animal or animal to human could be applied involuntarily by an enemy or assumed voluntarily by magical powers.

Druids also believed in the immortality of the soul, not in the sense that our contemporaries believe—that the soul lives eternally with God—but that the soul passed on to another body after death in reincarnation or multiple reincarnations. The Celtic mythological tale of Cerridwen illustrates reincarnation and shape shifting.

Cerridwen (also Caridwen, Ceridwen, Cereduin)

The Celtic Great Mother or Grain Goddess comparable to Ceres kept the cauldron in the underworld. Her cauldron contained a magical elixir of all knowledge, which when consumed, preserved her omniscience. Gwion, instead of guarding the cauldron as assigned, tasted the magic potion and immediately possessed all knowledge. The two became enemies. To get away, Gwion transformed into a hare, and

Cerridwen changed into a greyhound in pursuit. Gwion transformed into a fish, but Cerridwen changed into an otter and continued the chase. This transmigration lasted until he transformed into a grain of corn and Cerridwen became a hen and greedily swallowed him. In a bizarre twist, he was later reborn to her as a boy and the reincarnation cycle continued.

The goddess/sorceress Cerridwen possessed dark, prophetic powers and manifested herself violently, more so than the Greek Muses, who theoretically inspired poets and musicians. Welsh poets at one time called themselves sons of Cerridwen. Howbeit, her symbol, the sow, indicated her protection over her swine people whom I discuss next.

From where did these swine people come? Totemism, another feature of druidism, associated clans and families with animals or objects. It essentially taught that misshapen ancestors combined animal and human features long before the human form triumphed. Specific clans or families linked by common descent from one of these melded primitive ancestors might be wolf people, cat people, oak people, rock people, or any imaginable combination. Not many centuries removed from Babylon, they may have had acquaintance with Dagon, the fish-god of the Philistines, whose name meant "grain" or "wheat" and was associated with harvest (see 1 Samuel 5:1–5). As you may remember, Dagon had the body of a fish and the head and hands of a man.

The totem represented a bond of unity within the group; consequently, totem creatures couldn't be harmed in any way. Whatever their ancestral spirit, it protected the clan from hunger or disease. A totem symbol could be engraved on weapons, tattooed on the body, or carved onto poles. If a clan had a bovine totem, that clan couldn't kill cattle.

Sacrifice: Animal and Human

As northern Europeans descended deeper into transgression, worshipping the creature rather than the Creator, more abominable rituals occurred. Prisoners of war and criminals were kept specifically to be offered in sacrifice, and when the supply of criminals had been depleted, innocent wives or children might be offered to expiate guilt, to pacify a god or goddess, or in anticipation of a better crop. In certain areas, it was acceptable to offer criminals but forbidden to offer innocents. Christians, of course, were not considered innocents; they were thought of as intolerant, stubborn troublemakers. To sacrifice them served a twofold purpose: it cleansed society of undesirables and fertilized the soil with nutrient-rich blood flowing into the earth, resulting in a super abundance of grain. In this abased thinking, grain may have been the lowest thing to which a creature could descend before working its way back up life's ladder.

Groves

The Bible is replete with references to idol worship taking place in groves, 1 Kings 14:23, 2 Kings 16:4, and 2 Chronicles 28:4 to name a few. Celtic groves ranged from being simple places of reverence for ancestor trees to open sanctuaries dedicated to a specific god or gods. Each tree had its own ancestral spirit, so Celts commonly buried their dead in a hollowed trunk of an oak, the most important of trees. Second in importance, the almond (translated "hazel" in Genesis 30:37), prized for its nuts, inspired creativity and encouraged fertility.

Groves from Syria to Britain were carefully tended. Gathering wood from the gods' plantations was illegal. Local magistrates gathered fines from freeborn offenders and whipped slaves who couldn't afford the fines. Eunuchs and slaves tended the trees under supervision of a priest or priestess. Christians, known for felling these groves, showed determination at both ends of the Mediterranean.

> St. Martin was remembered for killing some great old
> trees in Gaul, and in the east, in the sixth century, John
> of Ephesus made several assaults on Asia's sacred timber.
> The triumph of Christianity was accompanied by the
> sound of the axe on age-old arboreta.[45]

The word *grove* sounds innocent enough, but in reality, groves were places of degenerate wickedness. They were generally situated on hilltops so night revelers could easily view the first rays of their sun god. Groves displayed tree trunks stripped of branches and leaves that were carved into phallic symbols, the upright pales representing procreation of life. In the Old Testament, the pale represented the goddess Asherah and was erected beside Baal's altar. Such foulness provoked the Lord to anger, for He wrote they "put the branch to their nose" (Ezekiel 8:17).

Other groves consisted of a sacrificial altar, a *cromlech*, in the center surrounded by idols, probably totems carved from tree trunks. The more prosperous overlaid the idol or totem with silver or gold.

Stones and other materials also were used to represent the "image of the male" (Ezekiel 16:17). The *menhirs* standing in British Isles today are descendants of the Asherim of Canaanite nations.[46]

From Totems to Temples

In time, worshippers erected temples to these lifeless idols, though some believe idols may have been energized by demonic activity. Apparently, these temples were of sound structure and esthetically pleasing, for Pope Gregory in AD 601 gave instructions to Abbot Mellitus that the idols were to be destroyed but not the temples. The temples themselves were to be aspersed with holy water and dedicated to God. This had a twofold motive: to show the former and present idol worshippers that they would be welcomed to the same places of worship as they had previously, and that the shift of worship would be to God. Further, no longer would oxen be killed for the Devil but for feasting and giving thanks to God. Gregory reasoned,

> If the people are allowed some worldly pleasures in this way, they will more readily come to desire the joys of the spirit. For it is certainly impossible to eradicate all errors from obstinate minds at one stroke, and whoever

wishes to climb to a mountain top climbs gradually step
by step, and not in one leap.[47]

As early as AD 61, Roman ruler Suetonius Paulinus had begun
to outlaw the bloody practice of human sacrifice among Celtic tribes,
although Roman Caesars never fully gave it up, reserving that privilege
for themselves. Rome did break the power of the druids, but the
coming of Christianity with its good message of the one true sacrifice
for humanity's sins negated their need for sacrifice. Yet it was hundreds
of years before Christianity dissipated druidic influence.

Early believers in Christ attempted to exterminate druidism and
paganism, but they were never completely successful. Many pagans
simply went underground into less-noticeable activity. Just as Christianity
has many denominations and sects, so does modern paganism, and
today, followers of druidism are practicing openly throughout the world
in the form of neopaganism, Wicca, druidism, or by other names.

Many modern druidic groups and groves welcome all who wish
to share "the attitudes of our ancestors."[48] In fact, some modern
practitioners view this worship as a means of learning about ancestors
and understanding genealogical roots. Nevertheless, at least one,
the Bohemian Grove, a 2,700 acre, exclusive retreat in Monte Rio,
California, is off limits to common folk. Only elite, male, political and
media personalities are welcomed to this top-secret grove.

English

Long before the translation of the Hebrew and Greek Scriptures
into the language of the common peasant, many ethnic groups vied for
territory in the British Isles. Scots from Ireland made raids across the
Irish Sea, while Jutes, Saxons, and Angles swarmed across the North
Sea. Savage Picts from the southern tip of the Scandinavian peninsula
invaded the interior. Danes attacked from the north, and Romans
invaded from the south. Each ethnic group brought its own pantheon,
and each had its own version of the Earth Mother.

Nerthus (Hretha)

No one knows for sure when the Earth Mother concept developed in England, but it seems that from the earliest times, the English had great reverence for a female goddess who possessed an exaggerated sexual organ. England's early Earth Mother was known as Nerthus or Hretha. The *h* is probably silent, so her name would sound like "Eartha" (Old English spelling, Eortha). (In most other languages as well, the earth is considered the feminine Mother Earth in contrast to the masculine Sky Father.) The name may mean "fury," a good reason to think of her as a battle goddess.

Hretha's image remained veiled within a sacred cloth in a sacred forest on an island, perhaps what is now Burgsee (*Herthasee*), an island in the Baltic Sea. She was approachable by only one priest, who knew when Hretha in her oxen-pulled cart would appear at any one village. When she did appear at the spring equinox, great happiness, peace, and calm reigned; no wars were fought, and many weddings were performed.

Roman historian Tacitus informed us that Nerthus was

> worshipped with orgies and mysterious rites at night by Teutonic tribes. Her veiled statue was moved from place to place by sacred cows. After the rites, the image, vestments, and vehicle were bathed in a lake.[49]

The washing ritual completed, Hretha disappeared into the water. The cart-pulling slaves who had viewed her holy figure were put to death by drowning, thus disappearing along with Hretha. Those who had not looked directly on her image stored the sacred cart until its next needed appearance.

A similarity exists in means of transportation between Cybele and Hretha. Cybele proceeded through the streets of Rome in her lion-pulled cart silently blessing her worshippers; Hretha traversed the English countryside bestowing her blessings.

Ostara, Eostre, or Easter?

We previously cited pagan day names. Not only were the days of the week named for pagan gods, two of the Anglo-Saxon calendar months were also named for goddesses. In AD 730, the Venerable Bede, England's first historian, recorded the only information we have about that calendar. According to him, the equivalent of our March, Hrethmonath, honored the goddess Hretha. Our April would have been Eostremonath in honor of Eostre, a Teutonic goddess of Germanic tribes.

The Anglo-Saxon year had two seasons: six months of summer and six months of winter. Hrethmonath was the last winter month; after enduring months of snowy or gloomy weather, the people looked forward to Eostremonath, the beginning of summer and the new year with its indulgent celebrations.

Believe Bede or Not?

Currently, a move to discredit Bede seems underway. A few modern critics charge him with being a meddling monk who just wanted to mess up pagan history. They accuse him of developing the goddess Eostre to suit his theological purposes because history books and early manuscripts were devoid of mention of any such goddess. It is not questioned that the lunar month around our April in the Julian calendar was called Eostremonath. However, the critics have no suggestions or alternatives for the origin of the Eostre in Eostre's month.

Some things cannot be proven. Do you remember as a child having grandparents or perhaps older neighbors who didn't speak the same as you were taught in school? Did they have speech mannerisms and old-fashioned expressions you considered quaint and strange? Some of those expressions you have never seen written in any short stories or novels, nor will you. If you should repeat these old phrases to a philologist, he could tell you quite sincerely that these expressions never existed because he has not found them in any old English literature. Your grandparents and older neighbors have long ago passed away, so you cannot tape record these words. What do you do?

In a similar vein, we cannot prove Bede correct, nor can we or others prove him incorrect. We know in German oral tradition, according to Jacob Grimm's *Deutsche Mythologie* published in 1835, Ostara was worshipped on hilltops at dawn and had a month named after her, Ostaramanoth, and a holiday, Ostern. He stated matter-of-factly that their goddess, Ostara, took her name from the goddess Eostre (who never existed?). It should be understood that by his own admission, Grimm was not trying to prove anything but was simply recording oral tradition as he knew it, just as he and his brother, Wilhelm, recorded the now famous but then oral fairy tales. Grimm noted the parallels between the Eostre and Ostara and implied a common origin, but what was it? If Bede originated it, he certainly came up with a worldly winner. Multitudes of pagans and Christians from antiquity to the present celebrate Eostre's Day!

Two questions arise: First, did the Anglo-Saxons worship two earth mothers? It appears they may have had many, for Bede translates the night following New Year's, Modra Niht, as Mothers Night. We know that Freya also was an earth mother whose partner, Frey, was the Norse god of fertility. Protection to one's tribe or clan rested on these mother goddess's shoulders.

Second, if Hretha was worshipped at the equinox, how and when was she displaced by Eostre, who was worshipped in our April? The Anglo-Saxon fourth month, Eostremonat, would have begun late in what we now call March. Consequently, Eostre might have been associated with the equinox as well. Another possible conjecture is that Eostre replaced Hretha when her celebration on the first Sunday after the full moon following the vernal equinox replaced the Passover (communion) celebration among early believers.

Suggested Etymologies of Eostre

To this all scholars agree: the word *Easter* was never used in the original Greek manuscripts. It has no biblical association with the death, burial, and resurrection of Jesus Christ.

On the issue of Eostre, Bible believers have sometimes been accused of creating fake-lore when trying to reconstruct pagan history and looking for a goddess who never existed. This is genuinely perplexing considering modern pagans perform equinoctial rituals to Eostre associated with a goddess of dawn who brings forth fertility and renewal of life. Part of the ceremony includes carrying Eostre's eggs around the symbolic circle and offering them on the altar to Mother Earth and Angus Og (Lad of Love) with incense and holy water.

Do modern pagans keep Eostre's name because they like the poetic sound of it, or has Eostre's identity been preserved through oral tradition from antiquity? Until a biblical archaeologist or an ecclesiastical history professional can show us differently by some as yet undiscovered evidence, we must continue our process of etymological word association to try to determine from where this "nonexistent" Eostre came.

According to many Bible scholars, Eostre is a heathen term derived from the Phoenician Astarte of 1 Kings 11. She has been identified with the Semitic Ashtoreth, consort of Baal, in the Old Testament and the Sumerian Inanna. Moabite neighbors of Israel worshipped Ashtar-Chemosh. In 1 Samuel 31:10, the Philistines killed Saul and put his armor in Ashtoreh-Astarte's temple.

Likenesses also exist among the Egyptian Isis, the Greek Aphrodite, and the Roman Venus along with Ceres, Cybele, and Artemis previously cited. Perhaps most convincing is the phonetic similarity of Eostre to the Babylonian and Assyrian goddess Ishtar, whom biblical linguists pronounce "Easter."

Linguists also note a similarity between Eostre and the Greek word transliterated *heoos* (pronounced with the rough breath, *he-ō-os*), meaning "at early dawn" or "eastern" and the Latin *eos* meaning "dawn" and its cognate *eous*, meaning "belonging to the morning" or "eastern." In Old English, adding suffixes *er*, *re*, or *ier* denoted a person's occupation, as in farmer or furrier. Likewise in Latin, adding *or* denotes person performing the action. Imaginations do not need stretching to see the relationship of these roots—a goddess whose name means "east" and whose occupation among other things (*er*) is bringing forth the sun.

Was Eostre Beautiful?

Contemporary movie or television viewers are satiated to the point of nausea with descriptions of actors or actresses being spoken of as sex gods or goddesses. As a sex or fertility goddess, one wonders how Eostre would compare; probably not well in our eyes. Anglo-Saxon myth depicts Ostara/Eostre as a personification of the rising sun having a hare's head or ears. Neopagans believe she possessed a hare's head. This, of course, cannot be verified but just speculated on based on knowledge of druidic belief in animism.

Sunrise in Babylon and Beyond

Reread Ezekiel 8 to glimpse the scene in the inner court of the Lord's house and view the disgusting, abominable practices of idolatry: creeping things and pagan idols in forms of abominable beasts. Imagine! In their small minds shrunken by degeneracy, they thought the Lord couldn't see them!

> The Lord seeth us not; the Lord hath forsaken the earth (Ezekiel 8:12).

> And he brought me into the inner court of the Lord's house, and behold, at the door of the temple of the Lord between the porch and the altar, were about five and twenty men, with their backs toward the temple of the Lord and their faces were toward the east: and they worshipped the sun toward the east (Ezekiel 8:15-16).

119

What they were worshipping was Baal along with his female counterpart, Asherah. Does this sound like a contemporary Eostre service?

The names of the goddesses varied with locality, but practices were much the same: sacrifices and orgies. Goddesses received worship through prostitution of castrated males and/or women prostitutes. Herodotus recorded the Babylonian custom that every woman, rich or poor, must sit in the temple of Ishtar and at some time in her life have sexual intercourse with a stranger as her religious duty.[50] Shame was not a consideration; the rite symbolized divine union between goddess and man. As in Ephesus, seaports with temples maintained a large staff of "religious prostitutes" to accommodate sailors visiting the ports.

Back to Bede

Not in defense of Bede's theology but in defense of his character, it's intriguing that on his dying day in 735, the Venerable Bede completed his translation of John's gospel. This resembles more a man secure in his faith than a man intent on bolstering it by fabricating yet another goddess.

CHAPTER 12

Traditions of Past Easters

Though scholars scoff and declare no Eostre existed, it is common knowledge that celebrations of spring rites were held in the British Isles during Eostremonat in the pre-Christian period at or near Passover. To whom specifically these were dedicated is conjectural.

Fire Festivals

Specific yearly events honored the fire god or goddess of the locale. After Constantine usurped the prerogatives of the local Christian churches, predominantly Catholic countries continued the fire festivals, bringing sun deities and fertility traditions into the "state" church, professing to honor Christ, but doing so under the name of the same old pagan goddess. In British lands, Eostre's name predominated.

Imagine a generally devoted husband bringing an expensive anniversary gift to his wife, Roberta, but the present is engraved with Esther's name. His flattering excuse: "You've always been such a good wife, so kind and understanding, and Esther really is a nice name that I knew you wouldn't mind." But Roberta knows that Esther is an ex-girlfriend. Would Roberta be jealous? Would this marriage endure? If Roberta reacted as many would react, hubby would be fortunate to escape uninjured.

Imagine how Christ must feel when we profess to love Him but continue substituting another deity's name for His in a service theoretically dedicated to Him. We are not left clueless; He told us how He feels: "For thou shalt worship no other god; for the Lord whose name is JEALOUS, is a jealous God" (Exodus 34:14). When Bible believers celebrate a Resurrection Day and call it Easter, are we provoking Christ to jealousy?

The agglomerated pagan/"Christian" fire-ritual week followed a traditional agenda. On the Saturday before Easter Sunday, all fires were extinguished from the churches and relit from the Easter candle. From the new candle flames, bonfires (originally from Middle English, *bonefires*) were kindled. These bonfires, by tradition always lit on the same hills, resulted in those hills being named Osterberg, or Easter Mountain. Rival villages competed to have the greatest bonfire. From the ashes of bonfires, people carried charred oak, walnut, or beech sticks home to relight their candles and hearths.

As the fires burned, villagers observed the drift of ashes. At planting time, seeds were sown where ashes had blown, and supplicants beseeched God to protect the fields from vermin and natural disasters. As the bonfires died, young and old jumped over the flames, exposing their reproductive organs to absorb warmth and ensure fertility. Cattle also passed through the fire for the same reason.

A straw man, Judas, went up in flames in the church graveyard on Easter Sunday as people chanted his blazing. However, women and young girls were not allowed near the Judas fire and could observe it only from a remote location. It has been speculated that only men were allowed to absorb the might and fertility of the gods when they participated in this particular rite.

In some areas, the burning of the Judas man occurred between nine and ten at night on Easter Sunday. A complicated racing contest determined which young man earned the privilege of lighting the flames, but no one under eighteen could partake in the ceremony, probably a primitive version of our contemporary "adults only" shows.

Burning Judas in effigy had replaced the practice of human sacrifice. Julius Caesar described the human sacrifice as a "wicker man," a compartmentalized cage containing small animals and slaves or criminals offered for burning.

Besides ensuring fertility, repelling witches served another of the fires' purposes. Farmers blamed witches for many of the ills of the time: cattle diseases, poor crops, stealing milk from cows, hail, thunder, lightning, and just about anything otherwise unexplainable. Flaming discs hurled into the air, burning wheels rolled down hills, both ignited hovering witches flying low on their broomsticks.

On Easter Monday, eager planters gathered ashes from the fires and strew them on fields soon to be planted.

The *Catholic Encyclopedia* informs us,

> The bishops issued severe edicts against the sacrilegious Easter fires (Conc. Germanicum, a.742, c.v.; Council of Lestines, a. 743, n.15), but did not succeed in abolishing them everywhere. The Church adopted the observance into Easter ceremonies, referring it to the fiery column in the desert and to the Resurrection of Christ; the new fire on Holy Saturday is drawn from flint, symbolizing the Resurrection of the Light of the World from the tomb closed by a stone.[51]

So here we have an official admission that the origins of Easter fires are pagan.

At the risk of being judgmental toward less-informed people, we have an example of groups untutored in God's Word and trying to serve two masters, the old fire god or goddess and Christ. "No man can serve two masters: for either he will hate the one and love the other: or else he will hold to the one and despise the other. Ye cannot serve God and mammon" (Matthew 6:24).

Easter Bunnies

We have seen that Eostre/Ostara, the personification of the rising sun and a symbol of fertility, may have had either a hare's head or ears. Other European fertility gods and goddesses also associated with rapidly reproducing hares: Cupid, Venus, the Norse goddess Freyja, the Siberian goddess Kaltes, and England's Andraste were often depicted with hares as companions.

Because of reincarnation beliefs, killing or eating hares was forbidden; it was, after all, a serious matter to run the risk of eating one's own grandmother. That restriction, however, was lifted at Eostre's Monday feast featuring hare pie. Handfuls of the greasy pie were thrown into a drunken, raucous crowd as it lapsed into further preposterous conduct.

In 1790, one rector tried to stop this aspect of Eostre's festival, but his parishioners wrote on the walls of his vicarage, "No pie, no parson." He succumbed to their demands, and the hare pie party continues yet today on Easter Monday and is advertised in Leicestershire, England— with the added convenience of modern beer kegs.

The hare, a prolific breeder, has a gestation period of thirty-one days. One doe can produce as many as forty-two young a year. The young grow rapidly to adulthood and continue reproduction, thus, the natural connection of hares and rites of spring. During mating season, they leap wildly, and their observers compared them to witches dancing. The expression, "Mad as a March hare" derives from comparing crazed people to mating-time behavior.

Hares are native to Europe, and when the Europeans brought pagan Easter customs to the New World, rituals associated with them easily transferred to animals most resembling them, native American rabbits.

The disinformation of Easter bunnies laying and hiding eggs for innocent children to find completes the modern tale of Easter for most children, many of whom know not Christ died and rose again for them.

Easter Eggs

Throughout world cultures, the egg symbolized many things. To some, it symbolized resurrection or the world's creation. To others, eggs continued to be a symbol of fertility and were associated with the fire festivals in enhancing men's virility. Other than at fire festivals, the sickly or weak were encouraged to eat more eggs. Eating eggs at Easter assured an upcoming healthy year, especially if eaten just before sunrise. As in the past, some cultures today use eggs emblematically in marriage rituals.

An assortment of pagan mythologies attribute the world's creation to an egg: an Egyptian legend presents the bennu bird, the phoenix, having hatched from a gigantic egg produced by chief god Geb, the earth, and Nut, his wife, the sky. According to legend, when it reached the end of its five-hundred-year life, it set fire to its nest. From the dead bird's ashes, a new phoenix came to life, continuing the cycle of representing the sun dying each night and rising each morning.

In Hindu fables, the gold world egg hatched Prajapati, father of all gods and creatures. Hindu sacred writings relate a creation story in which the world developed from an egg. Mountains formed from the outer membrane, clouds from the inner membrane, ocean from the fluids, and the sun from the yolk.

Early inhabitants of the largest Hawaiian island believed their island formed from the bursting of a gigantic bird's egg, while druidic creation tales are much the same as the Sumerian creation story: the world hatched from a divine primeval egg. In Babylonia,

> An egg of wondrous size is said to have fallen from heaven into the river Euphrates. The fishes rolled it to the bank, where the doves having settled upon it, and hatched it; out came Venus, who afterwards was called the Syrian Goddess—that is, Astarte or Easter.[52]

125

Babylonians believed in reincarnation and taught that Astarte survived the flood by floating in an egg containing the world. After the waters receded, the world itself emerged.

Again from the *Catholic Encyclopedia*,

> Because the use of eggs was forbidden during Lent, they were brought to the table on Easter Day, coloured red to symbolize the Easter joy ... The custom may have its origins in paganism, for a great many pagan customs, celebrating the return of spring, gravitated to Easter.[53]

As for coloring eggs, originally the decorations and artwork on them were based on folktales and religious myths such as those cited. For the most part, egg decorating today is basically harmless, clean fun—except for the serious craft worker who has raised the skill to an art form and those who present eggs to their goddesses, such as eggs presented to Eostre in Alban Eiler offerings.

The secular aspect of Easter is promoted in the United States by the practice of egg rolling by children on the White House lawn and egg hunts sponsored by towns and cities across the nation.

Lent

We have seen how pagan spring worship and nominal Christian practices became jumbled, pagans and Christians each doing what they considered right. That proved not enough for Satan. He next stirred something else into the mix, Lent.

By definition, Lent is the penitential season preceding Easter. The name comes from the Middle English word *lente*, meaning spring or the lengthening of the daylight hours. It begins on Ash Wednesday, forty days before Easter. Well-meaning penitents observe forty days of fasting or abstinence in memory of Christ's forty days of fast in the desert preceding Passover.

One generally thinks of Lent as a time of giving up something held dear to please Christ, for instance, chocolate, cigarettes, alcohol, meat, and so on. Some have given up bad habits altogether after going for forty days without. For example, some penitents have thought, *If I can go without a smoke for forty days, I can do it for good.* So without doubt, Lent has proved beneficial to some.

> Forty has long been universally recognized as an important number, both on account of the frequency of its occurrence, and the uniformity of its association with a period of *probation, trial,* and *chastisement*— (not *judgment,* like the number 9, which stands in connection with the punishment of enemies, but the chastisement of sons, and of a covenant people).[54]

Examples of forty days abound in Scriptures.

- Forty days Moses was in the mount (Exodus 24:18)
- Forty days of the spies (Numbers 13:25)
- Forty days of Elijah in Horeb (1 Kings 19:8)
- Forty days of Jonah and Nineveh (Jonah 3:4)
- Forty days Ezekiel lay on his right side to symbolize the forty years of Judah's transgression (Ezekiel 4:6)
- Forty days Jesus was seen by His disciples (Acts 1:3)

Where do the Greek Scriptures enjoin us to observe forty days of fasting and denial before a pagan feast? For that matter, where do the Scriptures enjoin us to observe forty days of fasting before the celebration of the resurrection? One can diligently seek the Hebrew and Greek Scriptures and find not one reference to believing Jews or Christians ever having been commanded to observe such a period. From where, then, did this practice originate? Let us look to ancient Canaan and Syria.

> The Canaanites were enslaved by one of the most terrible and degrading forms of idolatry, which encouraged

their immorality. Discovered in 1929-37, Canaanite religious literature from Ras Shamra (ancient Ugarit in North Syria) reveals the worship of the immoral gods El and Baal and the sacred courtesans Anath, Asherat, and Astarte.

Cult objects, figurines and literature combine to show how sex-centered was Canaanite religion with human sacrifice, cult of serpents, sacred courtesans and eunuch priests excessively common. The sordid depths of social degradation to which the erotic aspects of Canaanite cults led can scarcely be imagined.[55]

Ugaritic tablets of the fourteenth or thirteenth century BC describe Asherah as the consort of El, chief god of the Canaanites. She was also referred to as 'Elat, feminine form of El and the Mother of the Gods. The Bible represents her in three ways: as an idol, as a green tree, and as asherim, tree trunks. Israelites were instructed to cut down, root out, and burn these according to Deuteronomy 16:21 and Judges 6:26.

Coming forward in time, Baal replaced El in name as the chief god, and Ishtar replaced 'Elat. Judges 6:25 and 2 Kings 21:3 ordered that the altars of Baal be removed along with Asherim/Ishtar.

Ishtar was known as Inanna in Sumeria. Early Sumerian literature describes her as a heartless mate who destroyed her lovers, of whom there were many. Her sexual attraction lured men to their doom, and men feared her while being attracted to her. If she could not seduce them, she might take vengeance on them.

Inanna was paired with Dumuzi or Dumuzid. Many erotic poems celebrated their marriage. Dumuzid in Sumerian translates to Tammuz in Hebrew, and there is only one reference to the name in the Old Testament. "Then he brought me to the door of the gate of the Lord's house which was toward the north and behold there sat women weeping for Tammuz" (Ezekiel 8:14).[56] Information regarding Tammuz must therefore be gleaned from various secular accounts.

One version of the story states that Tammuz, sometimes called Bel or Baal, met his death because of his love for Ishtar although she was not the direct cause. According to legend, a wild boar killed him when he was forty. Ishtar, along with males and females accompanied by the *kinnor*, a sort of lyre, mourned Tammuz forty days, one for each year of his life. Some Bible commentaries fix the days of mourning at seven and consider the event a funeral feast.

Finally, Ishtar descended to the Land of No Return, braving all the horrors of hell to rescue Tammuz. During her absence, all sexual attraction is gone, and all procreation ceases. Poetry and lamentations written to her in frank, clear language describe activities that do not happen among animals and humanity that normally produce offspring.

Another version has Inanna/Ishtar descending through seven gates to the underworld. At each gate, she had to take off an article of clothing or jewelry. By the seventh gate, she was naked, but she dared to sit down on her sister's, Ereshkegal's, throne. The judges of the underworld condemned her to death, and she was hung on a meat hook.

She begged for a replacement of herself to be sent back to earth, but instead, she was mercifully resurrected only to find Dumuzid/Tammuz seated on her throne. Being the vengeful goddess, she set the demons on Dumuzid/Tammuz, who murdered him. In the end, Inanna changed her mind and restored her lover to life.

In both versions, each year thereafter, Tammuz died and descended to Hades. During his absence, mourners wailed for the dead to return, played musical instruments, and fasted the whole month of Tammuz, our June-July.

There are other renditions of the Ishtar and Tammuz relationship. Some are gruesome, and others are erotic. What it boils down to is that Ishtar was a religious prostitute, the leader of the harem, Tammuz, a personification of Satan.

What Tammuz stood for in the popular mind is varied: to some, he was the mighty sun god. To others, as the god of vegetation, he represented the cutting of perfect fruits or the celebration of the death and resurrection of seeds.

In Asia Minor, Egypt, Syria, Babylonia, and elsewhere, it is incontestable that the identities of deities were very much alike in their main characteristics, many having to do with solar worship or power over vegetation. It is also indisputable that Tammuz and the Greek Adonis were the same. An Orphic hymn refers to Adonis as hermaphrodite. We know the cult of Tammuz had primarily a feminine following, so the question arises, was Tammuz considered a hermaphrodite? We also know that Satan hates God's pure traditional role for men and women and will subvert their thoughts when possible and lead them into gross perversions. In the words of the goddess Ishtar, "I turn the male to the female. I am she who adorneth the male for the female; I am she who adorneth the female for the male."[57]

Whether masculine or feminine, infamous practices accompanied Tammuz worship. For seven days, the women succumbed to weeping. Along with their lamentations, they were obligated to shave their hair or to sacrifice their chastity.

Similar mourning, mock burial, and sexual ritual repeated itself in cults over the Euro-Asian geographic area in the forms of Astarte in Phoenicia and Syria, Astoreth in Israel, Ishtar in Sumeria and Babylon, Cybele in Phrygia, Artemis in Ionia, Ceres in Poseidonia, Venus in Rome, Anaita in Persia, and dare we say Eostre in England? Think of them as a single drama performed on pagan stages in many countries by different actors and actresses wearing indigenous costumes, speaking different dialects, but all with the same satanic plot.

It would be tiresome and overkill to go into more detail, for all themes concerned death, lamentation, and resurrection, and most were celebrated around the time of the Jewish Passover. The period of Lent before Easter undeniably came from these pagan practices.

CHAPTER 13

Should We Celebrate Easter, Passover, or Resurrection Day?

We have determined the pagan origins of Easter and examined some of the Ishtar/Easter customs, but how did those get confused with Passover, which had been instituted by God?

There are seventy-six references in the Bible that have been translated "Passover" in our English versions of the Scriptures. Twenty-eight of those are in the New Testament; of these, only one is translated as Easter (in Acts 12:4). Because of this most unfortunate translation, sincere believers have been swirling in confusion for centuries.

The First Passover

Let us start with the first Passover. In Exodus 12, Jehovah instructed the Israelites to kill a male lamb without spot or blemish on the fourteenth of Abib (Nisan), our April, and smear its blood on the two sides and the upper doorpost. They were to hastily eat the sacrificial lamb wearing their clothes and shoes, ready to depart at the signal. That night, the Lord smote all the firstborn in Egypt, those who lived in houses with no blood on the doorposts. Much sorrow ensued, for not one house of the Egyptians was left where the firstborn was not slain.

Pharaoh sent a message in the night for Moses and Aaron to come to him. He ordered all Israelites to take their flocks and herds and leave Egypt immediately. The Egyptians gladly gave the Israelites silver and of gold and any raiment the Israelites desired to be rid of them because the Egyptians feared they would all be killed. Such an eventful day served as a memorial, and the Jews were to keep this ordinance to the Lord throughout their generations.

> Seven days shall ye eat unleavened bread; even the first day ye shall put away leaven out of your houses: for whosoever eateth leavened bread from the first day until the seventh day, that soul shall be cut off from Israel. And in the first day there shall be an holy convocation to you; no manner of work shall be done in them, save that which every man must eat, that only may be done of you. And ye shall observe the feast of unleavened bread; for in this selfsame day have I brought your armies out of the land of Egypt; therefore shall ye observe this day in your generations by an ordinance for ever. In the first month, on the fourteenth day of the month at even, ye shall eat unleavened bread, until the one and twentieth day of the month at even. (Exodus 12:15–18)

Deuteronomy 16:1–8 instructs that the month of Abib would be observed "for the Lord thy God brought thee forth out of Egypt by night." The observant will note that the Passover was not celebrated at sunrise but in the evening. Passover and the days of unleavened bread were all referred to as the Passover. Note also that although the verse says to "observe the month of Abib," it was not a month-long celebration.

Hebrew to English Transliteration

Before we consider Acts 12:3–4, let us look at the word in question, *Passover*, and how it came to be. The first complete English translation of the Bible by John Wycliffe was handwritten in 1385. There was no word in English to represent the Hebrew word we call Passover, so he didn't translate the word but simply transliterated it to read "paske."

Later, in 1522, Martin Luther translated the Greek Scriptures into German. He knew the word *pasca* referred to the death angel passing over, but he decided that the word should be translated Ostern, a well-known festival occurring around the same time.

William Tyndale in 1534 translated the same Greek word as *ester, easter, easterlambe* and *ester fest*. When he later translated the Old Testament into English, he soon realized that the word *Easter* didn't fit, that it was totally inappropriate. At this point, he coined a new English word, *Passover*. His translation of the New Testament was never revised, so Passover remained translated as Easter in each instance.

All Greek texts including Stephanus's *Textus Receptus*, Scriveners' *Textus Receptus*, Aland-Metzger's fourth edition, Nestle, Westcott and Hort—*all* extant Greek texts—use the Greek *pasca*, "paske" when referring to Passover.

Summary of Acts 12

Chapter 12 records events regarding Herod's persecution of the converted Jewish believers in Jerusalem during the apostolic Acts era. This specific Herod is Herod Agrippa I, the son of Aristobulus and Berenice, the grandson of Herod the Great, and the nephew of Herod Antipas.

After Caius Caligula ascended the throne, he gave to Herod Agrippa I the tetrarchy of Philip, which consisted of Batanea, Trachonitis, and Aurantitus. He also gave him the tetrarchy of Lysanius along with the title of king. Shortly thereafter, Herod Agrippa received the tetrarch of Herod Antipas consisting of Galilee and Peraea. And, lastly, after the Emperor Claudius began his reign, he gave to Herod the areas of Samaria and Judea. Like his grandfather, Herod the Great, he ruled over all Palestine.

Herod Agrippa's reputation was less than honorable by normal Jewish standards. He gloried in his power and the authority bestowed upon him. Agrippa patronized pagan games, gladiatorial contests, and pagan music fests. However, on the exterior, he made a pretext of observing the Mosaic feasts and rituals, and he promoted the Jewish religion so that through him, the Jews regained some confidence in their national identity. Like many modern politicians, he took advantage of any event that could advance his agenda.

The prevailing sentiment involved the persecution of Christians. Agrippa had caused James, the brother of John, to be executed by the sword. Viewing the approval of the crowd, Agrippa seized Peter also with the intention of holding him in prison to be guarded by four quaternions of soldiers until after the week of Passover and then to have Peter's trial.

> Agrippa, who was exceeding fond of theatrical shows, intended to convert that trial into an exhibition for the amusement of the people. (*Anagine* is applied to the act of conducting any one before the public on an elevated stage.)[58]

Neither the solemnity of the occasion nor fear of the crowds but the evil arrogance of Herod Agrippa compelled him to hold Peter until after Passover week ended to make a show for his own glorification. Agrippa's intended flaunting never transpired due to the unceasing prayers of intercession by the assembly of believers and God's miraculous intervention and deliverance of Peter from prison. Of course, Peter's release highly displeased Herod, who then commanded the execution of the guards.

According to Josephus, Herod went to Caesarea with entertainment for Emperor Claudius Caesar. On the second day of the shows, Herod wore a robe woven of silver threads. At sunrise, he went to the theater for his oration. The rays of the sun reflected an intense, blinding glare from his robe. Herod's flattering followers deified him declaring, "Be thou propitious to us! If we have hitherto feared thee as a man, we shall henceforth own thee as superior to the nature of mortals."[59]

Herod Agrippa, wrapped in his huge ego, allowed his subjects to worship him when that praise should have been redirected to God. As a result, "the angel of God smote him because he gave not God the glory, and he was eaten of worms" (Acts 12:23). The church historian Eusebius gave more details: "At length, overpowered by the pain of his bowels, for four days in succession, he ended his life in the fifty-fourth year of his age and the seventh of his reign."[60]

Acts 12:4—Should It Be Easter or Passover?

One school of thought believes the King James Version was directly inspired by God and maintains that the word *Easter* is the correct one, that King Herod intended to jail Peter until after Easter was completed.

As much as we revere and respect the KJV, we must step back and look at it realistically. It is a translated version of God's holy Greek and Hebrew Scriptures. The translators worked by authority of King James and under his constraints. One limitation involved the use of the word *church*. It is based on the Old English *circe*, which means "the house of a god." The translators were not allowed to translate *ekklesia* as "assembly of believers" or as "congregation of believers." Unfortunately, many people have been misled into thinking that "church" is a building rather than God's called-out ones, the body of Christ.

No, we are not about to throw out the KJV because there are some mistranslations or some archaic word usages, but we must be aware of them and continue to do as Timothy entreated: "Study to show thyself approved unto God, a workman that needeth not to be ashamed, rightly dividing the Word of Truth" (2 Timothy 2:15). We trust Luke, the Gentile physician and companion of Paul, to have written the word correctly as *paske*, Passover, in Acts 12:4 just as the Holy Spirit had led him (2 Peter 1:21).

Christ was crucified on the day of Passover and rose the third day according to the Scriptures. Jewish converts celebrated the resurrection immediately after the Passover, and by their usual calculations, that would occur on a different day of the week from year to year. Gentile converts commemorated Christ's resurrection on the first day of the week, Sunday. By their calculations, Resurrection Day would occur on the same day of the week but on different dates from year to year. Thus, the eastern Jewish congregations in Syria, Cilicia, and Mesopotamia and the western ones in Alexandria and Rome celebrated it at different times. Disputes arose regarding the correct day to observe the new Christian Passover, now known as Communion or the Eucharist.

The Roman conquest of Jerusalem in AD 135 prodded the controversy more sharply. Greek bishops appointed by Romans to oversee Gentile Christian churches observed the Roman "Easter," thus challenging Jewish believers who observed Passover as they had before.

Church historian Eusebius tells us that Polycarp, who had observed Passover with the apostle John, traveled to Rome to end the controversy among those observing on Passover and those observing on a pagan feast day. Polycarp's meeting with Anicetus ended amicably with neither convincing the other.

However, the issue didn't go away. During the time of Victor of Rome (AD 189–199), Victor tried to force the pagan holiday time observance on the other bishops in the East. Polycrates answered Victor's threats of excommunication, informing him that he had never deviated from observing the Pascal festival and would continue to do so in spite of threats replying, "We must obey God rather than men!"

Council of Nicea, AD 325

By 325, the Roman Empire had become extremely anti-Jewish. Constantine, himself a Jew-hater, attempted to change the date of Passover from the biblically assigned time to that of the Roman sun gods and goddesses occurring near the same time. He convened a council of 318 bishops in Nicea. The council had several items on the docket, but the Passover question is the one I will address.

The Hebrew word for *Passover* was transliterated into Latin so that the pronunciation would be significantly similar to the Hebrew sound, whereas the word *Easter* was not used at all. The bishops definitely debated when Passover should be observed. Probably with some arm twisting by Constantine, the bishops came to an agreement. Constantine wrote to the bishops who had not been in attendance and gave specific instructions as well as indulging in some haranguing against the Jews. Portions of *The Ecclesiastical History of Eusebius* are translated by Isaac Boyle as follows.

> In the first place, it seemed to every one a most unworthy thing that we should follow the custom of the Jews in the celebration of this most holy solemnity, who, polluted wretches! having stained their hands with a nefarious crime, are justly blinded in their minds ... They boast that without their instructions we should be unable to commemorate the festival properly ... They do not perceive the truth ... They commemorate the Passover twice in the same year ... It was agreeable to the common judgment of all that the most holy feast on Easter should be celebrated on one and the same day ... One day has our Saviour set apart for a commemoration of our deliverance, namely, of His most holy Passion ... Regard yourselves bound to accept what has gone before, and arrange for the regular observance of this holy day ... that I may be able to celebrate with you this holy festival upon one and the same day.[61]

The time designated by Constantine for the Christian Passover would be celebrated on the first Sunday after the full moon following the vernal equinox. If the full moon should happen to be on a Sunday and coincide with Passover, it would be commemorated on the next Sunday. Feasts of the Christian Passover and the Jewish Passover must be avoided. Christians were exhorted to distance themselves as much as possible from the Jews.

Problems didn't disappear after the Council of Nicea. Faulty calculations sometimes resulted in the Romans placing the full moon too soon and the Alexandrians placing it too late. Thus, in assorted years, the Romans and Alexandrians celebrated on different days. In AD 387, Theophilus, Bishop of Alexandria, devised a chronological table of the festivals based on work done by the church there. This seemed necessary because the observances in France and Egypt were thirty-five days apart!

The date AD 457 is also significant in regard to calculating the festival date. Roman archdeacon Hilary ordered Victor of Aguitaine to devise new calculations that would make the eastern Churches' and the western Churches' festival day uniform.

No one seems to know for sure just when the Christian Passover or observance of the Lord's communion table began to be called Easter, but it was unquestionably very early. We can conjecture that it may have been shortly after the Council of Nicea, when the vernal equinox became involved in calculations. At that point, Easter replaced Passover, superstition replaced Scripture, Ishtar's name coexisted with Christ's, and a paganized-Christian doctrinal mix further diluted truth.

At least three religious elements fomented in this mixture. First, there were certainly among the sincere Jewish converts Judaizers who wished to observe Jewish rituals and ordinances and to take the early body of believers back into the bondage of law. Second, others willingly left the freedom of grace to conform to the decrees of men and went after Ishtar/Easter's day. Third, many denied the dispensation of the mystery as revealed to Paul. No surprise there, for even during Paul's lifetime, they had rejected it, as he told us in 1 Timothy 1:15. But some, faithful to the Scriptures, understood that He had "broken down the middle wall of partition" (Ephesians 2:14), that Paul had closed the gates to the kingdom in Acts 28:28, and that in God's eyes, there were no more Jews, no more Gentiles, but *all* who acknowledged Christ as their head were united in the one body.

As we know, most conformed and tagged along with the ecclesiastical entourage who led away from strict adherence to Pauline Scriptures. Consequently, with the introduction of the Gregorian calendar in AD

1752, western countries such as England, Ireland, and the United States also began celebrating Easter on the same day.

Actually, not much if any Easter celebrating occurred in the early settlements of the American colonies. Many settlers were Puritan of strict Calvinistic persuasion. They eschewed the pomp and pageantry of organized Catholic or Anglican churches, and they knew clearly the origins of Easter.

Puritans and early Calvinists have been unjustly accused of practicing denial of any pleasure the year-round. Be that as it may, laws on the books of the Massachusetts Bay Colony in 1659 forbad observing Christmas or other days considered pagan. Offenders would risk paying five shillings for every offense. Not until after the Civil War, nearly three hundred years later, did Easter begin to be celebrated.

Because Easter affects many people religiously and secularly, proposals have been made and efforts were initiated as long ago as 1926 to fix a date for Easter just as Christmas is always on a specific date. There were suggestions of declaring the first Sunday in April the official Easter, making it easier to remember. Do you suppose that the rulers of this world would ever assign Easter to Nisan 17? If we had been instructed to celebrate the Passover as Christ's resurrection day, certainly Nisan 17 would be the correct time. However, celebrating resurrection day at all is debatable.

Rightly dividing Bible believers will recognize that history and practice as recorded by secular and "official" state-church historians is not necessarily the same as instructions directly from the Lord. Researching practices of the early churches can make one wonder if they had thrown away Ephesians and Colossians! Those early believers, about whom much is documented, seemed determined to practice a mix of Judaism and Christianity. On further thought, twenty-first-century believers seem determined to do likewise!

Rituals and Ordinances

God instituted the first Passover and the old covenant exclusively for the Jews; He forbad Gentiles to partake of it in Exodus 12:43. The new covenant as prophesied in Jeremiah 31:31–35 was introduced in Matthew 28:26. Christ partook of the "cup" at the Passover signifying the new covenant, and He instructed the disciples to partake of it until He returned to set up His kingdom.

The new covenant, also, was exclusively for the Jews. Hebrews 8:8–12 quotes the Jeremiah 31 verses. See also Luke 22:20, Mark 14:24–26, and 1 Corinthians 10:16. To whom was Christ speaking? The disciples were the ones receiving instruction to partake of the bread and the cup until Christ returned to set up His kingdom, which they had good reason to believe would occur very shortly.

After Acts 10, Gentiles began to be grafted onto the kingdom. Paul explained the purpose in Romans 11. His listeners would have been familiar with the dendrologist's practice of grafting a wild olive branch onto an old, unproductive olive tree to get it producing again. Israelites hadn't taken advantage of their unique position under the new covenant; they weren't producing fruits of their calling as a priestly nation. Some of its branches had been broken off, so they weren't living up to their holy potential. God, therefore, gave the Gentiles the opportunity to be blessed through Israel by permitting grafting into Israel, but they were not considered as equals.

In 1 Corinthians 11:2, Paul instructed us "to keep the ordinances as I delivered them to you." Verses 23–26 are commonly used in today's Communion services. "For as often as ye eat this bread and drink this cup, ye do show the Lord's death 'til he come" (1 Corinthians 11:26). But the coming spoken of here is the *parousia*, the presence of the Lord. The parousia had been prophesied and promised as far back as Abraham. The Jews were looking for Christ to come and set up His kingdom and the fulfillment of 1 Thessalonians 4 with Christ fighting His way through the heavens to reign on earth. "For the Lord Himself shall descend from heaven with a shout [command, snort of a warhorse], with the archangel, and with the trump of God: and the dead in Christ shall rise first" (1 Thessalonians 4:16). This is what the kingdom people knew; this is *all* they knew.

Those promises made to Moses and the prophets have nothing to do with us. Furthermore, we aren't grafted onto the nation of Israel. These things belong to a past dispensation. In Ephesians, we have a new dispensation, one not prophesied. Yes, to some, *dispensation* is an almost dirty word, but Paul spoke it clearly, distinctly, and emphatically.

Before God through Paul dismissed the Jewish nation at Acts 28:28, Jews and Gentiles didn't congregate together in the temple. A stone wall, *chel*, approximately fifty-four inches high, separated the court of the Jews from the court of the Gentiles. God was deadly serious regarding this separation. Upon the wall of this enclosure was a tablet bearing a Greek inscription.

> No one being a foreigner may enter within the enclosure around the holy place. Whoever is apprehended will himself be to blame for his death which will certainly follow.[62]

What a change with the writing of Ephesians!

> But now in Christ Jesus ye who sometimes were far off are made night by the blood of Christ. For he is our peace, Who hath made both one, and hath **broken down the middle wall of partition** between us; having abolished in His flesh the enmity, even the law of commandments contained in ordinances; for to make of Himself of twain one new man, so making peace (Ephesians 2:13-15).

The Jew was first while the wall stood; with the abolishing of the wall, Jews and Gentiles became equal (see Ephesians 3:6).

Humanity had long lived in the shadows, but after Christ's completed work on the cross, He exposed the infamy of ordinances, which were a shadow of things to come. (See Colossians 1:15.) The shadows are gone, but those who refuse to acknowledge Christ as Head are still worshipping shadows. Why would we want to make ourselves subject to ordinances when Christ through Paul commanded, "Let no man therefore judge you in meat, or in drink, or in respect of an holyday, or of the new moon, or of the Sabbath days" (Colossians 2:16). The answer is too obvious. Some of us love our rituals and the good feeling we experience from them more than we love Christ and the unspeakable bounty we possess as body members.

The Jews of the kingdom age looked for Christ's parousia. We of the one body look for His *epiphaneia*. "Looking for that blessed hope, and the glorious appearing of the great God and our Saviour, Jesus Christ" (Titus 2:12). In the epiphaneia, Christ appears in the heavens but doesn't set foot on earth. He takes His body members up to be with Him. At this appearing, there are no angels, no trumpets, no warfare in the heavens. The parousia was prophesied (see Daniel 12:2 and Malachi 3:2); the epiphaneia was not. It was part of the mystery hidden in God and revealed to Paul. (See 1 Timothy 6:14, 2 Timothy 4:8.)

Celebrate Easter? Definitely not. Celebrate Passover? Not unless we are in a time warp and have been transported back to the last century BC or the first few years AD. How about Resurrection Day? Surely no one can object to that. If we choose to celebrate Resurrection Day, what day will we set aside? Ishtar's Day? Nisan 17? First Sunday in April?

We need to prayerfully consider and ask ourselves what will please the Lord. His standards for us are found in Ephesians, Colossians, and 1 and 2 Timothy. Perhaps our answer is given in Ephesians 5:10–11: "Proving what is acceptable unto the Lord, And have no fellowship with the unfruitful works of darkness, but rather reprove them."

As Bible believers, we should not even discuss Ishtar's Day, Easter, but rather always refer to it as Resurrection Day and treat it as such.

Christ's earliest followers after His resurrection considered every Sunday a "little resurrection" celebration. In the early churches, one of the distinct differences was the lack of ceremonial observances when compared with the Jews or any of the heathen systems surrounding them. In truth, a genuine believer in Christ's resurrection celebrates Resurrection Day every day!

CHAPTER 14

May Day

Origin of May

In the old Julian calendar, May was the third month and was originally called Maius, but it became the fifth month in the revised Gregorian calendar currently in use. There are at least three prevailing theories regarding the origin of the name of the month of May. One theory is that it was named to honor Rome's senators, who were called *maiores*, the Latin word for older men. (May was a sacred month for older men just as June was for junior, *juvenior* men.) A third and possibly more plausible theory is that May was named for a Roman goddess, Maia, the mother of Mercury in Roman mythology. Maia Majesta, the goddess of springtime and flowers, was also known by the names of Fauna and Flora. In Rome, the festival of the unhappy dead and the festival of the goddess of chastity, Bona Dea, were both celebrated in May. Thus, May came to be regarded as a bad month for marriage, which also accounts for the popularity of June for weddings. Because the cows could be milked three times a day during this season, the Anglo-Saxons called the month Thrimilce.

Origin of May Day Celebrations

Some historians believe that celebrations on May Day began with the tree worship of the druids. These pre-Christian Celtic peoples divided the year into two main seasons. Winter, the beginning of the year, began on November 1, which they called Samain. (See further elaboration in the "Halloween" chapter.) The middle of the year and hence summer, began on May 1, known as Beltane (also spelled Beltine). For some reason, it was thought that the boundary lines between the supernatural and the natural worlds were dissolved during these times. Witches and fairies roamed at will, and humans took measures to guard against their sorcery.

Beltane is first mentioned in a work attributed to Cormac, bishop of Cashel and king of Munster, who died in AD 908. His explanation of the word's origin was that it was a combination of *bel*, from the god Belenus, and the old Irish word *tene*, meaning "fire." One proposed meaning of Belenus is Bright One; this gives us new understanding of 2 Corinthians 11:14: "And no marvel, for Satan himself is transformed into an angel of light." Perhaps this explains why various ancient cults practiced religious devotion to fire as divine or sacred. For example, the Aztecs worshipped the fire god Xiuheucti, Greeks had their Hephaestus, while the Celts offered prayers to Ceridwen, who was later Christianized to St. Bridget, patroness of fire and fertility. A perpetual fire was kept in Bridget's honor until AD 1220, when it was forbidden.

Specific references to Bel are in Isaiah 46:1, Jeremiah 50:2, and Jeremiah 51:44. The ancient Accadians, the inventors of cuneiform writing, worshipped a trio of gods: Anu ruled over heaven, Bel ruled over earth (some accounts have him as ruling the air), and Ea ruled over the sea. Bel is the same as the Phoenician Elu. During a time of difficulty, Elu had offered his firstborn son "the beloved" on a high place, by fire. In sacred biblical history, God commanded his chosen people to not let their children be sacrificed by such fires as in the fires of Molech (Leviticus 18:21).

Bel is also a variation of the Babylonian Baal, which figures prominently in Scripture. Baal was combined with many other names to produce the names of idols: Baal-berith (lord of the covenant), Baalzebub (lord of the flies), place names and personal names such as Baalah (Joshua 15:9), Baaleth-beer (Joshua 19:8), Baal-hamon (Solomon 8:11), Jezebel (1 Kings), as well as Hasdrubal and Hannibal of secular history. Bel's three children were Shamas, the sun god; Sin, the moon god; and Ishtar, goddess of fertility.

The practice of sacrificing the firstborn to the god of fire had passed to the Semitic nations. Understanding the commonality of this practice makes it easier for us to understand Abraham. He had undoubtedly witnessed others honoring their heathen gods in this way, and perhaps he felt he could do no less than offer Isaac for the one true God. (Isaac would have been thirty-three during this incident and obviously a willing participant.)

The worship of Baal under the names of Belenus or Bel was practiced in Italy, the Alps, Gaul, and the British Isles. The great fire festival, Beltane, in Celtic lands, was primarily a fertility celebration. Also, at that time, cattle were driven between two fires as a means of protecting them and purifying them before they were put out to summer pasture.

Irish folklore and mythology tell of a summer god being released from his bondage on May 1; other stories tell of a summer maid lured from her father, Earth Giant at that time.

The custom of the maypole fertility dance came from Germanic traditions surrounding the feast of the goddess, *Walpurgisnacht*. A phallic pole, stripped of its branches, would be planted in the earth. Red and white streamers attached to the top were woven about the pole until it was completely covered with the variegated ribbon. Another custom was for young people to spend the eve of May 1 in the fields and woods. This sometimes led to irate parents demanding "greenwood" marriages, probably akin to our "shotgun" marriages.

Undoubtedly, the druid religion had an influence throughout the northern European areas concerning May Day. However, an influence of equal importance seems to have come from Rome. As Roman armies moved north and conquered tribes and lands, they brought with them the worship of Flora and contributed to the legacy of licentiousness throughout Latin and Germanic lands.

Flora's festival dates to 238 BC, when a temple to her was dedicated on the slopes of the Aventine Hill. Before that, her worship was practiced in the house of a consul or praetor. No males were allowed in the house while the services conducted by the Vestals were in progress. (The Vestals were virgin priestesses who vowed to remain chaste.) The Floralia normally took place from April 28 to May 3. The priests of Vulcan made sacrifices to Flora on the first day of May, but as a prophetic goddess, she revealed her oracles only to females. Sacrifices were offered on behalf of the whole Roman Empire during the Floralia. Prostitutes, who considered this their special season, were readily available. Public entertainment by actors consisted of mimicked lewd, immoral dramas.

Each community's celebration reflected unique customs of the locale, but a common thread throughout vast areas included processions of people carrying green branches, garlands, or small trees. A May king and queen were appointed, and dancing around the maypole ensured fertility for crops, cattle, and humans. The queen, who represented the goddess Flora, generally wore a crown of flowers.

During medieval times, May Day became a major holiday. In English villages, people decorated their homes and churches, sang spring carols, and exchanged gifts. Robin Hood also received homage on May Day, the traditional day of his death. Italian boys serenaded their sweethearts, while in Switzerland, young men placed pine trees under their girlfriends' windows. German boys secretly planted May trees in front of the windows of the girls they hoped to win, as did young men in Czechoslovakia. In France, the month of May was sacred and dedicated to the Virgin Mary. May Day itself became a religious holiday with May queens leading processions in honor of the Virgin Mary. This is another example of well-intentioned people changing a pagan holiday to a religious one.

May Day in Colonial United States

The Puritans well knew the history and background of May Day festivals. They eschewed them as pagan, which indeed they were. In

1660, Governor Endicott of Massachusetts led a group of men to Merrymount and chopped down a maypole. He renamed the place Mount Dagon after the Philistine idol. Because of the Puritan influence, May Day was not celebrated with the same enthusiasm in the United States as it had been in Europe.

May Day in the Early 1900s

In the 1890s, safety in the workplace, child labor, and work hours were unregulated. The American Federation of Labor declared a national strike on May 1, 1886, to demand an eight-hour workday. A total of 350,000 workers nationwide went on strike. Stockyards, railroads, and other businesses were forced to close. Of particular notoriety was the Chicago Haymarket Square Riot, during which several police officers were slain and others injured by a bomb tossed in their midst. Police retaliated by wounding 200 citizens while firing randomly into the crowd of strikers. Eight revolutionary labor leaders were arrested, and four were executed. As news of executions spread, protestors rallied around the world. (See "Labor Day" chapter.)

In 1889, the Socialist International, an assembly of Socialist and Labor parties, declared May 1 as a day of demonstrations. After the Russian Revolution in 1917, May 1 became a major holiday in Soviet Russia and other Communist countries. It was habitual that tanks and mobile missile-launchers would parade in Red Square in Russia and that May Day would cause riots in Europe and elsewhere.

Labor advocates in the United States urged a national labor day holiday on May 1, so celebrations occurred on that day for some time. Eventually, our official Labor Day became the first Monday in September. This compromise honored workers and upheld family values without advocating the militancy and subversive activity that had been connected to earlier May 1 celebrations.

In 1947, the U.S. Veterans of Foreign Wars renamed May 1 as Loyalty Day in an effort to defuse left-wing labor tendencies; Congress made the title official. Its celebration flourished until the unpopularity of the Vietnam War led to a decline in participation of patriotic activities on that day.

May Day Today

Over the years, May Day festivities lost their original significance and came to be a simple day of innocent rejoicing that warm weather had come once again. Art teachers in search of creative activities instruct their students in the painting or weaving of paper May baskets. In many communities, May Day celebrations are in connection with the annual Spring Fling, an attempt by hard-pressed working parents and teachers to raise money for school activities. Probably neither the children nor their parents have any concept of the former significance of May Day or the maypole.

On the flip side of the May Day coin, in keeping with satanic influence, you can expect riots, needless damage, or violence on May Day. After all, it is still Beltane. "Why do the heathen rage, and the people imagine a vain thing" (Psalm 2:1).

CHAPTER 15

Mother's Day

Biblical Basis

The basic biblical structure of the family is built around the father and mother despite modern notions to the contrary. Even though the word translated "father" appears 979 times as compared to the word translated "mother," which appears 245 times, the role of motherhood is of no less importance.

One of the Ten Commandments given to the Israelites, "Honour thy father and thy **mother:** that thy days may be long upon the land which the LORD thy God giveth thee" (Exodus 20:12), was reiterated by Paul: "Honour thy father and mother; (which is the first commandment with promise)" (Ephesians 6:2). The sinless Son of God honored His mother, who is pictured in prayer and supplication with other women in Acts 1:14.

Students of Paul's epistles are well aware of his praise for two believing women. He extolled them because they brought their children up in the teachings of the Lord. "When I call to remembrance the unfeigned faith that is in thee, which dwelt first in thy grandmother Lois and thy **mother** Eunice; and I am persuaded that in thee also" (2 Timothy 1:5).

A beautiful Scripture reference of motherhood delayed is in 1 Samuel 1–2. Hannah, despondent over her barrenness, went to the temple weeping. Moving her lips silently, she agonized in prayer. Eli, the priest, thought she must have been drunk with wine. Upon his investigation, she told him of her heart's desire for a son, and Eli promised her that God would grant her petition. In due time, Hannah bore a son, Samuel, whom she in turn lent back to the Lord as soon as she had weaned him. Samuel's name means "asked of God" or "God heard."

In 1 Samuel 2:1–10, we read Hannah's song of praise to the Lord. "There is none holy as the Lord; for there is none beside thee; neither is there any rock like our God" (1 Samuel 2:2). "And Eli blessed Elkanah and his wife, and said, The Lord give thee seed of this woman for the loan which is lent to the Lord" (1 Samuel 2:20). Hannah lent Samuel to the Lord; subsequently, the Lord blessed her with three sons and two daughters. He quintupled what she had originally asked for!

Countless references could be given to exemplify good mothers. Perhaps one of the most beautiful in praise of the virtuous woman concludes, "but a woman that feareth the Lord, she shall be praised. Give her of the fruit of her hands; and let her own works praise her in the gate" (Proverbs 31:31). Earlier in the passage, we are told that her children rise up and call her blessed. This virtuous woman's important job title is "mother."

Some tell us that the earliest Mother's Day celebrations were in honor of Rhea, the ancient Greek mother of the gods. If the reader is not a student of Greek mythology and has time to spare plus a strong stomach, he could look up this character. To make a long story short, Cronus swallowed his six children. Rhea, his wife, outwitted him, and he later disgorged them. I prefer to believe that Exodus 20:12 predates that far-fetched myth, and it's definitely not nauseating to read.

Possibly a precursor to our modern day celebration was "Mothering Sunday" dating back to 1600s England, when many poor children worked as servants for the wealthy. Because distances were difficult to travel, these child servants lived at their employers' houses during the week. On Sundays, they returned home to spend the day with their mothers. Church activities later blended in a special Mothering Sunday on the fourth Sunday of Lent.

Campaign for National Holiday

In our own country, Julia Ward Howe organized meetings in Boston in the 1870s to honor mothers, but it was much later that Anna Jarvis began her campaign to initiate a national Mother's Day.

Anna Jarvis's father had served as a minister in Philadelphia and Grafton, West Virginia. Her mother had staunchly supported him in his work. As a child, Anna helped with the vegetable and flower garden, mainly white carnations. Anna Jarvis persuaded her mother's churches in Grafton and Philadelphia to celebrate a day in honor of her mother as well as other mothers on the second Sunday of May 1907, the second anniversary of her mother's death. West Virginia's governor William E. Glassock declared the second Sunday in May as Mother's Day in 1910.

After that, things began to snowball. People bombarded ministers, businessmen, and politicians with letters seeking to establish a national Mother's Day. By 1911, Mother's Day had become quite popular. President Woodrow Wilson made it official in 1914 by proclaiming Mother's Day as a national holiday to be held on the second Sunday of May.

Another Day Gone Commercial

Anna Jarvis wanted every mother in her mother's church, Andrews Methodist Episcopal in Grafton, to feel special. She sent five hundred white carnations, her mother's favorite, to be distributed. The appreciated gesture didn't go unnoticed, and thereafter, the giving of carnations became traditional. In fact, Mother's Day became so commercialized that Jarvis, disillusioned with the practice, disagreed with the floral industry over selling flowers for Mother's Day.

In 1923, Jarvis was arrested for disturbing the peace at a mothers' convention because of her objection to the exploitation of holiday sales of carnations.

In the 1930s, the postal service planned a Mother's Day stamp with *Whistler's Mother* and a vase of white carnations on it. Jarvis objected strenuously and campaigned against the stamp. President Roosevelt removed the words *Mother's Day* but left the white carnations.

Melda Eberle

Mother's Day Traditions

Today, wearing a white carnation honors a deceased or an estranged mother, and white carnations are often placed on deceased mothers' graves. Wearing pink or red honors a living mother.

Giving gifts to mothers is popular, and young children honor mother by homemade cards or simple, store-bought items she cherishes until they wear out or fall apart.

Restaurateurs experience this day as the busiest of the year, giving mother a break from the kitchen on her special day.

Surrogate Mothers

Obviously, the Bible doesn't command a national or international Mother's Day, but mothers should be honored, special day or not. Unfortunately, today, many mothers have reneged on the job due to addictions, self-centeredness, or ignorance of their God-given blessing: "Children are an heritage of the Lord, and the fruit of the womb is His reward" (Psalm 127:3).Others are taking the responsibility for rearing the hapless children.

It would seem fitting, therefore, to recognize any mother figure, whether stepmother, aunt, or grandmother, who is helping fill the void in the life of one of God's defenseless little ones, for honor should be given to whom it is due.

Some may feel disdain rather than honor for a less-than-honorable mother. Howbeit, she gave the gift of earthly life, so perhaps by kindness and love, she may be brought to the One who said, "I am the Way, the Truth, and the Life" (John 14:6), our Head, Christ Jesus.

Wouldn't it be encouraging to see a revival of genuine motherhood, one worthy of receiving the honor that God so long ago commanded? This can happen only if present-day Loises and Eunices continue training sons and daughters by word and example their unfeigned faith in our Savior.

CHAPTER 16

Memorial Day

The Origins of Memorial Day

As with many holidays, Memorial Day's origins have several versions. Women's church auxiliaries of the North and South helped families bereft of fathers and husbands after the Civil War; these auxiliaries supplied food and clothing for widows and orphans during and after the war. Along with performing Christian charity toward the living, the ladies' auxiliaries helped preserve grave sites and decorated them in memory of the fallen war dead. The Northern states celebrated various days in memory of their dead while the Confederate women set aside May 30.

One story credits Cassandra Oliver Moncure, a Virginia woman with French ancestry, for naming May 30 as the date. That date corresponded with the Day of Ashes in France, a commemoration of the return of the body of Napoleon Bonaparte to France from St. Helena.

Another story credits Major General John A. Logan, who desired a more uniform celebration throughout the states. On May 5, 1868, Logan, of the Army of the Republic, issued an order designating a specific day to be set aside "for the purpose of strewing with flowers or otherwise decorating the graves" of Union soldiers. This official observance became known as Decoration Day.

At the time of Logan's proclamation, Arlington National Cemetery held 20,000 Union dead as well as several hundred Confederate soldiers, making it the logical site for the first large memorial service.

This first celebration consisted of verandas draped in mourning at the former homes of Generals Robert E. Lee, Ulysses S. Grant, and other important Washington officials. After appropriate speeches, prayers, and hymns, children from the Soldiers' and Sailors' Orphans Home scattered flowers on Union and Confederate graves.

Claims to Be First

At least twenty-five cities claim to be the original birthplace of Memorial Day; among them, Macon, Georgia; Columbus, Georgia; and Richmond, Virginia claim to have begun the tradition in 1866. Boalsburg, Pennsylvania, claims to have begun its celebrations in 1864. Carbondale, Illinois, home of Logan, also makes claim to the title, citing its original celebration date of April 29, 1866.

New York became the first state to recognize the holiday in 1873, and by 1890, all Northern states recognized it. The South refused to join the North in this celebration and honored their war dead on separate days until after World War I. By that time, Decoration Day had expanded to honor all who had died in any American war.

President Johnson Decides Which Was First

Congress and President Lyndon Johnson in 1966 named the official birthplace of Memorial Day to be Waterloo, NY. Their reasoning included the assertion that the other cities had only one-time celebrations or were unofficial events. In Waterloo, flags had first flown at half-staff and businesses closed to honor the war dead on May 5, 1866, and had continued the practice yearly. Besides flying the flag at half-staff, the townspeople also placed small American flags on veterans' graves, a practice that continues today.

Some Southern States Have Own Celebrations

Mississippi, Alabama, Florida, and Georgia celebrate Confederate Memorial Day on the last Monday of April, North and South Carolina on May 10, Tennessee and Louisiana on June 3 (Jefferson Davis's birthday), and Texas on January 19.

Red Poppy Tradition

Moina Michael, the first person to wear a red poppy on Memorial Day in 1916, originated the idea after reading the poem tribute "In Flanders Fields." The blood-red poppy memorialized the blood of fallen heroes. Ms. Michael sold poppies, giving the proceeds to benefit servicemen, war orphans, and widows. Other countries followed her example by selling artificial red poppies. The Veterans of Foreign Wars sold poppies nationally in 1922, and by 1924, disabled veterans were making artificial poppies for sale through their "Buddy" Poppy program. For her conception and instigation of the national poppy movement, the postal service honored Moina Michael by issuing a red three-cent stamp with her image on it in 1948.

Dim Remembrance

The same act of Congress in 1971 that gave us three-day weekends declared Memorial Day to be a federal holiday and placed it on the last Monday in May. Some feel that this diminished the meaning of the day and caused new generations to be ignorant of its true meaning. Rather than being a day for somber thankfulness and remembering loved ones, friends, or ancestors who gave us the blessings of liberty, the day has become the entrance to summertime fun. Memorial Day should instead be considered a day of national mourning, and the flag should fly at half-staff until noon.

To remind us all of the true meaning of Memorial Day, in December 2000, Congress passed PL 106-579, the White House Commission on Remembrance. Its stated ten-year mission—to educate younger and future generations in our history and to honor the sacrifices of our fallen heroes—has an annual budget of $250,000. The Commission is committed to uniting the country in the "National Moment of Remembrance." This simply asks each of us to observe in our own way a moment of remembrance at 3:00 p.m. to reflect and honor those who gave their lives in service to our country.

Worship or Tribute?

We as a nation don't worship our ancestors or military heroes. True ancestor worship involves placating the dead for fear they will cause disease or other bad luck if not worshipped properly. Our Memorial Day is a reminder of our heritage of freedom, a legacy we have because of what our veterans have done for us, and specifically those men who didn't come home and aren't with us to celebrate. We are who we are and have what we have because of the rich blessings of God and the sacrifices of those who died on our behalf. May we always remember those who didn't return to the good life, and may we be always thankful to God for His mercies.

> Except the Lord build the house, they labor in vain that build it: except the Lord keep the city, the watchman waketh but in vain (Psalm 127:1).

> Righteousness exalteth a nation, but sin is a reproach to any people (Proverbs 14:34).

Let us keep our nation in constant prayer while meditating on these verses.

CHAPTER 17

Father's Day

The Bible contains 1,718 references to the word *father* and its possessive, *father's*, plural *fathers* and its possessive, *fathers'*, and 43 references to *fatherless*. Judging by this large number of Scriptures, we must conclude that God considered fathers important.

To choose from such a large selection is difficult, but we will look at a few significant verses. Proverbs, the book of wise sayings for an earthly people, speaks timeless wisdom across all God's dispensations: "A wise son makes a glad father: but a foolish son is the heaviness of his mother" (Proverbs 10:1). "Train up a child in the way he should go, and when he is old, he will not depart from it" (Proverbs 22:6). Added counsel to fathers in the Church who is His body speaks: "And ye, fathers, provoke not your children to wrath, but bring them up in the nurture and admonition of the Lord" (Ephesians 6:4). "Fathers, provoke not your children to anger lest they be discouraged" (Colossians 3:21). In giving instruction to Titus on selection of elders, qualifications included "having faithful children, not accused of riot or unruly" (Titus 1:6). Any man who succeeds in following the above verses is a real man and worthy of honor.

Father's Day Origins

With Father's Day, we have another oxymoron of a secular holiday. It is not a holy day required by the Lord but a man-made celebration, a secular day we can celebrate without pangs of guilt or worry in regard to possible pagan derivation. Although God doesn't command a day of celebration, He does write as the fifth commandment, "Honor thy father and thy mother: that thy days may be long upon the land which the Lord thy God gives thee" (Exodus 20:12). Paul's letter to the Church who is His body confirms this necessity: "Honor thy father and mother; (which is the first commandment with promise)" (Ephesians 6:2).

When did Father's Day begin?

Two traditions exist regarding the beginnings of Father's Day as a public celebration.

Tradition One: Fairmont, West Virginia, 1908
The lesser known evolved from a coal mining disaster on December 6, 1907, at the Monongah mine near Fairmont, West Virginia. Of the 361 men killed in the disaster, 250 were fathers. In 1908, near her father's June birthday, Grace Golden Clayton, saddened by the memories of her late father and concerned for the many fatherless children around her, determined that these fathers would be remembered and honored with a special day.

Her congregation liked the idea, so they paid homage to fathers with a Father's Day church service at the Williams Memorial Methodist Episcopal Church South in Fairmont. At that time, the area residents didn't try to influence other congregations to follow suit, but many years later, they wished they had been more proactive and wanted to be recognized for having had the first Father's Day celebration. This is certainly a believable claim since the site of the first Mother's Day celebration was at Grafton, West Virginia, about fifteen miles away.

Tradition Two: Spokane, Washington, 1910

The best-known Father's Day tribute honored a widowed father, William Jackson Smart, who reared six children, including an infant. After Sonora Smart Dodd reached adulthood, she realized the tremendous sacrifices her father, a farmer and Civil War veteran, had made to keep his family together and well cared for.

In 1909, she suggested to her minister and others that a special service be dedicated to her father and other fathers. She proposed the date June 5, her father's birthday. That didn't give the minister enough preparation time, but on June 19, he spoke at a special service honoring all fathers. After the service, fathers accepted small gifts of appreciation from their children. From that time forward, the state of Washington kept the third Sunday in June as Father's Day.

The current tradition of wearing a red rose to honor a living father or a white rose for a deceased father began in Spokane also.

An Arduous Journey to National Holiday

Organizations over the United States lobbied Congress to declare Father's Day a national holiday. President Woodrow Wilson approved, and his family celebrated the day privately with him in 1916, but it took eight years before the event gained recognition.

A perhaps not-so-meek gentleman by name of Harry C. Meek in the 1920s, while president of the Chicago Lions Club, campaigned enthusiastically for the idea of a Father's Day to be held on June 20, his birthday. President Coolidge recommended and supported the day, making it a national event in 1924, but he didn't declare it a national holiday.

The National Father's Day Committee, founded in 1926 in New York, promoted traditional values and sound family relationships. One of their goals encouraged national and international observance of a day honoring fathers.

A Joint Resolution of Congress in 1956 recognized the observance of Father's Day. Ten years later, President Lyndon Johnson proclaimed an official national holiday. However, it was another six years, 1972, before President Richard Nixon signed into law a permanent United States Father's Day to be observed on the third Sunday of June.

What Should Be the Father's Role in the Family?

The father is to be the head of the family because he has been given this role by God. There is an order that God has established that cannot be violated with impunity. This order is God in Christ, Christ in man, man over woman, and woman over children. The father brings the spiritual identity to the family. Until the early 1960s that role was being filled; then government welfare programs took the father out of the home. Now, mothers are in charge, and this has reversed the God-ordained order. This has brought evil into the black family, with disastrous results.[63]

The above words, written by a godly, Christian minister, ring true for all races, for Satan hates all fathers. The father in the home is the earthly representation of our heavenly Father. Thus, removing the father from the home makes Satan's work so much easier, for that is one less frame of godly reference with which Satan has to battle in his war against God.

Status of Fatherhood Today

According to government census statistics, the number of single fathers in 1970 was 393,000. As of this writing, the estimate is 2.3 million. Ten percent of those are raising three or more children under age eighteen. Divorced fathers represent 42 percent of that number, while 38 percent have never married.[63]

How Can We Eliminate Some of These Statistics?

The only solution to any problem of any magnitude is a return to Christ, individually and as family. True men must stop being wimpy and accept responsibility for the lives they have sired in or out of wedlock. Children must be accepted as "an heritage of the Lord: and the fruit of the womb is His reward" (Psalm 127:3) rather than as trophies for bragging rights.

In my former position of correctional educator, I heard many young men boast of having three or four babies by as many different "mamas." They assumed this assured their masculinity. When I challenged them to take responsibility because every child deserves a father, they were incredulous at such a preposterous (to them) idea. Admittedly, when one's procreative life is so out of control, it is humanly nearly impossible to rectify those unfortunate situations.

Honor to Whom Honor Is Due

If fatherhood isn't respected and a father doesn't accept responsibility for his children, someone else fills the gap. Any man, stepfather, uncle, grandfather, or mentor who steps forward to accept the challenge of helping an abandoned child deserves honor on Father's Day. Just like the godly biological father rejoices when his child does right, so also the surrogate father rejoices when his "child" succeeds. "The father of the righteous shall rejoice: and he that begets a wise child shall have joy of him" (Proverbs 23:24).

CHAPTER 18

Flag Day

Origin of Flags

An Assyrian statue dating from 671 BC represents a soldier with the standard of his unit. The standard, a solid object fixed to the top of a staff with streamers attached, became the forerunner of our cloth flag. We now refer to cloth flags as standards, but the two have differences. Standards generally bore symbols sacred to certain groups. Cities and city states adopted their own symbols; for example, some flags from Egyptian cities had the sign of the sphinx; Greek cities had Pegasus or other mythological figures. By order of G. Marius, a consul of Rome, Roman legions carried only the eagle. Warriors carried these distinctive standards in advance of approaching royalty.

Predating these, the Old Testament contains three words transliterated, *degel, nace,* and *owth,* "standard," "banner," and "ensign" in our English Bible. In sacred and secular history, the purpose of each has been military. We will consider illustrations from the Old Testament.

Standards

Standards signified specific tribes and families: "Every man of the children of Israel shall pitch by his own **standard**, with the ensign of their father's house: far off about the tabernacle of the congregation shall they pitch" (Numbers 2:2).

When issuing a proclamation concerning judgment about to be carried out by the military, the standard was prominently displayed: "Declare ye among the nations, and publish, and set up a **standard**: publish and conceal not: say, 'Babylon is taken, Bel is confounded, Merodach is broken in pieces; her idols are confounded, her images are broken in pieces'" (Jeremiah 50:2).

Ensigns

After the standard or ensign became visible, war trumpets blew. "All ye inhabitants of the world, and dwellers on the earth, see ye, when he lifts up an ensign in the mountains; and when he blows a trumpet, hear ye" (Isaiah 18:3).

Another example of the use of the ensign in warfare was when Jehovah warned the Israelites that their alliance with Egypt will be futile: "And he shall pass over to his stronghold for fear, and his princes shall be afraid of the **ensign**, says the Lord, Whose fire is in Zion, and his furnace in Jerusalem" (Isaiah 31:9). Isaiah assured the Israelites of victory over Assyria if Israel renounced its idols. The victory would be by the Lord's might, not by Israel's, but at the sight of Israel's ensign, the Assyrians would disappear in cowardly flight.

A rallying point against foreign invasion also required an ensign: "And He will lift up an **ensign** to the nations from afar, and will hiss unto them from the end of the earth: and behold, they shall come with speed swiftly" (Isaiah 5:26). The sight of a standard, banner, or ensign assures God's presence and protection, a comfort to Israel but consternation to her enemies.

Banners

After "Joshua discomfited Amalek and his people with the edge of the sword" (Exodus 17:13), "Moses built an altar, and called the name of it Jehovah-nissi" (Exodus 27:15). Jehovah-nissi means "God is my banner."

Ensigns and banners representing each of the tribes were probably embroidered or by some means ornamented with the name of the tribe and its mazzaroth (zodiac) sign.

We know that when Israel camped in the wilderness under God's direction, Moses divided the people into four groups with the excluded Levites in the center. Even though each tribe had its own banner, God organized them under the banner of the leading tribe in each group of three. To the north, Dan's banner presided over Asher's and Naphtali's; to the south, Reuben's banner presided over Gad's and Simeon's; to the east, Judah's banner presided over Isaachar's and Zebulon's; to the west, Ephraim's banner presided over Manassah's and Benjamin's. (For complete details, see Numbers 1.)

Today, we can buy banners purporting to represent each of the tribes of Israel. All the same, such modern representation must be considered speculation due to the fact that God never told us what writings the banners or ensigns carried. Rabbinical tradition is the closest we can get to their descriptions. Nevertheless, a serious study of the book of Ezekiel will lead us in the right direction for conjecturing what insignias might have been on the banners.

Feudal Europe

Tribes and ethnic groups other than Israel also carried standards and banners. European feudal nobility developed distinct heraldic and genealogical insignia displayed on poles and over armor as tabards or surcoats boldly declaring proud heritages. As the feudal system gave way to the concept of nations, national flags preempted family or tribal banners.

I have used the words *standard* and *banner* interchangeably, but there are differences according to medieval as well as modern usage.

From Standards to Flags

With the rise of Constantine and the Roman State Church, flags commonly bore the sign of a cross. During the twelfth-century Crusades, crusaders clearly showed for whom they were fighting by the cross depicted on their flags. The English and Germans adopted a white flag with a red cross—commonly known as the cross of St. George; the French carried a red flag with a white cross.

Other national flags developed during the late 1200s and early 1300s were influenced by those flags. Denmark's flag is a white cross on a red field; Sweden's is a yellow cross on a blue field; Scotland has a white cross on a blue field—known as the cross of St. Andrew; Ireland's is a red cross on a white field—known as the cross of St. Patrick. Britain's current Union Jack is formed by a combination of the crosses of St. George, St. Andrew, and St. Patrick.

In contrast to the Christian flags, Islam prohibited images on its plain, colored flags. Mohammed allegedly carried a solid black flag, black signifying vengeance.

Later Islamic dynasties carried flags of solid black, white, or green. Not until 1453, when the Turks conquered Constantinople, did the crescent moon and star, that city's existing flag, became associated with the Muslim world. Several modern Muslim countries continue using the crescent moon and a star or stars symbol while other Muslim countries reject the symbols as ancient pagan icons.

A Flag's Purpose

During and after the Crusades, flags had several forms and performed a variety of functions. Before modern communications systems, flags coordinated soldiers' movements, signaling where to rally or when to charge. Soldiers cherished their flags and looked with disdain on the enemy's. Shame and derision accompanied the poor fellow who lost his flag or even let it touch ground. According to their purposes, flags were known as streamers, standards, banners, guidons, and pennons.

The streamer measured twenty to sixty yards long and about three yards wide. Created for use by warships, it could be easily identifiable by friend or foe from a distance. Today, the pennant replaces the streamer.

Of those flags carried on land, the first in importance and the largest, the standard, generally remained stationary. Its long, tapering, two-pointed end marked a palace, ship, or the presence of a king or noble and always preceded royalty in parades or reviews.

Next in rank, the square or oblong banner bore personal or family genealogical insignia. Privileged royalty or noble soldiers carried banners into battle. Banners hung vertically from a horizontal pole, whereas flags were positioned horizontally on vertical staffs or halyards.

Knights of lesser rank, who were not entitled to carry banners, carried guidons, a rounded flag with two round swallowtails.

Least in size and importance were the small triangular pennons, one of which adorned the top of each knight's lance. They possibly served as warning flags much as today's small red flags attached to extended loads warn vehicles from following too closely.

History of the United States' Flag Day

Our founding fathers declared the thirteen colonies freed from England by the Declaration of Independence on July 4, 1776. Almost a year later, June 14, 1777, the Continental Congress decided to adopt a national flag. They resolved that a new constellation would be born, that the flag of the United States would be thirteen stripes, alternate red and white, with thirteen white stars on a blue field.

The U.S. flag changed over the years to keep up with the growing nation. As new states were added, new stars were added. Union soldiers fought under a thirty-three-star flag. Even though some of those states had broken away, President Lincoln would not let the stars of the seceded Southern states be removed. When Kansas became a state in 1861, the number of stars became thirty-four. Union soldiers fought under a thirty-five-star flag when West Virginia broke away from the Confederate state of Virginia. Today's flag contains thirteen red and white alternating stripes and fifty white stars on a blue field.

The Fourth of July had always been celebrated as the birth of our nation, but 108 years later, men began to see the need for an annual day to celebrate the flag itself. Credit for establishing a National Flag Day is given, with good reason, to several major supporters of the idea.

Perhaps the least known is that of George Morris of Hartford, Connecticut. During the Civil War, Hartford observed a patriotic day in 1861 in which he expressed concern for the preservation of the Union and offered prayers for the success of the Union army.

In 1885, schoolteacher Bernard J. Cigrand began a campaign that lasted several years. He made speeches urging the adoption of a Flag Birthday or a Flag Day. His students in Fredonia, Wisconsin, celebrated such a day before he left for dental school. He continued speechmaking and publishing articles urging a national flag day.

As prime organizers of the Illinois organization, American Flag Day Association, Cigrand along with Leroy Van Horn received recognition as those most responsible for 300,000 children celebrating Flag Day in five city parks in Chicago on June 14, 1894.

Other supporters included Colonel J. Granville Leach of the Pennsylvania Society of the Sons of the Revolution, along with its sister organization, the Colonial Dames of America. On April 25, 1893, they adopted a resolution requesting Philadelphia's mayor to display the flag on June 14 with appropriate patriotic exercises and to give each assembled schoolchild a small flag. This resolution resulted in the superintendent of the city's public schools, Dr. Edward Brooks, directing such Flag Day exercises in Independence Square on June 14, 1893.

The Flag Day concept had taken hold in New York State; in 1894, Governor Roswell Flower ordered the flag to be displayed on June 14. This stemmed indirectly from the effort of George Balch, a teacher in New York City who had planned patriotic flag displays for his kindergarten students a few years earlier.

Some credit for Flag Day goes to William T. Kerr, Pittsburgh, who organized the American Flag Day Association of Western Pennsylvania in 1888 and served fifty years as its national chairman. During those years, he wrote articles, delivered radio addresses, and spoke to thousands in his quest for having a day to honor our flag.

It took several years' work, but from the combined efforts of such people as well as Kerr's efforts, on May 30, 1916, President Woodrow Wilson issued the proclamation officially establishing June 14 as Flag Day.

Over the next thirty years, many bills were introduced in Congress asking for June 14 to be a legal holiday, but all were defeated. Finally, in 1949, the 81st Congress introduced Public Law 203 that designated June 14 of each year as Flag Day, though it is not a federal holiday as far as closing post offices or other federal institutions.

As final vote on PL 203 neared, Senator Herbert R. O'Conner of Maryland informed William T. Kerr by letter that the bill he had sought for so long would pass. After its passage, Senator Francis J. Myers, Pennsylvania, telegrammed Kerr that the resolution had passed. President Truman called Kerr to the White House to participate in the signing of the law on August 3, 1949.

By that time, Kerr was in his eighties and in failing health, but he participated. President Truman presented Kerr with the pen used to sign the document and afterward invited him to chat.

After passage of PL 203, Kerr received numerous honors from patriotic, civic, and educational organizations, a fitting closure to his lifelong, successful quest.

A Few Tips for Proper Flag Display

Various flag codes have been enacted or amended by Congress. The Flag Protection Act of 1989 imposed fines or prison terms for mutilating or defacing any U.S. flag. The Supreme Court declared the law unconstitutional in *United States v. Eichman* on June 11, 1990. In spite of that, there are still right and wrong ways to treat and display the flag. Many rules of flag etiquette exist, but below are a few of the basics.

- Fly the flag from sunrise to sunset. Raise the flag quickly; lower it slowly and respectfully.
- Do not fly the flag in rain or inclement weather.
- If the flag is flown at night, it must be illuminated.
- After the death of a president or other high government official, the flag is flown at half-staff on land, half-mast at sea for thirty days. Other occasions for half-staff are May 20, Peace Officers Memorial Day, when the flag flies half-staff until noon, and December 7, National Pearl Harbor Remembrance Day, when the flag flies half-staff until sunset.
- Never allow the flag to touch the ground.
- The flag should never be draped over any vehicle. When displayed on a car, it must be clamped to the right fender or fixed firmly to the chassis.
- The flag should never be used as a covering for any statue, not even for one about to be unveiled.
- When used to cover a casket, the flag must be placed so that the union (the stars and blue field) is at the head and over the shoulder, and it is never lowered into the grave.
- When the flag is passing in a parade or in review, everyone except those in military uniforms should face the flag and stand at attention with the right hand over the heart. Those in uniform, of course, give the military salute.
- No other flag should ever be placed above the U.S. flag.
- A worn-out flag should be burned or buried. A special ceremony for burning the flag is performed routinely by patriotic organizations as well as the Boy Scouts.

I pledge allegiance to the flag of the United States of America, and to the Republic for which it stands, one nation under God, indivisible, with liberty and justice for all.

American schoolchildren have the right to pledge allegiance to our flag, and they will have this right until someone becomes offended by the word *God*. How God must be amused at such sensitivity! His amusement will one day become laughter.

> Why do the heathen rage, And the people imagine a vain thing? The kings of the earth set themselves, and the rulers take counsel together, against the Lord and against his anointed, saying, "Let us break their bands asunder, and cast away their cords from us." He that sits in the heavens shall laugh. The Lord shall have them in derision. (Psalm 2:1–4)

God's Great Banner

Psalm 60 relates the account of the great battle of the valley of salt. It encouraged the Israelites to trust in God and do right to be victorious over the Edomites. "Thou hast given a **banner** to them that fear thee, that it may be displayed because of the truth" (Psalm 60:4). There is only one banner upon which victory is always poised: the truth of God's Word in the power of His hand.

Francis Scott Key recognized that when he witnessed an American flag surviving battle in Baltimore Harbor during the War of 1812. Filled with emotion, he penned the words to what became our national anthem. The Museum of American History in Washington, DC, displays this flag.

The Star Spangled Banner

> O thus be it ever when free-men shall stand
> Between their lov'd home and the war's desolation;
> Blest with vict'ry and peace, may the heav'n rescued land

Praise the Pow'r that hath made and preserv'd us a nation!
Then conquer we must, when our cause it is just,
And this be our motto: "In God is our Trust!"
And the star-spangled banner in triumph shall wave
O'er the land of the free and the home of the brave!

Our flag has a proud history; thousands have died for its preservation
and honor. If it were just another piece of cloth, it would not excite so
much furor or fervent devotion. The stars and stripes displays a silent
statement of our national ideals of freedom and justice; it represents
a unique form of representative government—a government "of the
people, by the people, and for the people"—a grand experiment in
freedom unheard of heretofore in history.

Henry Ward Beecher stated it well in 1861, and his words are as
true today as then.

> Beginning with the Colonies and coming down to our
> time, in its sacred heraldry, its glorious insignia, it has
> gathered and stored chiefly this supreme idea: Divine
> right of liberty in man. Every color means liberty; every
> thread means liberty; every form of star and beam or
> stripe of light means liberty; not lawless, not license;
> but organized institutional liberty.—liberty through
> law, and laws for liberty. It is not a painted rag. It is
> a whole national history. It is the Constitution. It is
> the government. It is the free people that stand in the
> government of the Constitution.[64]

CHAPTER 19

Independence Day

Whether it's called the Fourth of July, Independence Day, or just the Fourth, the day is a federal holiday. It celebrates our formal declaring of independence from England on July 4, 1776. The postal service, the federal court systems, and other federal offices not necessary for the safety of our citizens are closed for the celebration.

Our most important secular holiday, the Fourth, is generally not celebrated by religious services, that is, unless the day falls on a Sunday, although often, time is given to honor God. Patriotic parades, fireworks displays, picnics, ballgames, and family reunions are customary ways of celebrating; patriotic Americans participate in many commemorative ways.

The road that led thirteen loosely aligned colonies possessed by England to self-governing, united American states took several long and sometimes painful detours. During the early colonial period, most people contented themselves with being subjects of King George III. Unfortunately, several significant governmental acts that were impossible to ignore or even to compromise with fueled smoldering resentments eventually leading to the Declaration of Independence.

> When in the course of human events it becomes
> necessary for one people to dissolve the political bands
> which have connected them with another and to assume

among the powers of the earth, the separate and equal station to which the Laws of Nature and of Nature's God entitle them, a decent respect to the opinions of mankind required that they should declare the causes which impel them to the separation.

We hold these truths to be self-evident, that all men are created equal, that they are endowed by their Creator with certain unalienable Rights, that among these are Life, Liberty and the pursuit of Happiness—that to secure these rights, Governments are instituted among Men, deriving their just powers from the consent of the governed.

This document, written by Thomas Jefferson, proclaimed that the American colonies had had enough and were breaking away from England. But just of what had they had enough? Throughout the late 1600s, as untamed wildernesses beckoned or as settlers populated the seaboard, able men and women relied on themselves rather than governments ruling from a distance. They valued freedom and ruled their communities and churches without fear and distrust. However, the English Parliament, controlling from afar, wished to tax at whim and rule a subservient people. The colonists refused to think of themselves as lower than their English peers. Let's examine a few of the unendurable situations the colonists faced during the 1700s that led to the final revolt.

The Stamp Act

On March 22, 1765, the British Parliament under leadership of George Grenville, Chancellor of the Exchequer, passed the Stamp Act. This new tax required all American colonists to pay tax on every piece of paper they used. Newspapers, licenses, legal documents—everything from playing cards to academic degrees were subject to this new tax.

England had a standing army in the colonies, primarily to keep the colonists in line, but the ostensible purpose of this tax was to pay the expense of ten thousand troops stationed on the frontier near the Appalachian Mountains to defend the pioneers in that area.

The method authorized for the taxes proved offensive to the colonists, for it was a direct tax imposed upon them without their consent. Prior to the Stamp Act, any taxes on colonial trade were for purposes of regulating commerce. The Stamp Act had one purpose though it wasn't acknowledged by England: to raise revenues for the treasury of England. It was the foot in the door, so to speak. If England could impose this tax without approval of colonial legislatures, what would they tax next?

Common people, who at first felt helpless to do anything about the situation, had revived hope as the various legislatures adopted resolutions defying the tax. Virginia led the way by the Virginia House of Burgesses adopting Patrick Henry's Stamp Act Resolves. These resolves stated that the colonists possessed rights equal to the British and that the colonies could be taxed only by their elected representatives. Further, colonists should not pay taxes imposed upon them by the English. Anyone who agreed with Parliament's right to tax the colony was henceforth an enemy of the colony.

The speaker of the House of Burgesses interrupted Patrick Henry's speech with the shout, "Treason!" Patrick Henry rejoined without pause, "If this be treason, make the most of it."

Several men throughout the colonies had been appointed stamp agents, but the majority declared opposition. A Stamp Act Congress met in New York in October 1765 to assure allegiance to the king but insubordination to a Parliament that had overstepped its authority. As a result of that Congress, colonists "persuaded" stamp agents to resign their commissions. On the day the Stamp Act became effective, no stamps were available, so business went on as usual with unstamped documents.

In December 1765, Parliament backed down on this issue and repealed the Stamp Act. Nevertheless, on the day the Stamp Act was repealed, Parliament passed the Declaratory Act, which in effect reiterated Parliament's authority to declare tax on the colonists.

Townshend Duties

For a couple of years, it seemed as though the British had backed away from the tax question. Unfortunately, the government, plagued by debts from previous skirmishes, needed money. A new chancellor of the exchequer, Charles Townshend, favored raising money from the colonies. Under his leadership, Parliament passed a series of acts in 1767. The most egregious, known as the Townshend Duties, placed a tax on imports of paper, lead, glass, paint, and tea. The act specified that the duties must be paid in silver; further, the money would first be used to pay for the colonies' governance, and anything left over would go the British treasury. Customs officials also had what amounted to blank search warrants, writs of assistance, to go into any shop, house, storehouse, or any other place to search and seize untaxed goods. This sharply restrained trade because colonists weren't permitted to buy those goods elsewhere.

To the rescue came John Dickinson, a true founding father, sometimes known as the Penman of the Revolution. He published newspaper articles and wrote letters denouncing the Townshend Acts. He wrote with wisdom, suggesting first that petitions be sent to Parliament, and if those didn't get results, a boycott of all British goods. He emphasized that if the British could tax paper or glass, they could also tax property.

Following Dickinson's advice, the colonists petitioned for redress of grievances regarding the import tax. Their petitions were rejected. Importers and shippers closed all major ports by adopting nonimportation agreements among the various colonies. Shipments fell drastically, and in the face of Britain's deficiency in the treasury, that government became more conciliatory.

In 1770, under the leadership of Lord North, Townshend's successor, the Townshend Acts were repealed on all items except one. To show Americans that Parliament retained the right to tax them, the tax on tea remained in effect. Tea, after all, brought great revenue to them.

Boston Massacre

The heavy British military presence, including the practice of quartering soldiers in private homes, created much hostility among the colonials. That, together with existing resentment of the Townshend Duties, resulted in scuffles and brawls among civilians and soldiers. On March 5, 1770, unruly colonials pelted soldiers with snowballs, sticks, and trash in front of the Boston Customhouse. British soldiers who fired into the crowd killed five civilians and wounded six. The day after the massacre, to prevent further violence, British soldiers went to a fort on Castle Island in Boston Harbor.

In spite of the fact that he was an American patriot, lawyer John Adams defended the soldiers in court. The jury acquitted six soldiers; two others were punished by having their thumbs branded. The jury believed the soldiers had felt endangered by the headstrong mob. Indeed, a deathbed testimony given to a doctor and passed on to the court confirmed the jury's verdict.

Tea Act of 1773

Because of the boycott of British goods, the East India Company had warehouses full of tea and faced bankruptcy. Faced with this prospect, the British government devised the solution to satisfy everybody, or so it thought. The Tea Act of 1773 allowed East India Company ships to sail directly to America rather than going to England first. Tea delivered to America was taxed less than it had previously been, but now it could come only on East India Company ships and could be sold only by chosen consignees. This created a much-resented monopoly.

The colonists, agitated to the point of resistance, took action. Hundreds of chests of tea shipped to America were not unloaded at the docks due to intervention of such groups as the New York Sons of Liberty and other concerned patriots. The best known of these interventions, the dumping of tea into Boston Harbor by Bostonians disguised as Mohawk Indians, occasioned the memorable Boston Tea Party.

What was the consequence of these tea shipment rejections? Americans became coffee drinkers. From the British point of view, upstart Americans hadn't cooperated and Bostonians had to be punished. In fact, the whole of Massachusetts would be humbled by force if necessary.

Intolerable Acts

Between March 31 and June 2, 1774, Parliament passed the Coercive Acts. Of the four bills, two primarily affected Boston and Massachusetts. The Boston Port Act closed that port until the colonists reimbursed the East India Company for the destroyed tea. In response to Britain's men-of-war anchored around Boston, shopkeepers draped stores in black and church buildings were filled with supplicants praying for safety.

The Massachusetts Government Act allowed King George III to appoint members of the governor's council in place of those elected by the colonists as they had previously been. In addition, the sheriff would choose all juries. In short, Massachusetts's local government was taken from it.

Perhaps most unbearable of all were two acts applicable to all colonies. The Administration of Justice Act allowed certain people accused of crimes to be tried in England, and the Quartering Act empowered Britain to quarter troops in private homes. To the colonists, these Acts were not coercive; they were intolerable.

King George III declared the colonies must "submit or triumph." The line was drawn. The colonists determined to be free or die. In their minds, to submit amounted to slavery.

Responses to the Intolerable Acts were unusual and unexpected; jurors stood up and refused to be sworn. Church congregations refused to sing and walked out. Citizens refused the king's appointments. Patriots ignored the ban on free speech and assembly. Their objective was orderly but complete disobedience of the Intolerable Acts.

First Continental Congress

After the English closed Boston's port in revenge for the Boston Tea Party, twelve of the thirteen colonies sent fifty-six delegates to the First Continental Congress, which convened in Carpenters Hall in Philadelphia on September 5, 1774. The assembly's purpose was not to seek independence from England but to air grievances, to right the wrongs inflicted on the colonies, to have their rights respected, and to present a unified colonial voice Parliament would hear. To ensure Parliament's attention, delegates agreed to stop trading with England until it restored the colonists' right of self-government.

In response to the Congress's appeals, the British ordered Governor Gage of Massachusetts to enforce the Coercive Acts and to stop colonial insubordination by whatever means necessary. On April 18, 1775, General Gage ordered seven hundred soldiers to Concord to seize the patriots' hidden arms. Paul Revere and William Dawes rode from Boston to Lexington to warn Sam Adams, John Hancock, and others of the approaching soldiers.

In anticipation, numerous men had previously pledged to fight at a minute's notice. Farmers, woodsmen, or townspeople, they were at home with guns, and most owned their own. These citizen soldiers had trained throughout the fall and winter months. On the dawn of April 19, the Minutemen faced the British. An unordered shot by an unknown colonial defender, ever after known as "the shot heard round the world," began the Revolutionary War.

Second Continental Congress

The Second Continental Congress convened in Philadelphia on May 10, 1775, with all colonies represented. It elected John Hancock as its president. In June, the colonies decided to join forces to create a Continental Army and appointed George Washington commander in chief.

Even throughout months of fighting, the Second Continental Congress entertained thoughts of reconciliation. On July 5, 1775, the Olive Branch Petition appealed directly to King George III, but he refused to look at it. Instead, he declared the Americans to be in "open rebellion."

Congress established the navy in November 1775 and sent a secret delegation to Europe asking for help from France. By December, help was pledged, but it didn't arrive until May 1, 1776, when France contributed a million dollars in arms and munitions.

Not everyone hoped for reconciliation. Thomas Paine published a fifty-page pamphlet, "Common Sense," in January 1776 that criticized the king and argued for American independence. His widely read arguments struck responsive chords and undoubtedly influenced the delegates of the Second Continental Congress.

The months of June and July 1776 proved eventful in two significant ways. On one hand, citizen soldiers and sailors were, for the most part, barely holding their own on land and sea against professionally trained military; on the other hand, congressional delegates busied themselves with brainstorming and prayer in regard to this highly momentous decision of whether to declare independence. On June 7, 1776, Richard Henry Lee goaded the undecided with this resolution.

> Resolved, That these United Colonies are, and of right ought to be Free and independent States, that they are absolved from all allegiance to the British Crown, and that all political connection between them and the state of Great Britain is, and ought to be, totally dissolved.

The decision process consisted of heartrending thought and prayer. Theirs was not a small civil rights protest, nor was it a protest against society. To dissolve allegiance to one's own country was contrary to all reason. Consequently, they realized England would see it as high treason and could impose the death penalty—hanging. The decision to declare independence was postponed until July.

In the meantime, the Continental Congress appointed a committee to draft an acceptable document of intent to separate from England. The committee consisted of Thomas Jefferson, Benjamin Franklin, John Adams, Roger Livingston, and Roger Sherman. No doubt the ideals contained in it had been ruminating in his mind for a long time, for Thomas Jefferson composed the first draft in one day. After a few suggested changes by Adams and Franklin, they presented the document to the congressional delegates at the end of June.

Serious delegates debated the issue in secret behind locked doors for fear of British reprisal. On July 2, twelve of the thirteen delegations approved Lee's resolution for independence from the Kingdom of Great Britain. On July 4, Jefferson's Declaration of Independence received endorsement, and a copy signed by the president of the Congress, John Hancock, and Charles Thomson, its secretary, was released to the printers.

The first public readings were held on July 8 to celebrations and bonfires modeled on previously held celebrations of the king's birthday. Some towns held mock funerals for the king that symbolized the death of tyranny and the birth of freedom.

On July 19, 1776, Congress commissioned a fine, handwritten copy on parchment in preparation for a symbolic signing by all delegates set for August 2.

Signers of the Declaration

With the exception of Benjamin Franklin, all the signers were young men who could have normally looked forward to living many more years. Twenty-four delegates were lawyers or jurists; eleven were merchants; nine owned large land areas; and some were doctors, members of the clergy, or other professionals.

If England won the war, these men knew that if they were not hung for treason, their professional lives would be over. What started as resistance to unfair taxation without representation had developed into other matters involving principles and honors for which they were willing to give up their professions, their "lives, land, and sacred honor."

John Hancock's famous lavish signature ensured that King George III would be able to read it without his glasses. "There! His Majesty can now read my name without spectacles, and can now double his reward of five hundred pounds for my head. That is my defiance!" Some modern historians deny that John Hancock ever said that, that it is only legend. Legend or not, the signing was in itself an act of defiance.

Hancock further stated, "There must be no pulling different ways. We must all hang together." To which Benjamin Franklin replied, "Yes, we must all hang together, or most assuredly, we shall all hang separately."

Most of the fifty-six delegates signed on August 2 at what is now known as Independence Hall;[65] however, we celebrate the Fourth of July, the date on the Declaration of Independence parchment.

Articles of Confederation

Shortly after the adoption of the Declaration of Independence, the colonies began work on the Articles of Confederation to bring together in a "league of friendship" what amounted to thirteen separate nations. Our present word *state* meant about the same thing then as an independent nation. Americans wished to present to the world a united front by so confederating. Under the Articles of Confederation, ratified during the years 1778–79 by all (except Maryland, which ratified it in 1781), there were neither a separate executive nor courts. Nevertheless, that Congress had power to make war and peace, coin money, establish weights and measures, and make treaties and alliances.

Victory at Last

Like a bell that cannot be unrung, the shot at Concord couldn't be reversed; the stage had been set for a drama of brutal, epic proportions with an unpredictable grand finale. The war seemed interminable. It had, after all, been dragging on for seven years. Historians have devoted innumerable chapters to the final battles of this war: the deadly cat-and-mouse maneuvering throughout the Carolinas, the sizeable professional British military versus the small-scale volunteer Continental forces, and the fact that General Cornwallis just didn't understand his infuriated enemy.

Britain knew that if it conquered Virginia, its claims to all lands west of the Alleghenies would be assured. At the time, Virginia claimed lands almost as far north as Lake Erie and to the west as far as the Mississippi. General Cornwallis commanded the largest army in America, much larger than the Americans could muster, but he had lost too many men; therefore, he chose a base near the sea, intending to be supported by the British Navy. He camped at Yorktown, Virginia, on the York and James Rivers, which empty into the Chesapeake Bay. It became the site of the decisive battle.

Patriots gave credit to Providence for letting all aspects of this critical battle fall into place. The French naval commander arrived at a propitious time, luring the British fleet to sea, successfully engaging them, and occupying their attention to the point they couldn't concern themselves with the army on land.

General Washington and General Comte de Rochambeau's united Continental and French forces had previously marched from New York to Chesapeake Bay, ferried across to Virginia, and dug fortifications around Yorktown. Cornwallis, surrounded by water on three sides with no navy to support him and bombarded with heavy artillery from the formidable force of Continental and French under the leadership of General Washington, knew his situation was hopeless. A British squadron arrived off the Virginia coast, but for Cornwallis, it was too little, too late.

Through the deafening fire of seventy cannons, a British drummer boy sounded the "parley," meaning, "Let's talk terms." No one heard him. After what seemed a considerable time, a British officer stood and raised a white handkerchief. It was over. Cornwallis was surrendering.

On October 19, 1781, British soldiers marched through a mile-long column of Colonial and French soldiers to stack arms and surrender, but it was two years before an official signing of a peace treaty.

Treaty of Paris

It has been said that the Articles of Confederation's greatest achievement was the Treaty of Paris of 1783, which specified terms of settlement with Britain. The treaty described boundaries, specified fishing rights in British North American waters, made provisions for restitution of confiscated Loyalist property, and promised speedy withdrawal of all British armies, garrisons, and fleets from the United States. Of prime importance:

His Britannic majesty acknowledges the said United States ... to be free, sovereign and independent States; that he treats them as such, and for himself, his heirs, and successors, relinquishes all claims to the Government, proprietary and territorial rights of the same, and every part thereof.

Fate of the Signers of the Declaration of Independence

Before the conclusion of the War for Independence, the brave signers of the Declaration of Independence gave up much to give us more than we can grasp. They fought their own government to establish a free and independent America. In the process, some of them gave their lives and many their fortunes. It would be a daunting task to list all fifty-six signers and their fates, but here is a sampling.

Every signer was hunted and condemned to death as a traitor. Five were imprisoned and tortured before they died. Seventeen lost everything. Nine died from wounds or other injuries while fighting the Revolutionary War.

George Walton and Button Guinette of Georgia and Edward Rutledge of South Carolina had properties looted or vandalized. William Hooper's property in North Carolina was destroyed, and he was ruined financially.

Thomas Nelson Jr.'s Yorktown, Virginia home had been commandeered for British headquarters. Dead horses and soldiers lay all around it, but Nelson noticed that his home had been untouched. When he questioned why it was intact, he learned it had been spared out of respect for him. Nelson urged General Washington to open fire on it rather than let the British occupy it. Colonial soldiers destroyed the house, killing all inside before Cornwallis surrendered. After the war, Nelson died bankrupt.

George Clymer's wife and children in Pennsylvania hid in the woods as British soldiers burned their furnishings. Lyman Hall's rice plantation in Georgia was seized and burned. Thomas Heyward's fields in South Carolina were burned, and his slaves were stolen and sold in Jamaica. While he was imprisoned, his young wife died. Arthur Middleton's South Carolina home was ransacked and vandalized but not burned. However, valuable paintings were slashed, and slaves and silver were stolen.

John Hart's New Jersey farm, house, fields, and gristmill were destroyed. For a time, he lived in caves and forests. William Floyd's New York estate was looted and stripped of anything of value. British soldiers in New York took Lewis Morris's livestock for food; his tenants were driven from their homes.

Robert Morris of Pennsylvania lost one hundred and fifty ships and his personal funds and died a poor man.

Carter Braxton of Virginia had been a wealthy sea merchant. The British seized his cargoes and ships and burned his house at Chericoke along with all his papers and furnishings. Not only was he ruined financially, but two of his sons-in-law, who had cosigned notes for him, were also ruined. After his death, relatives contributed to his widow's survival.

Thomas McKean of Pennsylvania reported being hunted like a fox and forced to move his family from place to place. He lost all his possessions. Benjamin Harrison's shipyard on the James River in Virginia was burned. Francis Lewis of Whitestone, New York, was not home when the British came to call. An aging Elizabeth Lewis was forced to watch the looting of her fine china, clocks—everything that could fit into saddlebags. She also was carried away on horseback, locked in a filthy, unheated room under guard, and forced to sleep on a cold floor. By the time she was released, her health had deteriorated; she died within weeks.

After the War

Most signers survived incommunicable hardships, and many lived into their seventies. The oldest survivor, Charles Carroll of Maryland, died at ninety-four.

All suffered financially from the burden of war. None accepted the king's offer of immunity or his money if only he would break his pledge. All put emphasis on principle rather than expediency. Some died in poverty while others became prosperous. A few finished out their lives in obscurity, but numbered among the surviving signers were prominent judges, senators, state delegates, mayors, community leaders, and governors. Best known were John Adams and Thomas Jefferson, our second and third presidents. (Coincidentally, Adams and Jefferson died on the same day, July 4, 1826, the fiftieth anniversary of the signing.)

Benjamin Harrison's third son, William Henry Harrison, became our ninth president, and his great-grandson, Benjamin Harrison, became our twenty-third president.

Gone and Now Forgotten

The fearless men and women of the War for Independence era are in most cases forgotten. Like the Egyptians recorded in Exodus, new Pharaohs have forgotten the Josephs, the saviors of their people. Too many Americans are ignorant of our precious heritage and have frittered away hard-gained rights. As we celebrate the Fourth, let us pause to thank a merciful God for all we have, and let us earnestly pray that as a people, our godly citizens will present a unified stand for righteousness. Although the following verse was written for the Jewish nation, the dictum yet rings true: "Blessed is the nation whose God is the Lord, and the people whom He hath chosen for His own inheritance" (Psalm 33:12).

CHAPTER 20

Labor Day

Labor Day is a legal holiday in the United States and its territories, Puerto Rico, and the Virgin Islands. It has been celebrated on the first Monday in September since 1894 in honor of American workers and their economic achievements. (Communist and Socialist countries celebrate Labor Day on May 1.)

According to Samuel Gompers, founder of the American Federation of Labor,

> All other holidays are in a more or less degree connected with conflicts and battles of man's prowess over man, or strife and discord for greed and power, of glories achieved by one nation over another. Labor Day ... is devoted to no man, living or dead, to no sect, race, or nation.[66]

Working Conditions in Early Industrial America

Labor Day's tumultuous conception began in the early 1800s. Thousands of immigrants settled in coastal cities such as New York and Los Angeles as well as inland cities such as Chicago and St. Louis. They had emigrated from England, Scotland, Ireland, Germany, Holland,

France, or Spain, many to escape hunger in their homelands. By the 1880s, thousands of Jews had fled Russia, Hungary, Poland, Latvia, or Lithuania to escape religious persecution. Most arrived with not much more than the clothes they wore and a few meager possessions stuffed into well-worn suitcases or small trunks. They came seeking better lives for themselves and their children. Instead, many found disillusionment. Rather than instant prosperity, they experienced long-lasting hardship and poverty.

Commonly, five or six families lived in a house intended for one family. Crowded boarding houses lodged single men and women. In the absence of indoor plumbing and running water, sewage from outhouses attracted rats, which spread cholera, tuberculosis, and typhoid.

Unskilled coastal laborers worked ten to twelve hours at the docks or at other physically demanding jobs for seventy-five cents a day. Inland, men built bridges and canals, labored in the fields, or mined coal. The adventuresome headed west to the coal, silver, and gold mines.

Unskilled women generally worked as domestic servants or in factories. A demanding employer might require a maid to work sixteen hours a day caring for children, cooking, and cleaning.

Men, women, and children worked in factories or textile mills heated by hot-air furnaces. With poor air circulation, in such sweatshop conditions, sicknesses spread. One of the prevalent diseases in the sweatshops was commonly called consumption, a wasting away of the body due to pulmonary tuberculosis.

Able or not, the sick came to work for fear of being fired for missing a day. They realized that the unemployed were eagerly waiting for their jobs. Those fortunate enough to be employed in factories also worked eleven- to thirteen-hour days with only a short lunch break, and most worked seven days a week to eke out a bare existence. Women and children earned much less than did men. Sometimes, raises were given to men but not to women or children. Existing child labor laws, such as they were, were not enforced.

Even after laborers gained official recognition, sweatshop conditions continued. Workers in droves had headed for Los Angeles and its healthier climate, hoping to escape or be cured of tuberculosis. To keep workers in and union organizers out, the Triangle Shirtwaist Factory in New York kept its doors locked. In 1911, a fire killed 146, who burned to death or died jumping from upper floors that had no fire escapes.

Poor housing, long hours, low pay, job insecurity, and unhealthy working environments led to agitations and sometimes workplace disturbances across the country.

Frontrunners in the Emergence of Labor Unions

Workers formed small unions and sometimes went on brief strikes only to then see their unions disintegrate after their issues were addressed. Purportedly, one of the first unions formed was in 1825 by New York seamstresses, who formed a women's union and went on strike.

Sarah Bagly (1806–1848)

Seventy weavers at Middlesex Mills in Lowell, New Hampshire, walked off the job in November 1842. They protested having to work two looms instead of one. Economic depression reigned in Lowell from 1842 to 1844, and over a thousand workers left the city while employers decreased remaining workers' wages. When economic conditions improved in 1844, textile corporations raised wages but for male textile workers only. Partially in response, Sarah George Bagly organized the Lowell Female Labor Reform Association. Reforms requested included better working conditions and a ten-hour day.

In 1845, Sarah and her association presented the Massachusetts legislature with 10,000 names from throughout the state petitioning for a ten-hour day. The legislature investigated, said the matter was not in their hands, and passed the issue back to employers and employees to work out.

Political pressure prevailed, however, and the mills shortened the workday by thirty minutes in 1847. Sarah's employer fired her, undoubtedly because of her constant pro-worker agitations.

Kate Mullany (c. 1845–1906)

To gain some insight into the rigors of life in the 1860s, just think about the lack of labor-saving appliances—no automatic washing machines, dryers, steam irons, or spray starch; instead, scrub boards, clothes lines, flatirons heated on wood stoves, and starch cooked from water and wheat or corn flour.

Life became somewhat easier for women with the invention of the detachable collar in the 1820s. Women had grown weary of scrubbing and starching complete shirts when only the collars and cuffs showed signs of soil. One such wife, Hannah Lord Monteague, of Troy, New York, cut the collar off her husband's shirt, washed and starched it, and sewed it back on. A businessman liked the idea and turned collars themselves into a thriving industry. His collars were not sewn on; they were attached with two metal studs, one in the front of the shirt and one in the back.[67]

By the 1860s, the first commercial laundry in Troy supplied much of the nation with cleaned, starched, and ironed collars. The laundry employed approximately four thousand women washers, starchers, and ironers who worked in stifling heat as long as fourteen hours a day for $2 per week

A young Irish woman, Kate Mullany, organized the Collar Laundry Union, and along with two hundred coworkers, she went on strike in 1864, demanding better working conditions and a twenty-five-cent raise. The strike ended in a week after the women got their raise. Kate earned the distinction of being the first female appointed to a labor union's national office in 1868 when the National Labor Union honored her work.

William H. Sylvis (1828–1869)

Elias Howe's new lockstitch sewing machine, patented in 1846, strengthened factory production, which in turn led to the creation of standardized, proportion-sized clothing. With sewing easier and faster, mass production of Civil War uniforms became possible. Along with mass sewing production, sweatshop conditions accelerated as well.

Shortly after the Civil War, William H. Sylvis organized the National Labor Union in 1866. Diverse groups of workers united into a single union; however, it was more a political than a trade union, and it disbanded in 1870s, partly due to the panic and economic depression of 1873.

Continued problems affected American laborers, who responded by organizing secretive, sometimes violent, but short-lived labor unions. Among those emerging after Civil War woes were the shoemakers' union, Knights of St. Crispin,[68] Sovereigns of Industry, and the Molly Maguires, coal unionists who assaulted managers and foremen connected with the Pennsylvania coal fields in the late 1800s.

Uriah S. Stephens (1821–1882)

Around the time the National Labor Union disbanded, the Noble and Holy Order of the Knights of Labor came onto the scene and subsumed several unions. On Thanksgiving Day 1869, Uriah S. Stephens invited nine Philadelphia garment workers to participate in founding this new union.

The Knights based many of its secretive rituals and initiating procedures and concepts on Freemasonry, Odd Fellows, Knights of Pythias, and others fraternities to which Stephens belonged. Stephens named the new group Adelphion Krupton, Secret Brotherhood. Members were subjected to lectures on the nobleness of labor and the evils of working for slave wages.

Through the years, by election of the membership, Stephens progressed through the ranks of first master workman, first district master workman, and first grand master workman.

Dissension within the organization arose when Roman Catholic members voted in favor of omitting scriptural quotations from the rituals, editing ceremonies that were considered anti-Catholic, opening the organization to the public, and revealing the name of the order. At that point, Stephens resigned as grand master workman after having founding and guiding it for nearly ten years. The internal debate lasted nearly five years, but on January 1, 1882, the Knights of Labor became a public organization. Welcomed were all productive members of society who worked for a living, women included, and after 1881, blacks. Among those not welcomed were lawyers, gamblers, and liquor producers.

Militant Marxists and Socialists influenced the Knights and intensified disputes between skilled and unskilled trade unionists. Points on which all agreed were shortening the workday, ending child labor, and equal pay for equal work. Promotion of government ownership of railroads and telegraphs, passing an income tax amendment, and issuing paper money were also topics on their socialist agenda.

Two important successful strikes in which the Knights of Labor participated were the Union Pacific Railroad strike in 1884 and the Wabash Railroad strike in 1885. Two strikes ending in tragedy rang the death knell for the Knights: the Rock Springs Massacre (1885) and the Haymarket Square Massacre (1886). All four occurred under the leadership of Grand Master Workman Terrence V. Powderly.

Terrence V. Powderly (1849–1924)

Rock Springs, Wyoming, a growing coal-mining town, was the setting for one of our nation's worst racial and workers' union riots. The Union Pacific Railroad maintained a monopoly on coal production and transportation, enabling it to control prices for the coal and wages paid to those who mined it.

In 1875, the company reduced wages but didn't reduce merchandise prices at the company store. Workers protested such treatment by striking. The company immediately replaced striking workers with Chinese. Welsh and Swedish miners resented sharing the mines with Chinese workers and didn't conceal their contempt for the company and the Chinese. For ten years, ill will seethed among the miners.

On September 2, 1885, Rock Springs miners learned that miners in Colorado were receiving a raise but they weren't. Simmering over actual and perceived past injustices and then that, their fury reached explosive proportions. A union mob violently attacked Chinese workers and burned homes of approximately seventy-five Chinese families. Twenty-eight Chinese died immediately; fifteen were wounded, some of whom later died. Many Chinese escaped into desolate areas, and some were rescued by Union Pacific. Violence erupted again when remaining Chinese wouldn't cooperate by striking for higher wages. Federal troops arrived, restored order, and remained there until 1898.

An unsuccessful strike of the McCormick Harvesting Machine Company and the resulting Haymarket Riot or Massacre in Chicago the following year marked the beginning of the decline of the Knights.

On May 1, 1886, the Chicago Knights of Labor led by locals Albert and Lucy Parsons led 80,000 people down Michigan Avenue in support of an eight-hour day. In a few days, 350,000 workers nationwide went on strike at 1,200 plants.

Cyrus McCormick, of McCormick Harvesting Machine Company fame, had refused to accept a union to represent his employees and closed the factory only to reopen it later with new employees. McCormick granted an eight-hour workday and a half day off to celebrate his concession to lower working hours.

On May 3, 1886, August Spies, editor of *Arbeiter-Zeitung* (Worker Newspaper), spoke to a crowd of 6,000 and led them to McCormick's plant to harass replacement workers. As McCormick's new employees left the factory, they were greeted by abusive name-calling from the union and other strikers from across the nation who had congregated in Chicago. Several strikers were killed after challenging the police, who had been called to protect the emerging factory workers.

Local and foreign anarchists distributed provocative circulars printed in German and English promoting a meeting at Haymarket Square, then a thriving business center, now in Chicago's West Loop. The circulars urged workers to take up arms and get justice for the murdered strikers. Circulars also claimed police murdered strikers on behalf of business owners.

The night of the Haymarket Square rally, May 4, 1886, a peaceful rain was falling. A large number of police officers ordered to report to duty watched the proceedings from close by. Mayor Carter Harrison Sr., noting the calmness of the crowd, left early.

Much later, police officers ordered the crowd to disperse. Someone threw a bomb into the police formation, killing one policeman, Michael J. Degan, instantly. Seven others later died from injuries. Police opened fire, killing eleven and injuring dozens.

Police charged eight people with Degan's death, seven of whom were sentenced to death, the others to fifteen years in prison. This punishment, considered excessive by some, created heroes of the radicals in the labor organization and sparked worldwide protests. The case was appealed to the Supreme Court of Illinois and the U.S. Supreme Court.

After all appeals were denied, Governor John Peter Altgeld, the first immigrant to be elected governor of Illinois, commuted the death sentences of Michael Schwab, a German immigrant, and Samuel Fielden, an English immigrant. Both were pardoned in 1893. Another German immigrant, sentenced to death, Louis Lingg, committed suicide in his cell using a smuggled dynamite cap. On November 11, 1887, the following four were hanged in public: Albert Parsons, a United States citizen, and August Spies, Adolph Fischer, and George Engel, German immigrants. As they marched to the gallows in hoods, they sang the anthem of the international revolutionary movement, the French national anthem, *La Marseillaise.*[69]

Both tragedies, and specifically, the shameful treatment of the Chinese at Rock Springs, clearly defied the principles of the Knights of Labor as stated in its initiation ritual, and an investigation into the attack on the miners resulted in reparations for families of those killed or injured.

After Powderly was voted out of office in 1893, the Socialist Labor Party left the Knights to form the Socialist Trade and Labor Alliance, a Marxist organization. In 1905, many left the Knights to join the newly established Industrial Workers of the World.

Negative publicity from the tragic strikes and riots and dwindling membership rendered the Knights ineffective as a labor organization, though it continued to hold conventions until 1932.

Samuel Gompers (1850–1924)

Samuel Gompers emigrated with his parents from the Jewish slums of London in 1850. In the United States, one of his jobs was reading to illiterate fellow employees to help break the tedium of their everyday routine. As a reader, he was able to further his own education, enabling him to become a leader in his local union and of the national Cigar Makers Union.

In 1886, Gompers founded the American Federation of Labor, a federation of unions of skilled workers. At first, he shunned partisan politics and focused on union activities that promoted shorter hours and higher pay. With time, however, his views changed, and President Wilson appointed him to the Council on National Defense. He attended the Paris Peace Conference in 1919 as a labor advisor.

During strikes, his unions felt justified in using force because they felt their workers were being taken advantage of by their employers. While rank-and-file union members didn't condone Marxist doctrine, some Marxist philosophy came into play here: the workers contributed all the value to goods, but the capitalists kept a huge portion of the value for themselves when they had contributed nothing except the money to begin the business. Class consciousness and contending with capitalists (employers) for what they considered rightfully the workers' fruits of their labors were also stressed. Workers were encouraged to struggle in whatever way necessary to oppose their employers, the capitalists.

Gompers voiced concern that with the prevalence of machinery introduced into the factories, American craftsmanship would decline and skilled Americans would be reduced to begging.

Eugene V. Debs (1855–1916)

Pullman, Illinois, might be considered a clean company town in contrast to the dirty coal dust of a Rock Springs company town. George Pullman had designed the town to be a workers' paradise. Skilled craftsmen and assembly-line workers lived in identical row houses. Managers lived in Victorian-style homes while Pullman lived in a sumptuous hotel, where his suppliers and salesmen also stayed when in town.

Everybody in Pullman worked for the Pullman Company, lived in Pullman housing, had their rents deducted automatically from their Pullman checks, and cashed their weekly checks in the Pullman bank. This had been the routine from 1880 when the town was founded until 1893, when the financially unsophisticated and unprepared were caught in a nationwide depression.

George Pullman dismissed hundreds of employees and cut wages of those left after orders for Pullman sleeping cars sharply decreased. Even though paychecks shrank, rents remained the same. Pullman employees went on strike, demanding more pay and less rent.

In support of the Pullman strike, Eugene V. Debs led the American Railway Union nationwide to boycott trains carrying Pullman cars. Railroad cars were looted and burned as union and nonunion mobs pillaged and rampaged. With all railway service disrupted, the mail couldn't get through.

For this reason, President Grover Cleveland declared the strike a federal crime and sent 12,000 troops to end it. In Kensington, Illinois, near Chicago, U.S. marshals fired on protesters and killed thirty-six, thus bringing another strike to a tragic end.

The Pullman strike was officially over on August 3, 1894. Debs, after due process, went to prison for violating a court order during the strike. While in prison, he studied socialist literature and became a prolific socialist writer promoting industrial unionism.

Again, during World War I, he was sentenced to prison, but that time for espionage. In 1920, from his prison cell, he campaigned for president on the Socialist ticket and garnered nearly a million votes. While he was in prison, the American Railway Union disbanded.

John L. Lewis (1880–1969)

John L. Lewis witnessed mining conditions firsthand when he began working the mines as a youth of fifteen in Lucas, Iowa. As a young man, he also tried farming, construction work, and other work for a time before he found his niche in the labor movement.

He had joined the United Mine Workers, an affiliate of the American Federation of Labor, and rose through the ranks to become president of the UMW in 1920, a position he held until 1960. An autocratic despot, he held tight-fisted control of the union.

In an effort to unionize other workers in mass-production industries, in 1935, Lewis joined other AFL leaders and formed the Committee for Industrial Organization (CIO). He also served as its president from 1936 to 1940. In 1937, General Motors and U.S. Steel, two giants among mass-production industries, were forced to recognize the union and the power of collective bargaining.

Lewis and the UMW backed President Franklin Roosevelt's reelection in 1936, but he urged the UMW to support Wendell Willkie in 1940, citing uncertainty regarding Roosevelt's intention to involve the United States in World War II. When the union refused to support Willkie, Lewis left the AFL.

However, after the Pearl Harbor attack, UMW workers pledged to support America's war efforts by not striking. Their pledge was short-lived, and half a million workers walked off the job in 1943. Steel mills closed due to power shortages and weakened production. President Roosevelt seized control of the mines to continue maximizing war efforts.

Lewis campaigned against the Taft-Hartley Act of 1947, which specified unfair labor practices that would apply to labor unions and their employers. Among those practices specified, the act forbad closed shops, permitted employers to sue unions for damages done during strikes, and required unions to make their financial statements public.

Listed among Lewis's successes is the first Federal Mine Safety Act of 1952 and four national coal mine strikes between 1945 and 1950, which ultimately improved working conditions and guaranteed miners higher wages and better health and fringe benefits. In his own defense, he stated,

> I have pleaded your case from the pulpit and from the public platform—not in the quavering tones of a feeble mendicant asking alms, but in the thundering voice of the captain of a mighty host, demanding the rights to which free men are entitled.[70]

AFL-CIO

The American Federation of Labor's original intent was to organize skilled workers. In contrast, the Congress of Industrial Organization organized entire industries regardless of skill. Bitter arguments, antagonistic verbal attacks, differences in ideology, and vitriolic attacks by John L. Lewis on his AFL colleagues hastened the break between the two in 1936 when the AFL expelled the CIO from the federation.

William Green (1873–1952)

A native of Coshocton, Ohio, William Green labored in the coal mines from age sixteen. He joined the UMW and rose through the ranks to become its secretary-treasurer in 1912. In 1924, he became president of the AFL, leading the struggle against rival John L. Lewis of the CIO.

Perhaps Green's best-known accomplishment was witnessing the passage of the Norris-LaGuardia Act of 1932 during his presidency. In large part, due to his unions' backing, this new law abolished yellow-dog contracts, pledges requiring workers not to join unions as a condition of employment. This same act greatly limited the use of injunctions during labor disputes. The law proved ineffective in settling labor disputes. Moreover, in 1935, it was held to be unconstitutional.

Old antagonisms gradually disappeared when the two organizations began working together on problems that affected all workers, skilled or unskilled. Both began concentrating on organizing unions in areas and plants where there was no labor representation. After a nineteen-year estrangement, the two reunited into the AFL-CIO in New York on December 5, 1955.

George Meany (1894–1980)

Upon the death of William Green in 1952, George Meany was elected president of the AFL. Meany, from the Bronx, sought and worked for reunification of the AFL and the CIO, and at its unifying convention, the newly merged labor federation unanimously elected him president.

Under Meany's leadership, labor and capital cooperated more with each other. He was known as a strong anticommunist. Labor unions considered leftist were expelled or decertified. He also called for an end to all discrimination in the workplace. Americans who benefited from this promotion of working rights for all were women, minorities, and retirees.

Meany supported laborers in the United States and advocated independent unions for workers in Central Europe, Russia, South Africa, or anywhere else where he felt workers were exploited.

In 1979, Meany retired as president of the AFL-CIO, and the organization unanimously chose his executive assistant, Lane Kirkland, as his successor.

Lane Kirkland (1922–1999)

Lane Kirkland, from Camden, South Carolina, had long been active in the labor movement. As president, his dominating theme centered upon solidarity in the United States and abroad.

He was instrumental in channeling millions of dollars to Poland to end Communist Party rule and gain freedom for Polish workers. (Poland's highest honor, the Order of the White Eagle, was awarded him posthumously.)

Largely through Kirkland's efforts, organizations such as the UMW, United Auto Workers, Brotherhood of Locomotive Engineers, and the International Longshore and Warehouse Union all rejoined the federation, a triumph for solidarity. To oppose President Reagan's conservative policies, Kirkland organized a Solidarity Day rally in Washington, DC in 1981.

Kirkland increased the role of black Americans and other minorities in the AFL-CIO and nominated Joyce Miller, the first woman to serve on the AFL-CIO executive council.

Union membership declined tremendously, however, during Kirkland's tenure, perhaps due to the air traffic controller's strike in 1981 and the Hormel meat packers' strike in 1985.

In 1955, Congress had made strikes by federal employees illegal and punishable by a fine or incarceration. In 1981, almost 13,000 members of the Professional Air Traffic Controllers Organization (PATCO) went on strike; they wanted a four-day workweek of thirty-two hours per week and an across-the-board wage increase of $10,000 per year. In anticipation of a possible strike, the Federal Aviation Administration had a contingency plan in place. When members of PATCO rejected FAA's counteroffer and went on strike, the contingency plan fell into place, functioning smoothly and with a minimum of inconvenience.

On August 3, 1981, President Reagan issued a stern ultimatum for the strikers to return to work within forty-eight hours or be released from their jobs. Some controllers thought he was bluffing, but they found he was serious. PATCO leaders were jailed after ignoring court injunctions, and federal judges levied fines against the union. Eleven thousand strikers were fired, while 1,200 went back to work within a week. The public sided with the government and felt little sympathy for workers who were already earning wages far above the national average.

After the strike, a congressional committee recommended rehiring those who had been fired. The administration declined, and Transportation Secretary Drew Lewis refused to meet with PATCO leader Robert Poli to even discuss it.

President Reagan later pointed out that he was the first president to be a lifetime member of the AFL-CIO and that he supported the rights of workers to organize and bargain collectively, but under no circumstances as president could he tolerate an illegal strike by Federal employees. In the 1980s, long-established firms such as Armour, Swift, and Wilson were swallowed up by conglomerates such as Cargill, Occidental Petroleum, and Greyhound. Workers were laid off as plants closed only to reopen under new ownership that offered jobs at less pay with no benefits.

Hormel had not been subsumed by another corporation but had opened a new plant with new technologies in 1982 at its Austin, Minnesota headquarters. Workers complained of the high-speed disassembly line and prison-like regimen. Veteran workers who were eligible retired as soon as possible and were replaced by inexperienced workers who suffered from injuries due to lack of work experience in unsafe conditions. The straw that broke the camel's back was the 23 percent wage cut requested for plant workers after the company had declared record profits and had given a salary increase to its CEO. The United Food and Commercial Workers (UFCW) P-9 union organized the strike and prepared strategies.

The Hormel Meatpacking Plant strike began in 1985. Six months into the strike, thousands of strike supporters tried to block the plant's gates, but replacement workers crossed picket lines, thereby prompting riots. Democratic governor Randy Perpich called in the National Guard to escort replacement workers. About 500 Hormel workers reclaimed their jobs, crossing their own picket lines, and worked beside replacement workers. Calling the National Guard was not a good political move, and after public uproar, they were soon withdrawn from Austin. The strike was broken in June 1986 after ten months' duration.

Three hundred workers were fired outright for their behavior during the strike. Many were forced to retire or be placed on a rehire list. After the strike was broken, the national union ousted Local P-9.

The strike caused rifts among longtime friends that continue twenty years later. Some maintain that in spite of defeat, the strike forged solidarity as tens of thousands across the nation sent checks to help strikers and brought truckloads of food to help families survive during the long struggle when their own churches and schools turned their backs on Local P-9 in support of Hormel's corporate policies.

Thomas Donahue (1928–)

After Lance Kirkland retired in the spring of 1995, the executive council chose Thomas Donahue from the Bronx to fill out the remaining months of his term of office. However, at the AFL-CIO Convention in December 1995, after a hotly contested battle for leadership, the organization elected John J. Sweeney president.

Previously, from 1967 to 1969, Donahue had served under President Lyndon Johnson as assistant secretary of labor for labor-management relations. Within the AFL-CIO, Donahue had served as secretary-treasurer for sixteen years.

Donahue was instrumental in establishing the George Meany Center for the education of union members and workers, and he was a leading spokesperson against the passage of the North American Free Trade Association (NAFTA).

John J. Sweeney (1934–)

After John J. Sweeney's ascent to the presidency of the AFL-CIO, changes slanting leftward began to come. The Cold War policy of forbidding known Communists from holding leadership positions was reversed and a radical reorientation took its place. At this writing, the Communist Party USA and the labor organization are in complete accord. The leadership is moving toward creating a socialist international labor movement that includes the United States. Sweeney is not a Communist, but he is a member of the Democratic Socialists of America and a self-professed loather of capitalism.

Emergence of the Eight-Hour Workday

As early as 1791, workers were striking for shorter workdays. At that time, Philadelphia carpenters would have been happy to have had ten-hour days! Around 1836, labor publications began calling for eight-hour days. Bostonian ship carpenters achieved the eight-hour day in 1842.

Several laws were passed in the 1860s in various cities, and even Congress granted federal employees eight-hour days in 1868. However, all the laws had too many loopholes and were unenforceable and thus ineffective.

The turning point seems to have been in 1898, when the United Mine Workers won an eight-hour day. The Building Trades Council (BTC) followed suit in 1900. After arbitration of laborers and mill owners, the BTC won the eight-hour day, closed shops for skilled workers, and a permanent arbitration panel. Printing trades won their eight-hour day in 1905.

Ford Motor Company cut shift work to eight hours a day and doubled pay to $5 per day in 1914. However, it was not until 1916 that the first federal law, the Adamson Act, regulated hours of private industry workers and specified additional pay for overtime but for railroad workers only.

Three major pieces of congressional legislation affecting workers today were the National Labor Relations Act (NLRA) of 1935, the Fair Labor Standards Act of 1938, and the Taft-Hartley Act of 1947, which was an amendment to the NLRA of 1935 previously mentioned.

Labor had long agitated for government empowerment of unions so the scales would be tipped in their favor in disputes with employers. The

National Labor Relations Act of 1935 accomplished that by establishing the National Labor Relations Board. The NLRB was given power to investigate and decide on charges of unfair labor practices by employers and gave workers the right to decide if they wanted to be recognized by a union.

The Fair Labor Standards Act of 1938 established minimum wages and specified a maximum forty-hour week. Anyone working over that maximum would receive pay at one and a half times regular pay. Employment of children under age sixteen in factories was forbidden, and anyone under eighteen couldn't be employed in hazardous jobs.

Sarah Bagley, Kate Mullany, and other labor leaders from two centuries ago would find the contrast in working environments from their time to ours unfathomable.

Origins of Labor Day Holiday

There is some dispute as to who first demanded a holiday for laborers. Some believe Peter J. McGuire, a cofounder of the AFL, proposed the idea to his Central Labor Union in New York in 1882. That union organized a demonstration and picnic, and on September 5, 1882, he led ten thousand workers from city hall to Union Square in New York. Workers took an unpaid day to protest long hours, low wages, and poor working conditions.

Other sources credit Matthew Maguire, a machinist, with organizing and leading the protest march. What is certain is that the idea took hold and that by 1885, due in part to the growth of labor organizations, Labor Day was celebrated in various industrial centers in the United States.

Central Labor Union and Socialist leaders opted for May 1 as a workingman's holiday, but the majority wished to distance themselves from the tragedy of the Haymarket Riot of 1886; they followed the lead of the Knights of Labor and continued marching each September.

The first state to grant legal status to Labor Day was Oregon in 1887, followed by Colorado, Massachusetts, New Jersey, and New York.

Other states passed similar legislation until twenty-three states had granted recognition by 1894.

President Grover Cleveland's political popularity had suffered greatly after sending federal troops to quell the American Railway Union strike in Pullman, Illinois. To mollify national workers, the House of Representatives and the Senate rushed legislation creating a national Labor Day holiday. Six days after troops had broken the ARU strike, President Cleveland signed the bill into law.

Present Status of Unions and Workers

The AFL-CIO at present comprises fifty-four national and international unions representing such diverse professions as the Air Line Pilots Association and Writers Guild of America.

In 2005, the Service Employees International Union, the International Brotherhood of Teamsters, and the United Food and Commercial Workers International Union withdrew their membership in the AFL-CIO. Some issues causing their withdrawal included demands for reorganization of the federation, a reduction in its central bureaucracy, spending more money on organizing local unions, and eliminating smaller local unions. The loss of labor-backed presidential candidate John Kerry in 2004 intensified the debate and hastened their exit.

Although union membership represents over 9 million workers, membership has been declining for several years. Many reasons have been proposed, but perhaps the best reason is that unions have been victims of their own success. Increases in wages brought increases in prices. Companies simply resorted to sending factories overseas, taking advantage of less-expensive, foreign, nonunion workers while laying off stateside workers. Also, the majority of people now in the workforce are technological, professional, white-collar, service or governmental workers rather than low-skilled assembly-line industrial laborers of the past.

Perhaps most important, where unions once represented the common man and woman, they now represent the radical leftist ideology of sovietizing the United States into a workers' "all are equal" utopia. From this, many wish to distance themselves.

The Bible and Labor

Where does the child of God, the member of the one body, fit into this earthly scheme that declares employer and employee must always be pitted against one another? Is it true one will surely take advantage of the other? Does God's Word have any instruction on the matter?

The KJV gives eighty-nine references to labor. Many of these of course deal with how believers must labor in the Word or labor to live for the Lord, but many verses have practical application for us in everyday living. Christ is our great Counselor, and He has not left us clueless concerning earthly work.

Those of us at liberty in Christ desire freedom from interference in the marketplace. We like nothing better than to be left alone to tend to our business as God would have us to do.

As much as it is proclaimed today, we are not created equal. As much as we can wish or dream, we aren't all mentally capable of being doctors, lawyers, physicists, or concert pianists. All do not have the manual dexterity to become electricians, plumbers, or computer technologists. In the physical realm, all men are not as strong as Samson, and all women are not as strong as all men. The point is that whatever God gave us to work with, that is what He expects us to use. The parable of the talents in Matthew 25 illustrates this. Each man was given a number of talents according to what his master considered him capable of handling. The one with lesser ability was given less responsibility; nevertheless, he was expected to produce.

Unions must be given credit where it is due. They undoubtedly helped create safer work environments, for which we can be thankful. But how would the parable of the talents have been written if all the workmen pooled their resources and their labor and all received the same reward? The man with the most talents would have become a mediocrity because he wouldn't want to make the slothful one look bad. The slothful one would do a little work since the profits would be divided, and he wanted to say he had done his part. Misguided human reasoning would have affected them all in some way. Would the result have been as profitable for the master of the household? Unfortunately, forced unionism destroys freedom and individualism.

We must heed Paul's advice to us in Ephesians 6. Whether we are union or nonunion, we must do our work for our earthly employers as if we were doing it for Christ Himself, not always an easy thing to do.

According to Marxist teaching, it is inevitable that there will be class warfare. In the final analysis, either the employer (capitalist) will win, and we will all be subjugated to the slavery of the working class, or if the workingman wins, capitalism will be extinct, and we will all be living in the "equality" of a workers' utopia. Class warfare is one of the bogeymen that unions keep alive to breed our hatred and mistrust of each other.

Should we be a classless society? Can we be? If we were all taxi drivers, who would ride in our cabs? If all were teachers, whom would we teach? If all were students, who would teach us? The Bible speaks of servants and masters; it doesn't give excuses for slavery. God expects the teacher and student, the employer and employee, and the manufacturer and consumer to cooperate and live in harmony. "Knowing that whatsoever good thing any man doeth, the same shall he receive of the Lord, whether he be bond or free" (Ephesians 6:8). The words *any man* should be translated "each one," so this is directed to men and women alike. God will not condone riots in the street as an excuse for a classless society. In America, we have freedom of choice to escape the clutches of poverty, to aim high in any profession we choose, but we must follow our Head and do so with good testimony for Him.

Where in Scripture are we given the moral or scriptural right to strike? Employees certainly have the right to quit their jobs if they are dissatisfied with their hours or wages. We all, undoubtedly, know from experience that there are no perfect jobs and that on some days we'd be happy to walk away from ours. Why are we working in the first place? "He that labors, labors for himself; for his mouth craves it of him" (Proverbs 16:26). Hunger urges us on. We all like to eat, and we want to feed our families. Paul admonishes us, "Let him that stole steal not more; but rather let him labor, working with his hands the thing which is good, that he may have to give to him that needs" (Ephesians 4:28).

Under our present system, employers are coerced into submission, for they are not free to follow the husbandman's example of Matthew 25. The rights of the union minority who voted not to strike are ignored as well as the rights of those who would like to work without seizure of forced union dues.

Going on strike amounts to obtaining what is wanted by force, intimidation, or undue legal power, and that is the definition of extortion. God's Word has something to say on the matter; He rebuked an apostate Israel when He said, "In thee have they taken gifts to shed blood; thou hast taken usury and increase, and thou has greedily gained of thy neighbors by extortion, and hast forgotten me" (Ezekiel 22:12). Of the Pharisees, Christ said, "Woe unto you scribes and Pharisees! for ye make clean the outside of the cup and of the platter, but within they are full of extortion and excess" (Matthew 23:25).

In 1 Corinthians 5, Paul considered extortion in the same category as drunkenness, idolatry, and fornication. It may prove extremely difficult to choose between relying on the Lord for sustenance or living with a pure conscience knowing that your last raise was gained by extortion.

Employers shouldn't use similar coercive tactics to keep employees under control and must give fair wages. "Woe unto him that builds his house by unrighteousness, and his chambers by wrong; that uses his neighbor's service without wages, and gives him not for his work" (Jeremiah 22:13).

The Lord has not turned His back; He is watching and listening.

> Behold the hire of the laborers who have reaped down
> your fields, which is of you kept back by fraud, crieth:
> and the cries of them which have reaped are entered into
> the ears of the Lord of Sabaoth (James 5:4).

Like so many things in this world, we have in unions a mixture of evil and good. Those who are pro-union would say, "Unions are mostly good with a little evil mixed in." Those who are nonunion would say, "Unions are mostly evil with a little good mixed in." Both views must admit to a mix.

"That ye may approve things that are excellent; that ye may be sincere and without offence until the day of Christ" (Philippians 1:10). In this verse, the word translated sincere, *heilikrines*, means pure, unsullied, unmixed, found pure when unfolded and examined in the sun's light.

"Wherefore come out from among them and be ye separate, saith the Lord, and touch not the unclean thing: and I will receive you, and will be a Father unto you and ye shall be my sons and daughters saith the Lord Almighty" (2 Corinthians 6:17–18). This verse has often been used to urge believers to leave apostate religious organizations. Practically speaking, it can apply to the employer-employee, capital-labor relationship also.

For us to submit to membership in an organization knowing that our dues are working against our beliefs and that the end result may find us living in a totalitarian regime we helped install doesn't seem logical or the best stewardship of God's generosity. (See 1 Corinthians 4:2.)

CHAPTER 21

Columbus Day

Pre-Columbian Discoveries

Columbus Day commemorates the first sighting of land in the Americas by Christopher Columbus in 1492. In actuality, many explorers had reached the New World, a land inhabited by many tribes and ethnicities, before 1492, but their names are largely unfamiliar to many people.

Who Didn't Discover America?

As a child, you never heard this rhyme:

> St. Brendon departed County Kerry
> To spread his faith as a missionary.
> A seven year odyssey, he went far,
> In a wicker curragh covered with tar.
> ... And he discovered America (in the sixth century).

or

> Back in 1354, Knutson sailed from Norway's shore.
> To the Isle of Greenland he was bound.
> ... Instead, America he found!

or

> Back in fourteen twenty-one,
> Zhi Di's junks had just begun
> To search wild barbarous shores,
> Seeking gold to fill his stores.
> … And Admiral Zeng He discovered America!

But this rhyme, we were all taught.

> In fourteen hundred and ninety-two,
> Columbus sailed the ocean blue.

Who Was Here First?

Obviously, many countries with patriotic fervor claim the discovery of a land that was not lost but simply unknown in the Eastern Hemisphere. This land, according to paleographers, was once part of the super continent, Pangaea, which broke apart 300 million years ago into the super continents of Laurasia and Gondwana, which further broke apart into Eurasia and the Americas 15 million years ago, or so they would like us to believe.

Many Bible students prefer to think that the dividing of the continents occurred in Genesis 10:25 in the time of Peleg and that the nations were divided in the earth after the flood as stated in Genesis 10:32, not nearly so long ago. More important, Bible readers know the reason for the scattering of the different races.

However, the theory taught in the schools is that various groups made their way across the Bering land bridge connecting North America and Asia, that is, from Siberia to Alaska. Once there, the people advanced down the West Coast and spread east.

In the southern landmass, the Maya, Aztec, and Nazca developed complex civilizations, complex but obsessed with bloody religious rituals. It is estimated that 1,500 languages were in use in the Southern

Hemisphere before European contact. This is certainly evidence of many distinct tribes. To the north, over 700 different tribes occupied what are now Canada and the United States.

Both northern and southern landmasses were well populated. There is no disrespect intended here, but in the matter of semantics, it is difficult to ascertain what these natives should have been called. They were not Indians as Columbus supposed, nor were they Native Americans, for the Americas were not named such before 1504. In addition, these groups were not bound together by any encompassing confederation or name. This chapter will use both terms. More important than the name is the ever-debated question of who made the first European contact with them.

St. Brendon Discovered America in the 500s

St. Brendon was born in Ireland around AD 488 and died in 577 at age ninety-three. He was known for spreading the Christian faith and beginning monasteries around northwestern Europe, traveling by small boat. However, his most famous voyage was sailing across the Atlantic seeking the "Promised Land of the Saints."

"The Voyage of St. Brendon the Abbot," recorded in the ninth century from oral traditions, survives in texts in European monasteries. The legend gives detailed descriptions of his fragile *curraghs* sailing the Atlantic, "raised up on the back of sea monsters." St. Brendon and his group of handpicked monks saw "crystals that rose up into the sky." They were pelted with "flaming, foul smelling rocks by the inhabitants of a large island on their route." Drifting from island to island and coast to coast, they probably touched the shores of Virginia and possibly Florida. When their seven-year odyssey ended and they were safely at home in County Kerry, Ireland, they had samples of plant and animal life that were neither Irish nor European.

Cartographers of Columbus's time included St. Brendon's Island on maps, although no one knew exactly where it was other than that it was west of Europe. Spanish explorers even went as far as to proclaim it for Spain, wherever it was!

St. Brendon's voyage didn't seem plausible to many. However, on May 16, 1976, Tim Severin, a British navigation scholar, embarked from Brandon Creek on the Dingle Peninsula in a curragh much like those described by St. Brendon, "a light vessel with wicker sides and ribs covered with cow-hide, tanned in oak-bark, tarring the joints thereof." Severin smeared his hides with animal fat for protection against water. His replica voyage took him past Iceland's volcanoes, Greenland's iceberg belt, the Hebrides, and many other islands fitting Brandon's descriptions. On June 26, 1977, he landed on Newfoundland.

No one can say with certainly that St. Brendon landed on mainland American shores, but after Severin's journey, it can be said that it was entirely possible.

Eric the Red Discovered America in AD 982

Eric the Red, born Thorvald Asvaldsson (950–1000), was a violent man who had been exiled from Norway for murdering several people. As a result of his banishment, Eric and his family went to a Norse colony on Iceland's coast. He also roamed the seas as a leader of Viking exploration and is often credited as the first European to reach North America by reason of his contact with an island he named Greenland. (Perhaps he received credit because Eric was easier to pronounce than Gunnbjörn Ulfsson, whom Norwegian tradition credits with the first land sighting of the continent.)

During Eric's exile, he explored the island searching for any habitable, ice-free acreage. Murderers are generally not expected to be totally honest, and upon returning to Iceland after his required three-year exile, he regaled his listeners with tales of a wonderful green land. He ultimately convinced many people that opportunity was knocking, and a large group of colonists established two settlements on the southwest coast. The settlers who ventured to Greenland learned that farming there was not too great, but during summers, hunting for seals and beached whales near the arctic circle proved profitable.

Bjarni Herjolfsson Discovered America in AD 986

A fourteenth-century manuscript, *Flateyjarbók* ("The book of the Flat Island") is preserved in Reykjavík, Iceland. Completed in 1395, it chronicles the tales of an adventurer who was actually not an adventurer at all but a wary Norwegian merchant on his way to visit his father in Greenland, a place he had never before gone.

Bjarni Herjolfsson was born in Iceland, the son of Herjulf and Thorgerd Herjolfsson, who were early colonizers of that island. Bjarni lived primarily in Norway, although he alternated winters at home and visiting his father in Iceland.

In the summer of 986, Bjarni set sail for Iceland. Upon his arrival, he heard that his father had given up his farm there and had gone to Greenland with Eric the Red. When he learned of this, he refused to unload his cargo and decided to follow his father to Greenland even though neither he nor his crew had ever been there and were uncertain how to find it.

After sailing for three days, Bjarni and his crew drifted aimlessly, lost in fog for several days. When sun broke through the fog and they could determine their direction, they hoisted sail and continued until they spied land. Bjarni was afraid to go ashore, for it didn't look the way Greenland had been described to him. Instead of glaciers, he saw forested, low-lying hills delightful to behold, but he didn't know what might be lurking behind those trees. And he was, after all, on his way to visit his father with provisions and couldn't spare the time to explore an unknown land.

The ship continued for two more days before sighting another land. Again, they discussed the possibility that this might be Greenland. Bjarni decided it didn't fit the description. Turning north, the crew viewed an island covered with glaciers. It seemed closer to the right description, but they decided it didn't look hospitable enough to sustain life. Turning east, they sailed four more days before they reached Greenland. They soon found Bjarni's father living on the cape that later bore his name, Heriulfsness. Bjarni stayed with his father as long has his father lived.

In Greenland and in Norway, Bjarni reported his sighting of level, tree-covered land, but no one took him seriously.

(In February 1477, Christopher Columbus sailed to Bristol, England and possibly to Iceland and as far north as the arctic circle. The events recorded in the *Flateyjarbók*, the sagas of Eric the Red and Herjolfsson, continued to be extolled over mugs of ale and wherever boastful adventurers met. Columbus undoubtedly took the waterfront gossip and these glorious sagas seriously. Within a year after returning to Portugal, Columbus began seeking financial backing to cross the Atlantic to search for a direct route to the East Indies.)

Leif Eriksson (AD 975—1020) Discovered America in AD 1000

At age sixteen, Leif, the son of Eric the Red, left Greenland to go back to his family's original home, Norway. In Norway, King Olaf I warmly greeted and entertained him. The king also expounded Christianity to him, as was his custom for all visitors, and tradition says that Leif and his crew were baptized.

After a few months' instruction in Christianity, King Olaf wanted Leif to return to Greenland to convert the Vikings there. On his return to Greenland, Leif was blown off course. Instead of returning to Greenland, he came to a land covered with berries or *vinber*, which he named Vinland. Much debate swirls around what these berries might have been. They could have been cranberries, which grow well in our present northeastern states, or they could have been dewberries, blackberries, or grapes, all of which grow on vines. If grapes, he would have had to have sailed as far south as present-day Virginia.

The Saga of Eric the Red, recorded in AD 1387, gives another version. In it, Leif bought Bjarni Herjolfsson's ship to purposely retrace Bjarni's route. He hoped to find the level, heavily forested land Bjarni had spoken of. He didn't find it, but he found vinber instead. Some historians believe he landed in present-day Newfoundland.

Leif recorded meeting white-skinned natives during his journey, perhaps a remnant of St. Brendon's flock. Legend says that Leif went back to Greenland and spread the message of Christianity there.

Paul Knutson Discovered America in AD 1354

On October 28, 1354, King Magnus of Norway, Sweden, and Skåne sent an introductory letter with Paul Knutson. The letter gave Knutson authority to choose officers and men to accompany him to Greenland to determine why settlements were disappearing there. According to the king, the mission was for the honor of God and to bring pagans into the Catholic Church.

Farmers' properties had gradually become properties of the Catholic Church for payment of various fees, and the Norwegian population in Greenland is believed to have revolted and to have reverted to paganism due to this practice. King Magnus sent Knutson to get to the heart of the matter.

Upon Knutson's arrival, no settlers could be found, only a few neglected cattle. His mission party traveled west to the mainland of Vinland, onward to Hudson Bay, up the present-day Nelson, Red, and Buffalo Rivers, and camped at present-day Lake Cormorant. After being attacked by vicious Vikings who killed several of them, the remainder of the party fled south. The survivors are believed to have recorded their harrowing adventures on a rune stone now commonly known as the Kensington Runestone. A Swedish farmer, Olof Ohman, found the stone in 1898 while clearing his land in preparation for plowing. Since that time, professional archaeologists, historians, Scandinavian linguists, and interested amateur sleuths have debated the authenticity of the stone. No consensus has been reached as to whether the stone is a forgery or if it is authentic.

Paul Knutson did not return to Norway, but eight of his crew reportedly did.

Madoc, the Welsh Prince, Discovered America in AD 1170

The legend of Madoc (also spelled Madog or Madawg), tells that he was the son of Owain Gwynedd, who had thirteen children by two wives plus several more illegitimate children. When Owain died, his many heirs fought over his estate.

Rather than stay and fuss with his siblings, Modoc and his brother, Riryd, gathered a fleet and a hundred men and set sail to explore. They found a suitable and fertile land and returned to Wales to recruit colonizers.

Ten ships containing men and women probably landed at Mobile Bay (now Alabama). These Welsh settlers traveled up the river systems to the land of the Dakotas and intermarried with the native Mandan tribe. Unfortunately, warring savage tribes and smallpox seems to have almost obliterated them by 1849. Survivors joined the nearby Hidatsa and Arikara tribes.

Before they were wiped out, several expeditions recorded having met white, blue-eyed Indians with blond or brunette hair. In 1669, the Tuscarora captured the Reverend Morgan Jones. When Jones spoke in Welsh, the chief spared him, for the chief understood Welsh.

The Lewis and Clark Expedition didn't report finding any Welsh speakers, but they did report Indians with blue or green eyes and brown or blond hair with European features.

In 1832, frontiersman George Catlin lived among the Mandan in North Dakota. He reported that at least one-fifth of them were almost white with blue eyes. Catlin drew pictures of Mandan women with Nordic characteristics. He reported some peculiar beliefs the tribe had including a distorted version of the fall of man in Eden and one of a man born of a virgin who performed miracles. It was Catlin who first suggested the white Mandans were descendants of Madoc and his colonizers.

Many books have been written about Madoc, some defending his authenticity and others doubting he existed. If Madoc didn't exist, then another Welsh-speaking explorer had led the colonists. There has been too much documentation of Welsh-speaking Indians by early explorers to dismiss their existence.

In 1889, about forty miles south of Knoxville, Tennessee, near the mouth of Bat Creek, an inscribed stone was unearthed. Since that time, archeologists have been contending its origin. It was at first thought to be Cherokee. Hebrew archeologists argue that the inscription is Hebrew and that early Jewish explorers had left it. Those of the Madoc school of thought insist that the writing on the stone is Coelbren, an ancient British alphabet.

Perhaps the mystery will soon be solved. Researchers know the location of the burial places of Madoc's relatives in Wales. Through DNA profiling, they hope to determine if the remains found at Bat Creek, Tennessee, is Madoc. An inscription found next to the bones, written in Coelbren, allegedly reads, "Madoc the ruler he is."[71]

According to these particular researchers, Madoc sailed for America around AD 562 rather than 1170. Further, they assert that ancient British manuscripts and genealogies confirm Madoc was the brother of King Arthur II. Many are eagerly waiting for further developments regarding this Bat Creek mystery.

Chinese Discovered America in 1421

Perhaps the newest rival to the discovery of the lands in the Western Hemisphere is a claim by a former British Royal Navy submarine commander. Gavin Menzies spent fifteen years researching his hypothesis that China discovered the New World in AD 1421. His book, *1421: The Year China Discovered America*, gives credible evidence that Chinese junks navigated all over the world. Emperor Zhu Dhi had commissioned his fleet to find the world's barbarians, collect tribute from them, and convert them to Confucianism.

Several different types of evidence have been found purportedly supporting the Chinese discovery theory. Among them are claims of shipwrecked junks found in America, Australia, and Indonesia. Remains of ancient Chinese people have been claimed to have been found in

Peru. Linguistic similarities found in Peru and China influence many to believe Chinese were there before Europeans.

Menzies has his supporters who believe his research proves incontrovertibly that with ancient China's superior navigational and astronomical knowledge, they not only discovered America first but were also the first to reach Australia.

Critics of the Menzies theory question his nautical knowledge. They also maintain that the linguistic similarities between Chinese and various other languages are coincidental. Perhaps the biggest criticism is that Menzies didn't consult Chinese documents, which he claimed were destroyed by the Mandarins after 1421. All records were not destroyed, and some Ming dynasty documents have been used by historians such as Louise Levathes in her book *When China Ruled the Seas: The Treasure Fleet of the Dragon Throne 1405–1433.*

Menzies's theory of discovery is not widely accepted, and both sides of the controversy have empathizers lining up to share research to prove their points.

Columbus Discovered America in 1492

Even though many early explorers had touched islands or the mainland of North and South America, it will always be Columbus who gets the publicity and the glory for discovery, along with all the blame for the disastrous treatment of native populations. What was significantly different about his discovery?

It has been stated in various ways by secular historians that other than Jesus Christ—whom they see as relatively important but not as the Son of God—no other individual has made a bigger impact on the world than has Columbus. These earlier explorers, whose names we have touched on briefly, had very limited contact with the natives of the various islands or the mainland. After their brief ventures, few heard of them again.

In contrast, the first permanent European colony was established on Hispaniola within a year of Columbus's first voyage. Thus, there was established a need for commerce between Old World and New. For good, but often for evil, people in both hemispheres became aware that each other existed.

When Columbus set sail for the west, Europeans knew only of the continents of Europe, Asia, and Africa. They assumed only one ocean existed, the Atlantic. Without exaggeration, it can be said that the result of Columbus's "discovery" was an opening of an ocean thoroughfare. Multitudes flocked to the shores of the New World. Spaniards, followed by Portuguese, came seeking gold. Many English colonizers came seeking freedom to worship God after the dictates of their hearts, and of course, a myriad of other nationalities came for different reasons and continue to come.

Columbus: Inspired by the Holy Ghost and by Unholy Greed for Gold

Columbus seems to have been much like modern men and women. He was religious, frequently went to church services, and always went to church after returning from a voyage. He was quick to praise God for his safety and his successes, yet he had many glaring faults and obvious sins. In spite of these flaws, we should not label him as a mass murderer. Nor can he be held personally responsible for the mass destruction of the Native American population or the introduction of slavery into the New World.

Physical Features of Columbus

No portraits were ever painted of Columbus from life; all were painted based on what a particular painter theorized how he should look. He has been described and painted as having had blue eyes, a ruddy complexion, and blondish-red hair that turned to gray by his thirties.

Youth of Columbus

Even though many children's books have been written about Columbus, not much is actually known about his youth. The date of his birth is uncertain; it was possibly somewhere between the months of August and October 1451. He was born to Domenico Columbo, a wool weaver, and Susanna Fontanarossa, and he had at least two brothers, Bartolomeo, a cartographer, and Diego. He was from a Spanish-Jewish family settled in Genoa, Italy, but he was baptized Cristoforo Columbo, "bearer of Christ," in the Genoa church of Santo Stephano and was named for the Catholic patron saint of travelers, St. Christopher. At different times in his life, he signed his name as Colombo, Colomo, Colom, and Colón, but never the Latinized form Columbus.

Columbus grew up surrounded by violence in Genoa, where political upheaval was the norm. Contributing to that violence, Ottoman Turks had swept through to the Danube River with their mission of spreading Islam. Resisters were slain with the sword or sawn in half. All doors were barred at night, and fear of the dark prevailed among adults. In this environment, he learned to trust no one. During daylight hours, children roamed the streets, and like his peers, he was probably street-smart beyond his years.

Columbus first ventured to sea at age fourteen, a common occurrence for boys living in seacoast cities, but it is not until his twenties that he begins to come to life for us. On August 13, 1476, a Franco-Portuguese ship attacked the ship *Bechalla* while it was escorting a shipping convoy from Lisbon to England. The ship burned and sank, and Columbus was wounded, but he grabbed a long oar. By pushing the oar in front of him, he managed to swim six miles through enemy ships to Lagos, where he was treated well and taken to Lisbon.

This pivotal event marked a new beginning and new opportunities for him. His narrow escape from death convinced him that God was with him and had chosen him for glorious adventures. This is the first of many instances in his life that gave evidence of the hand of Providence upon him. Another evidence of the hand of Providence was his proximity in Portugal to the seamanship school of Prince Henry the Navigator.

Adult Education

Columbus spent seven years in Lisbon receiving instruction in Portuguese and mathematics. The bulk of his education occurred after he attained adulthood. While in Lisbon, he learned astronomy for celestial navigation. He taught himself Castilian and learned to comprehend scholarly Latin.

He could write in Spanish and Portuguese and completed one book, *The Book of Prophecies*, which quoted biblical passages and how he thought they applied to him. It is not often referred to by modern historians, perhaps because he does claim to have the leading of the Holy Spirit through the Holy Scriptures, and it reveals his personal faith.

In Lisbon, Columbus learned from master seamen how to handle a caravel, what provisions to take on long voyages, and the sort of cheap trinkets to carry to exchange with primitive people. All the while, he was becoming one of the greatest sea navigators of his time.

Columbus has been described as a self-promoting religious zealot and social climber. One reason for the observation as a social climber is evident in his choice of women and how he viewed them. He married a woman of Portuguese nobility, Felipa Perestrello Moniz, who bore him a son, Diego. Doña Felipa died during a subsequent childbirth in 1484, and Columbus raised Diego, later taking him to sea with him.

Columbus moved in with Beatriz Enriquez de Harana, a village shop owner who could read and write. Beatriz bore Hernando (Ferdinand) in 1488. While living with Beatriz, Columbus supported himself by making sea charts and dealing in the new printed books. He could not marry Beatriz because she was a commoner, and marriage to her would have impeded his climb into the proper social circles. There seems to have been no stigma attached to this relationship. He left Beatriz in 1491, but to his credit, he did make monetary provision for her after his New World successes.

Indies Obsession

During his stay in Portugal, Columbus became obsessed with raising money to find a westward sea route to the Indies. He never revealed to anyone what had inspired him this could be done. However, the sea route seemed necessary due to the Muslim blockade of 1453 and the Ottoman conquest of Egypt. The former prevented Christians from reaching the Orient overland, and the latter prevented use of the Red Sea route previously used to travel to trade for spices, silks, and ivory.

A rumor during his lifetime held that someone had been to the Caribbean and had mapped detailed information. It is believed that a shipwrecked pilot died in Columbus's presence and after his death, Columbus took ownership of his charts and pilot book that would have contained sketches of landmarks and detailed interior maps. This has never been proven, but it is certainly believable in light of many events that were credited to Providence.

That statement doesn't detract from the fact that God obviously guarded him from many dangers. If Columbus indeed possessed secret detailed maps and sketches, that in itself was providential. For reasons unknown to us, it is apparent that Columbus had been chosen by God to receive credit for the discovery of lands in the Western Hemisphere.

It is interesting to speculate on what would have been the fate of the Americas had they been colonized by the Vikings, the Welsh, the Chinese, or any number of other nationalities claiming to have discovered them. Would they have been any kinder to the natives? What would the predominant religion have been? Would the principles of the Constitution and the Bill of Rights ever have been espoused?

Of course, when requesting financial backing from King John of Portugal, he could not tell King John that he had secret maps if indeed he did. Had he done so, King John could have confiscated the materials and claimed them as his own, and Columbus could have been declared a traitor.

Becoming disheartened with Portugal's failure to give him financial help, Columbus traveled to Spain in 1485 and sought help from King

Ferdinand and Queen Isabella. At the time, they were embroiled in war with the Moors and unable to give aid.

In 1486, they appointed a commission of experienced mariners, the Talavera Commission, to study his proposal. After studying the situation for four years, in 1490, the commission decided that the voyage was impossible, that it would take three years to complete if it could be done at all, and that God would not hide an uninhabited land from His people for centuries.

But Columbus didn't give up. He requested another meeting with the queen. Juan Perez, Queen Isabella's confessor, sent Columbus 20,000 *maravedis* to buy new clothes so he would be presentable for his audience with the queen. At his meeting with her, Columbus had the audacity to ask to be made admiral of Castile, admiral of the ocean, viceroy and governor of all lands he found, one-tenth of all gold found, one-eighteenth of profit from trades, and the sole arbitrator of mercantile disputes. Isabella said no, and Columbus left on his mule.

Lawyer, Luis de Santangel convinced Isabella that the ten-year war against the Moors had depleted Spain's treasury. Perhaps investing in Columbus's journey would be profitable. He may also have revealed other secrets causing her to change her mind. Four miles north of Pinos, the queen's royal messengers caught up with Columbus as he crossed the bridge to Cordoba.

Four months later, on April 17, 1491, Columbus and the king and queen of Spain signed and sealed contracts that granted to Columbus everything he had so boldly asked for. The contract named no geographical sites but stated that he would be searching for islands and mainland to the west. After ten years of pleading for financial support amid much mockery, Columbus finally secured funds necessary to begin his westward quest.

Historians have told us Columbus was searching for a new way to China, Japan, and India, all of which were often referred to as India. Columbus loaded his ships with worthless trinkets to trade with any primitive people he might encounter, but he also took along Luis de Torres, a scholarly Jew who knew Hebrew, Chaldean, and Arabic just in case he met the great khan. Arabic was considered a universal language at the time, but it proved of no value in the New World.

Financial Resources

Three primary sources provided funds for the proposed journey. The town of Palos owed money to Spain's royal treasury for past smuggling offenses. The king arranged for the town to supply two caravels to Columbus instead of paying the fine.

Columbus invested 250,000 maravedis for the third vessel. A police patrol organization, the Holy Brotherhood, would advance other needed funds at 14 percent interest for two years, a loan arranged through Louis de Santangel.

The Fleet

Once permission was granted and resources established, the long-awaited exploratory journey of Columbus's dream neared its beginning. Royal orders commanded the caravels be ready to sail as soon as possible. It took about ten weeks for the crew to be assembled. Each crew member received four months' salary in advance. Full-fledged crew members earned the equivalent of $7 per month in gold, and the young boys around $4.60. All coastal towns were ordered to help equip and man the caravels.

Contrary to legend, nearly all the sailors were experienced seamen. A royal order pardoned any criminal who would join the crew, but only four men accepted the offer. One was an escaped killer, and the other three were his friends who had helped him escape.

Columbus renamed *La Gallega* the *Santa Maria*. It was a decked carrack that served as the flagship; it carried the royal flag of Ferdinand and Isabella. Their royal ensign consisted of a green cross with green initials of the king and queen under gold crowns, all on a white background. Second in command on the *Santa Maria* was Juan de la Cosa, owner and master of the ship. Staff included a secretary, the interpreter Luis de Torres, and a marshal along with forty men and boys. The *Santa Maria* carried approximately one hundred tons, the equivalent to what a couple of modern tractor trailers could haul.

Martin Alonso Pinzon commanded the *Pinta*'s crew of twenty-six. Cristobal Quintero, the ship's owner, accompanied his ship. The *Pinta* carried sixty tons. Martin's brother, Vincente Yanez Pinzon, commanded the *Niña,* which carried a crew of twenty and had a capacity of fifty tons. These two vessels were caravels, smaller but capable of swift movement under the right winds. The three captains sailed under their own personal flags as well as the royal flag.

The adept, skilled seamen represented various vocations. Aboard were carpenters, boatswains, coopers, goldsmiths, pilots, apprentice pilots, cabin boys, two physicians, and one surgeon.

The speed of these vessels varied with the wind, but they could travel as fast as eight knots and make ninety to one hundred miles a day, and two hundred miles on an outstanding day.

Victuals for the Voyage

Enough food for a year accompanied the crew. Jugs of earthenware contained olive oil. Everything else, such as molasses, raisins, rice, dry legumes, beans, salted or pickled meats (plus many other foods as well as water, wine, and vinegar) was stored in wooden casks. The cooper's job required him to keep all the casks tight, which was almost impossible. The pickling brine sometimes leaked out and seeped into the casks of dried foods. A good cooper definitely earned his pay.

Boiled foods were cooked in an open firebox with sand spread on the bottom over which a wood fire burned. Of course, stormy weather would snuff out the fire. On calm days, the sailors fished for food. If no fish were available, they prepared meat in a stew along with some of the dried foods.

The sailors had no forks or spoons, but each sailor had a knife. All ate from one wooden bowl using their fingers or stabbing pieces of meat with their knives.

Westward at Last

On August 2, 1492, the entire crew celebrated Mass at St. Georges at Palos, Spain. The next day before dawn, the small fleet set sail for India, thankful for favorable trade winds. Once at sea, the seamen rotated four-hour shifts of steering, calling compass, and lookout.

On the *Santa Maria*, the helmsman stood between decks. He could not see the sea or the sails; he would steer by orders from the watch officer on the top deck.

Columbus had few navigational instruments to help him. At his disposal were a half-hour sand clock, a mariner's compass, a quadrant for celestial navigation, sea charts, and a ruler. For timekeeping, a ship's boy turned the sand glass every half hour. The quadrant measured the height of the polestar above the horizon for determining latitude, but they had no accurate means of measuring longitude; the pilot estimated the ship's speed and distance as they went. To establish his daily position at sea and to trace his course across the unknown expanse of water, Columbus used dead reckoning. This method is now considered guesswork since it consists of laying down a compass course and estimating distances on the charts.

A recognized authority on Columbus, Samuel Eliot Morison, wrote,

No such dead-reckoning navigators exist today. No man alive, limited to the instruments and means at Columbus's disposal, could obtain anything near the accuracy of his result. Judged, therefore, not simply by what he did, but by how he did it, Columbus was a great navigator.[72]

Cookin' the Books

Today's business world uses this term to refer to corrupt bookkeepers or accountants who misrepresent or fake a second set of books to mislead the public. Despite the fact that Columbus believed God directed him, and at the top of every day's journal entry he wrote, "In the name of our Lord Jesus Christ."

He kept two journals; one gave false directions and distances sailed each day, which wasn't uncommon. Early explorers often concealed facts regarding their voyages, wishing to keep them secret from competitors. In fact, navigational records were state secrets. Anyone repeating information regarding their contents could be put to death as a traitor.

Portuguese navigators regularly disguised their true latitude, and Columbus had spent seven years learning his craft from the masters. The fake set his crew might see was the official log book, but he kept the true set in his back pocket. In case of capture by an enemy, it could be quickly thrown overboard. After completing his first trip to the New World, he inserted the true beside the false entries.

Evidence that Columbus knew where he was going more than the crew might have suspected was indicated by the entries in these journals. In the official journal, he recorded that they sailed west every day. Actually, they headed west for two days only, long enough to avoid King John's Portuguese caravels. After that, they sailed south and then west.

To further confuse any log reader, complete sentences were lifted from one day and put into another day. Patterns of the ocean currents were not what were penned in the log. Birds named in the log didn't fly in the specific areas where they were said to have been. Many map and chart makers and historians puzzled over the logs for years before unraveling them.

(On his second voyage, Columbus followed the southwest by west route, an indication that he probably followed that same route the first time rather than due west as had been claimed in the logs.)

Near Mutiny on the Santa Maria?

By Monday, September 24, 1492, grumbling sailors possibly secretly threatened to toss Columbus overboard. They were farther away from land than they had ever sailed and were ready to head home. The crew, mostly Spanish, didn't fully trust their foreign captain. However, journals kept by Columbus make no mention of mutiny. Perhaps sensing an undercurrent of unrest, Columbus summoned Martin Alonso Pinzon of the *Pinta* to approach his ship. He sent his sea chart to Martin Alonso to study. Apparently, some information in that chart convinced Martin to agree with Columbus to continue for eight more days.

The next day, Martin Alonso spotted land and claimed the reward the monarchs of Spain had promised to the first to sight land. Unfortunately, that night, the ship drifted forty miles, and the next morning, no sign of land could be found.

October 10 witnessed dissatisfaction and discord if not near mutiny. Thirty days out and 1,230 leagues from home, the crews assumed they were doomed. They saw birds but no land. The ships' captains were nearly ready to throw Columbus overboard. The Pinzon brothers decided to follow the birds, and Columbus had no choice but to tag along. He insisted they would sight land within three days and reminded the captains that the king and queen would punish them for treason if they didn't follow his command.

On October 11, crews from the *Pinta* and the *Niña* gathered a collection of items from the sea indicating land nearby: land plants, twigs, floating boards, flowers, carved sticks, and a stalk loaded with berries. Their spirits soared. Columbus ordered a change of course from west southwest to west. Some say he did this by hunch; others claim godly inspiration. The more-modern theory is the secret chart. Whatever the case, it proved to be the right course. At 10:00 p.m., crew members reported seeing lights flickering like many candles. They were nearing an island named Guanahani, an Indian name meaning "iguana." Crews of all ships anticipated sighting land, for theoretically, each crew member had an equal chance at the huge reward. Along with the coveted reward, an annuity of ten thousand maravedis, Columbus promised to give the discoverer a silk jacket. All eyes stared into the night blackness hoping to sight land and become rich.

On Friday, October 12, at 2:00 a.m., the lookout on the forecastle of the *Pinta*, Ridrugi de Triana, also known as Juan Rodriguen Bermejo, spotted land. The captains navigated their ships to the western end of the island and went ashore before noon. It is not certain where they landed. The three most likely possibilities are Watling Island, Santana Bay, or Grand Turk in the Bahamas, although some think it was Conception Island. Watling Island was renamed San Salvador in 1926 and proclaimed to be the island where Columbus had landed.

Columbus had committed himself on October 9 to persevere onward three days more. If land had not been sighted on the twelfth, the crew likely would have revolted and ended the voyage quite differently. Instead, the winds picked up, and they set a new distance record. Did God undertake in the winds? We know "even the winds obey Him" (Matthew 8:27).

Columbus didn't find anything resembling Marco Polo's descriptions of Oriental dwellings or pagodas. Instead, he found lush vegetation, unusual crops, and naked primitives.

The natives of the island at first ran for fear, but their curiosity brought them back to see whom the strangers were. The Europeans were met by naked, brown men painted red, white, and black. Columbus described them as gentle and friendly with attractive features. He described them as having short hair, which was coarse like a horse's tail. They had unusually broad foreheads. The Europeans later learned the forehead shapes were due to the Arawak custom of partially flattening their infants' skulls by pressing them between boards.

The native Arawaks, a branch of the Tainos, viewed the Europeans as birds from the sky that were folding their white wings (ships' sails). Some considered them heavenly beings visiting earth.

Many believe the landing on that particular island could have occurred by the grace of God. Had they landed on nearby islands where the Caribs were cannibals, their reception would have been quite different. Most likely, they wouldn't have lived to tell about their encounter.

Columbus Takes Possession

Columbus knelt and thanked God for their safe journey. He immediately erected two items of significance: a cross, which represented his faith, and a gallows, which represented Spanish justice. He claimed the land for Spain and renamed the Guanahani island San Salvador, "Our Holy Savior." If Columbus thought he was in China or Japan, why did he claim the land for Spain? Perhaps he only regarded these islands only as stepping stones, a means of approaching the Indies, open to whomever claimed them. Nevertheless, he called the natives Indians.

The primitive natives brought parrots, spears, food, cotton thread, and other worthwhile items to trade. In exchange, the Europeans gave them glass beads, broken crockery, or bits of broken glass. Eventually, Columbus forbad the crew to trade. This in effect cancelled the reason they signed on in the first place: to trade for gold or other valuables.

Columbus observed that the people were friendly, seemed to have no religion, and probably would make good servants while being converted to Christianity.

During their exploratory days through the islands, the *Santa Maria* became grounded and was destroyed on Christmas Day. They were stranded on the island Columbus had named Hispaniola. All the men couldn't fit into the remaining two ships. Therefore, what timber could be salvaged resulted in building Fort Navidad (the Nativity). Forty men were left to explore while Columbus readied to return to Spain. Columbus instructed the men to gather as much gold as they could before he returned.

The *Pinta* deserted him to search for an island reported by the Indians to have gold. Columbus's only recourse was to take command of the *Niña*.

Return to Spain

After ninety-six days in the Western Hemisphere, Columbus headed to Spain. Navigating through the islands, he sighted a high mound, a landmark he recognized (even though he has never seen it before!). He named it Monte Cristo (Mount of Christ).

Martin Alonso, who had sailed ahead in the *Pinta,* had also found Monte Criste and gold. Martin Alonso shared the gold with his crew and gave some to Columbus to give to the queen upon his arrival in Spain. Monte Criste later became famous as a gold-rush area.

A storm overtook the ships on Tuesday, February 12, 1493, as they neared the Canary Islands. Storms in this area over the years had sent hundreds of ships to the bottom, but the *Niña* ploughed on. To his shame, Columbus deserted the *Pinta* and sailed off on his own. Fearful he or his crew would be destroyed, he wrote down major events of their voyage, wrapped them in a waxed cloth, sealed them in a barrel, and threw them into the sea. The crew drew lots; whoever survived would make a holy pilgrimage and say prayers for the lost.

The *Niña* survived the storm only to be captured by King John for illegally entering Portuguese waters. King John's supporters urged him to kill Columbus, but instead, he released him. Again, God was merciful.

Columbus returned safely to Palos. Providential care is evidenced in yet another seeming quirk of fate. Martin Alonzo Pinzon had arrived on the same tide. He assumed Columbus had died in the storm and sent word to the king and queen of "his" discoveries in the New World. A mysterious disease struck Martin Alonzo, and he died in a matter of days.

Neither Europeans in general nor the Spanish royalty had seen canoes before Columbus returned. Neither had they viewed *hamacas,* string beds hanging from posts. Today, we call them "hammocks." Foods taken back to the Old World for display included pineapples, sweet potatoes, and maize. The nonfood item, scourge of the twentieth century, tabacos (tobacco), also made its first European appearance sometime after this voyage.

Celebrations and More Voyages

Columbus received a hero's welcome. Banquets given in his honor celebrated his accomplishments. The crown kept its promises to Columbus, granting him titles of nobility and monetary rewards. A special coat of arms was permitted on May 20, 1492. He received the appointment as admiral of the ocean sea and became the viceroy of newly discovered lands.

A significant character flaw reared its ugly head here. Columbus claimed the reward rightly belonging to Ridrugi de Triana. Ridrugi left for Morocco in disgust and disappointment at the loss of his anticipated ten thousand maravedis. The crown, ever eager to renew its gold supply, planned for more voyages.

Second Voyage

On the second New World voyage, seventeen ships left with nearly 1,500 crew. Adventurers eagerly signed on as well as women willing to accompany them. On this trip, Columbus established his stronghold in Hispaniola, explored as far as southern Cuba, and named the island of Dominica.

When he returned to Fort Navidad, he found it burned to the ground and the Spanish settlers killed. Columbus moved his new colonizers to the east and established the settlement of Isabella. Exploratory expeditions into the interior of the island encountered hostile tribes. The colonizers erected Fort Santo Tomas for protection against these cannibal Caribs.

Columbus now theorized that these islands were the outlying posts of eastern Asia and believed further explorations would lead him to China. He left the settlement in charge of his brother, Diego, and four counselors. He took three ships and spent five months exploring Cuba, Jamaica, and various smaller islands before setting sail for Spain.

On the second voyage, the first rape is recorded by Michele de Cuneo. Undoubtedly, some transpired before that date, but this is the first written record. The narrative is a vivid firsthand account of a beautiful young naked woman who resisted Michele's advances.

Third Voyage

On May 30, 1498, Columbus left with six ships from Sanlúcar, Spain. Upon reaching the Western Hemisphere, he sailed as far south as modern Venezuela and explored the mainland of South America. He was convinced he had reached the mainland of Asia. Friendly natives willingly exchanged pearls for trinkets, and Columbus left the Island of Margarita with three bags of pearls.

Columbus was a master navigator but a horrible administrator. He repeatedly dealt harshly with rebellious settlers and natives. His rule in the New World ended in disgrace brought about by his inhumane treatment of his European and native subjects and his having hanged some of his men for insubordination.

He sent word to Spain asking for help in ruling his new viceroyalty. He got more help than he wished, for the queen sent Francisco de Bobadilla with orders for Columbus to turn over the forts and all public property to him. He and his brothers had been accused of cruelty and gross mismanagement. The three Columbus brothers returned to Spain in chains on October 1, 1500, where they spent six weeks in jail until King Ferdinand had time to release them. The king commanded their confiscated wealth and privileges be returned to them except for one: Columbus could no more serve as governor. Instead, King Ferdinand appointed Nicholas de Ovando governor of the West Indies.

Fourth and Last Voyage

On his fourth trip, beginning May 11, 1502, his brother Bartolomeo and his thirteen-year-old son, Fernando, accompanied Columbus. The ostensible purpose of this trip was to find the Strait of Malacca to the Indian Ocean.

When Columbus arrived at Santo Domingo, Governor de Bobadilla denied him port permission, and he had to journey on to the mouth of the Rio Jaina. The governor also refused to listen to Columbus's hurricane warnings. As a result, Columbus's ships suffered minor damage, but twenty-nine of thirty ships of the governor's fleet were destroyed. Five hundred lives were lost, including that of Governor de Bobadilla. This same hurricane sank Spain's first treasure fleet carrying cargos of gold.

Shipwrecked and Forsaken

Columbus's mental and physical health began to deteriorate, and his judgment became more impaired. He had survived one hurricane, but other violent storms took their toll. On June 23, 1503, Columbus and his men sailed worm-eaten, sinking ships to Jamaica, where they were stranded for a year. His crews roamed the island, plundering and mistreating the natives. Understandably, the natives became more hostile and refused to give any help or supplies. Once more, Columbus's knowledge and experience as a mariner spared them. He told the natives the moon would refuse to shine if they didn't help his men. As predicted, there was an eclipse of the moon, after which the natives were once more compliant.

A relief expedition rescued Columbus and a remnant of his crew and delivered them to Spain on November 7, 1504. Because of his administrative failings, however, he lived in obscurity for his remaining short years.

The Book of Privileges

In 1502, prior to his final voyage to America, Columbus had commissioned the *Book of Privileges*. This unique preservation of thirty-six documents showed how he was to be remunerated for his New World explorations. It also contained an unofficial transcription of a papal bull of 1493 in which Pope Alexander VI in essence gave Spain rights to the newly discovered lands. Prior to this, Columbus had fallen out of favor with the monarchy, and he wished to make his position as secure as possible for himself and his heirs by publicizing these agreements under the watchful eye of judges and notaries in his hometown of Seville. Four copies were known to exist in 1502. Also, our Library of Congress has a copy that can be viewed online.[73]

On May 20, 1506, Columbus died as an old man at age fifty-one after suffering from malaria, arthritis, and gout. These were diagnosed posthumously from his daily journals.

His Burial

Columbus was buried on the grounds of a convent in Valladolid. In 1513, his body was reported to have been moved to a monastery in Seville. In 1536, Columbus and his son, Diego, were transferred to Santa Domingo in the Dominican Republic. In 1796, his bones were to have been taken to Havana. In 1896, the body supposedly went back to Seville.

DNA samples were taken from Columbus's grave in Seville in 2003 and compared with DNA from remains known absolutely to be Diego Columbus, his brother. In 2006, the forensic team led by Dr. Jose Antonio Lorente from the University of Granada announced a match, thus showing that at least a portion of Columbus's remains were in Seville.

History of Observance of Columbus Day

The first celebration of the discovery of America is believed to have occurred on October 12, 1792, in New York. By the time we celebrated our centennial in 1876, the Italian-Americans of Philadelphia had erected a statue of Columbus in Fairmount Park. San Francisco Italians first named the celebration Columbus Day in 1869. The

Columbian Exposition planned for 1892 in Chicago took place in 1893 and drew visitors from all over the world. Visitors could view replicas of Columbus's three ships as part of the festivities.

Colorado became the first state to proclaim an official observation of the day in 1909. Other states followed Colorado's lead. In 1937, President Franklin D. Roosevelt proclaimed October 12 as Columbus Day. The Uniform Holiday Bill of 1968 established Columbus Day as an official holiday. Since 1971, it has been celebrated the second Monday in October.

The day is usually observed by the post office, banks, government offices, and schools. For Americans in general, it is work as usual.

Anti-Western bias and the modern educational doctrine that all cultures are equal have resulted in anti-Columbus bias. As a result, the day might be known as Native American Day or Indigenous Peoples Day in some areas.

Is Columbus a Hero or an Archvillain?

Within thirty years, the Tainos were gone. Five hundred had been shipped to Spain. Others were killed or committed suicide due to the harsh labor conditions imposed upon them. The workers were required to produce a specified amount of gold every three months. Some resources state that three hundred thousand were killed. Since that culture had no periodic formal census, the number is probably a gross exaggeration and at best a wild guess. Still, every life is valued by God, and whatever the actual number, the loss is lamented.

Columbus is blamed for the conquest and destruction of the natives, and genocide is brought to mind. Genocide is defined as "the intent to destroy part or all of a cultural group." Columbus personally did kill some indigenous Americans, but he shouldn't be held personally responsible for all atrocities committed in the Western Hemisphere.

For those of us who are Native Americans or descendants of them, we need to keep in mind a few harsh facts.

1. Among the thousands of tribes, fighting on a regular basis was common, just as various ethnic groups in Europe and Asia constantly fought. Thus, they also contributed to their own destruction.

2. For thousands of years, little or no progress took place. Natives lived in unclean, unhealthy conditions. Yes, they had some knowledge of healing herbs, but they had made no significant progress in health or living conditions, and herbal healing generally went hand in hand with the superstitious pagan practices of witch doctors or shamans. Consider the mortality rate of Caucasian populations before the discovery that the simple act of washing hands could prevent spreading disease in hospitals. This was a small step, but it was progress.

3. Being isolated from the Old World and its diseases, the Indians had no resistance to European sicknesses. Exposure to measles and smallpox resulted in devastating depopulation. This of course was not purposeful behavior on the part of Columbus or the Europeans.

4. Populations in the Southern Hemisphere were highly advanced in mathematics and astronomy, but barbarous practices of human sacrifices to the gods were common. Untold thousands were used as blood sacrifices. Archaeologists regularly find evidences of this in their searches. Whether in colder climates or the lush, tropical forests, none was living in the paradise some have claimed. "Because that when they knew God, they glorified Him not as God, neither were thankful; but became vain in their imaginations, and their foolish heart was darkened" (Romans 1:21). They were far removed from Paradise.

Speaking in purely human terms, Columbus must be considered a hero for his nautical knowledge, skill, accomplishments, and dogged determination to reach his goal in the face of many years of opposition. On the other side of the coin, one must consider his character flaws. Administrative incompetence, greed for gold and social prominence, and the exploitation of uneducated primitives are less than heroic traits.

Rather than tangle with the leftists who choose to do political battle over the Columbus legacy, we must consider the Columbus holiday from the biblical standpoint. In the light of the scriptural knowledge you possess, how do you think Columbus compares with our biblical heroes of faith?

> And they that are Christ's have crucified the flesh with the affections and lusts. If we live in the Spirit, let us also walk in the Spirit. Let us not be desirous of vain glory, provoking one another, envying one another (Galatians 5:24-26).

CHAPTER 22

Halloween

What is Hallowed (Holy) Even and All Saints' Day?

The name Halloween is of Christian origin; it now refers to the evening before November 1, All Saints' Day or All Hallows Day. The evening before was referred to as All Hallows Eve, which became abbreviated to Halloween. Today, children hold parties and play games such as bobbing for apples. They dress up in costumes and go trick or treating. The underlying motive for this practice is something for nothing, but it was not always so.

May 13 had been the original Feast of All Saints; that was the date in AD 609 when Pope Boniface IV consecrated the Roman Pantheon to the Virgin Mary and all martyrs. This structure, formerly dedicated to Roman gods, was the third such structure in Rome dedicated to the gods.

The Pantheon

The first Pantheon occupied the marshy site where Romulus, Rome's founder, reportedly ascended to heaven. It was built by Emperor Marcus Vipsanius Agrippa in 27 BC. A fire in AD 80 destroyed the building, and Emperor Domitian (Titus Flavius Domitianus) had it rebuilt. The second structure burned after being struck by lightning in AD 110.

Hadrian commissioned the third and present structure in AD 120. This elegantly designed architectural wonder has three main parts: an entrance portico, a domed rotunda, and a linkage between the two. Builders used a powerfully bonding concrete made by grinding together lime and volcanic residue from Pozzuoli, Italy.

Building components consist of bricks, six different types of concrete from bottom to top, and variegated marble obtained throughout the Roman Empire. Supported by twenty-foot-thick walls, the 5,000-ton dome contains the only source of light, the oculus (eye). Originally, statues of the seven planetary gods stood in the vestibule. Each received honor from the sky god, Jupiter, as the sun's rays illuminated each during the course of the day.

Twenty-four columns supporting the front portico are estimated to weigh sixty tons each. Quarried in Egypt, they were transported by barge to Rome. Even though Hadrian's reputation was that of a self-centered, divinely inspired poet who considered himself a near deity, the columns support a pediment whose inscription attributes the building of the Pantheon to Marcus Agrippa.

When Michelangelo (1475–1564) first gazed upon it in the 1500s, he declared it to be a work of angelic design. Today, some believe it must be divinely protected for it to remain standing after 2,000 years.

In AD 609, Emperor Phocas transferred control of the Pantheon to Pope Boniface IV and gave the pope his approval to convert it to a Christian Church. The building, intended to honor all gods, including Venus, Jupiter, and Mars, was then consecrated and renamed Santa Maria and Martyrs. So many people had lost their lives for their faith in Christ that it was impossible to have a special day for all of them. This dedication made it possible to revere all known and unknown martyrs.

After transfer of allegiance from all gods to Mary and the martyrs, dedicated believers hauled twenty-eight cartloads of martyrs' bones from the catacombs and placed them in a porphyry basin beneath the altar.

All Saints' Day Changed

Sometime around AD 710, Pope Urban IV changed the observance of All Saints' Day to November 1. This change in date helped draw attention away from pagan celebrations and toward Christian devotion to God. Thus, October 31 became Hallowed Evening.

As we have seen, the organized Catholic Church adapted many pagan days and gave them new names and new emphases. We must assume that it did this in good faith and conscience to redirect the allegiance of the people. From our advantageous perspective, we surmise these changes were made without reference to Scriptures. After the Reformation, the Anglicans and other Protestants also kept this celebration.

What Was It before It Became Halloween?

It was definitely not hallowed or holy by our definition. When we think of the words *holy* or *hallowed*, we think of Christ's standard of piety or righteousness as set forth in the Scriptures.

When we do word searches into the Hebrew *qodesh* and the Greek *hagios*, we find the fundamental meaning of these words and their derivatives is "separation." These words have been translated as "holy." German and Dutch rendition of holy is "Heilig." In *Strong's Concordance*, Greek Lexicon #1506, "*hêilē*" means "the sun's ray." It has been suggested that Heilig comes from Heil, a Germanic sun idol, although my research doesn't confirm this.

Readers of World War II vintage or those viewing reruns of World War II movie newsreels will no doubt remember the odious, mindless, spineless salute of "Heil Hitler." This of course could be interpreted two ways: "holy" Hitler, or "to wish every blessing upon Hitler."

Today's spring and fall secular celebrations had their beginnings in religious fire ceremonies of sun worship and mystic rites from among the druids. As previously noted, the spring rites and festivals were associated with animal breeding and human fertility. As we shall see shortly, the fall celebration thrived on the death theme.

The druids were one of the elite classes of Celtic society. It is interesting to note the meaning of the word *druid* comes from the base *dru*, meaning oak or tree, and *wid*, meaning wise, or *he/she who knows*. Women were held in high regard in the druid society and could be priests, poets, and teachers as well as the men. Though much has been written about them, our knowledge of their doctrinal system is lacking. This of course is due to all instructions being passed down orally. Much of what we know about today's druids comes from those who have left their organizations and have turned to Christ.

Druids had a curious blend of belief in one supreme god along with belief in other lesser gods. Occult methods and what we would consider superstitions for determining the future accompanied these beliefs. Druid temples were dark oak groves; their practices were a mixture of observing refined ordinances and committing cruel savagery.

After Rome conquered Britain, it added some of its own fruit-harvest customs. But ruthless as the Romans were, even they were unfavorably impressed by the druid practice of human sacrifice. Because of these practices, Tiberius (Tiberius Claudius Nero) banned druids after Britannia became Romanized. The druid organization went underground only to resurface later. The druidic society is alive today and has its own Web site.

Druid Customs with Fire

Giant fire festivals took place four times a year, but May and November marked the two main times. Worshippers, all ages from children to adults, came in great numbers to these assemblies. Dusk to dawn, they sang, danced, ate, and chanted rites to the fertility goddess in spring and to the Lord of Death in November.

Between the two main festivals, smaller meetings occurred weekly or at least at short intervals. In each district, a band known as a coven of thirteen people, i.e., twelve people and their chief or leader "devil" served as the teachers, healers, and celebrants of the rituals. If any witchcraft were required, coven members were consulted. Human sacrifice occurred at intervals of three, seven, or nine years.

The time of the rising of the Pleiades constellation, or the seven stars, marked the official end of the growing and harvest season. It also marked the beginning of the long, dreary winter and the Celtic new year. The most important fire festival of the year, to Samhain, summer's end, and Lord of the Dead took place. The month of Samhain began with festivities on the eve of the first of the month. The veil between the living and the dead thinned. It could be considered a ghoulish family reunion.

Food and entertainment honored spirits of the dead. Places were set at the table for the deceased, and interaction between the living and the dead kept the families in unity. Sometimes, the dead were so far away, either in purgatory or hell, that they needed help to find their way home. Ringing bells and other loud noises helped them chart their homeward journey. (We continue ringing bells on New Year's Eve, but how many know where the custom began?) At this time also, another god, Lugh, the God of Light, passed through this thin veil. (Lugh had his special day on August 1, "Lughnasad.")

Ghosts, witches, hobgoblins, and demons of different kinds roamed about. Spirits came out of the cave of Cruchan in Connaught, the gate of hell. These spirits killed animals, stole babies and brides, and committed other vile deeds. To protect precious possessions, the druids lit fires to ward off the supernatural powers. Sometimes, they placated these spirits by burning animal and human sacrifices. From the piles of bones comes the phrase *bone fire*, now shortened to *bonfire*.

The Lord of Death, Samhain, oversaw the fate of the dead. Samhain sent the souls of the good into newborns, but the souls of the condemned entered bodies of animals for the next year. However, if enough gifts were given and enough prayers said to this Lord of Death, a wicked one's punishment could be reduced.

It was during this era that the custom of going door-to-door asking for food or clothing began. People clothed in animal masks and bear or wolf skins begged for items or "treats" for their kin's departed spirit. Beggars summoned demons. They pronounced curses and torments on the houses of those refusing to give. In exchange for protection, hapless householders gave food and sometimes children.

Once every three years at Talchtgah, County Mead, Ireland, festivities began by sacrificing human victims by fire to the gods. Along with this, all fires in the houses had to be extinguished that night and rekindled from the sacrificial fire of Talchtgah. For each relit fireplace, a tax was charged. Rekindling of fire meant that departed souls revisited their homes that day. Celebrations lasted two weeks, during which time the open-air parliament revised laws and updated genealogies.

In the highlands of Scotland on October 31, families carried lighted torches and marched widdershins around the fields, that is, from left to right. Thus, good crops would grow in the coming year. It also frightened witches from stealing milk and hurting cattle. Afterward, marchers threw the torches into a bonfire. Family members placed stones in the fire. After the fire burned out, they raked ashes over the fire. If any person's stone was misplaced or missing, he or she would die within the year.

Women who were normal during the rest of the year but who really had sold their souls to the Devil would meet the "devil" or coven chief at a prearranged place; he rode a goat and played dancing music on his bagpipe. Witches gathered the ashes from the devil's torch to make potent incantations.

Druids and other ancient people believed the human spirit resided in the head. If one could control the head of an enemy killed in battle, that enemy couldn't harm that person when the enemy returned to roam the earth at Samhain. For this reason, victors displayed beheaded enemies at Samhain. The spread of Christianity modified this practice to one of carving turnips and pumpkins into heads, an important symbolic gesture of enemy spirit control.

In a related celebration, around November 1, Rome honored Pomona, the goddess who blessed the fruit harvests. A featured entertainment there was horse racing. Fruits and nuts, with occult help, were used to foretell the future. Religious devotees of Pomona worshipped her with deviant sexual behavior in a grove near Ostia at the mouth of the Tiber River.

Another Word about Groves

The Bible as translated into English makes forty references to grove or groves. Only one reference, Genesis 21:33, where Abraham planted a grove of trees in Beersheba, refers to a grove of trees as we understand the common meaning of the word. All other references are from the Hebrew root word transliterated *'asherah* and are in regard to corrupted worship associated with trees. As previously noted, this grove worship was wicked and perverse. Is it any wonder Jehovah wanted these groves ground into dust and destroyed? (See Micah 5.) It is understandable why the early Church leaders eagerly changed names and practices of these ancient festivals.

Divination or Superstition?

It has been said that one man's religion is another man's superstition. Halloween customs seem to affirm this. Halloween is a celebration of devils and death. In past times, it was also a time of year for divination. The devils' help was sought for purposes of foretelling the future concerning marriage, health, and death. From our vantage point, it seems quite frivolous and a matter of quaint folklore; however, we have the blessed advantage of access to the translated Scriptures to guide us. The illiterate peasants of the Middle Ages and before didn't, so they believed much of the following.

Young people would get together for games to determine which of them would marry that year or who would marry first. Young men would winnow corn in the barns and wait for the spirit of the future wife to pass through the barn. Or young women might sow hemp seed at midnight, saying, "Hemp seed I sow, who will my husband be, let him come, and mow." If she looked over her left shoulder, she would see the figure of her future husband.

Scottish youngsters pulled cabbage stalks blindfolded. Stalks indicated the size and shape of their future mates. They placed the stalks over the door and numbered them. The girl who had number seven would get the seventh boy who walked in the door.

In Ireland and Scotland, various items such as rings, money, or dolls were baked in a cake. Whoever got the piece with the ring would marry, the finder of money would be rich, and the one who found the doll would have children that year. Of course, the night watchman at these parties was the jack-o'-lantern, often carved from turnips. His ugly, demonic face scared away evil spirits. Another account of the carved head comes from British folklore. In this tale, Jack O'Lantern had been a real person whose soul wasn't allowed to enter heaven or hell and had to roam the earth with his lantern.

What Do Witches Have to Do with a Holy Evening?

Our current Halloween celebrations generally have someone costumed in a black dress and hat and wearing a hag's face with a long nose. Somehow, the notion has prevailed that a witch must be ugly. The physical ugliness or beauty of the person involved is irrelevant.

The Bible has two specific references to witches and six to witchcraft or witchcrafts. "Thou shall not suffer a witch to live" (Exodus 22:18). A witch by biblical definition is a medium who delivers messages from the earthly world to the world of spirits or vice versa. Our word translated "witch" comes from the root word transliterated *kashaph*, meaning "to mutter" in reference to some demon.

> There shall not be found among you any one that maketh his son or daughter to pass through the fire, or that useth divination, or an observer of times, or an enchanter, or a witch (Deuteronomy 18:10).

Also relevant to this is Leviticus 19:31: "Regard not them that have familiar spirits, neither seek after wizards, to be defiled by them. I am the Lord your God." (This refers to evil spirits impersonating dead humans and attaching themselves to "mediums.") Perhaps in an attempt to dignify the practice, modern mediums refer to themselves as channelers.

Besides the quoted verses, there are also fifteen references to sorcerers and sorcery. It is evident that witches are real people who communicate with evil spirits and who have unusual powers given to them by those spirits. God's plain command: keep away from them!

Witches in Many Cultures

Ancient Egyptians, Romans, Brits, and early American Indians had witches. Of the hundreds of tribal groups of North America, the medicine man assumed a high position. His primary function consisted of healing those who had fallen into disfavor with a god or who through witchcraft or sorcery had developed sickness. Along with exorcising the evil spirit, he also used healing herbs and sometimes massages to revitalize his patient.

The early organized Church vacillated from saying that witches were only a delusion to affirming that there were such persons and condemning them to death. In England in AD 1603, Parliament, under King James, passed a law forbidding communication with witches. The law forbad using dead bodies or bones for use in any type of sorcery, charm, enchantment, or witchcraft. Anyone convicted of doing so would be put to death. Four hundred years later, can we assume that for such a law to have been enacted, graves must have been robbed for that purpose?

As often happened with a biblical truth or injunction, human interpretation got superimposed and truth became obscure. Thousands of people, mostly women, in Europe between AD 1450 and 1700 were tortured and slain after they had been accused of practicing witchcraft. Concerning the Salem witches' trials in our own country, it is believed by some, and with good reason, that Christians who opposed witchcraft were made the target of real witches. The falsely accused innocents burned at the stake while the true witches spitefully watched.

Similar to our modern bounty hunters, professional witch hunters identified suspects and were paid a fee for each conviction. One method of identification consisted of inserting the hand into boiling water to lift out a stone. If the hand wasn't burned, the person was innocent. Another method of identification consisted of throwing the accused into a pool of cold water. If she floated, she was guilty; if she sank, she was innocent. Every witch supposedly had a prick mark on her body put there by the Devil that didn't cause pain. If such a mark was found, it was proof she was a witch. The laws of Athelstan, the first king of England, had decreed these methods.

In early America, witches made wax images of their victims and stuck them with pins, causing pain or death for the victim. Sometimes, the waxen image would be melted in the fire, causing the victim to waste away. This tradition has been performed in Africa, by early American Indians, and in other cultures around the globe. Indeed, use of sorcery remains in India, Africa, and Latin America and is making itself evident in the United States via legal and illegal immigrants from these areas.

Modern Witches and Goddesses

What has been described is generally known as diabolical witchcraft. This supposedly contrasts with modern witchcraft, which had its resurgence beginning in the counterculture era of the 1960s and is generally known as Wicca. (Wicca may be an early Anglo-Saxon term for witchcraft.) Its modern dogma challenges biblical teachings of fixed standards of morality and stresses ecology, fertility religion, and the worship of human sexuality as in pre-Christian Europe. Some all-women's groups worship the goddess Diana and call themselves Dianic.

Other groups have revived the ancient Greek mythology personification of Mother Earth, Gaea (also spelled Gaia), or Ge, meaning "earth." In mythology, Gaea persuaded her son, Titan, to overthrow his father, Father Heaven, personified as Uranus. In the grisly account, Titan and his followers castrated Uranus, and from the blood spilled on the earth, giants and three avenging goddesses emerged.

In 1992, the United Nations held an Earth Summit in Rio de Janeiro. Ritual drummers sought to heal the earth, and radical environmentalists bowed to Gaea in supplication. The mainstream press treated this element of the conference as wacky but harmless. Perhaps it was. However, worship of Gaea as a mother goddess and a revival of pantheism along with aboriginal religions are present in global environmental circles.

Occult beliefs run the gamut from simple witchcraft, voodoo, and pantheism to secret, satanic societies that practice ritual human sacrifices. Many satanic societies will have the word *college* in their titles, not to be confused with state or private colleges. They may also have the word *Lucifer* or *Luciferian* in their Web site name or magazine titles.

Along with pagan religious revival, Hollywood has given us a spate of ghost movies featuring people who communicate with the dead. Mediums are no longer portrayed as frauds but as accurately portraying psychic phenomena. Each year at Halloween, old movies of this genre are rerun and new movies produced. The reason given for so many such movies is that people want to know about death. What a shame that Americans are turning to movies for their spiritual enlightenment rather than God's Word.

As at May Day or Beltane, so at Halloween or Samhain, you can count on Satan stirring up the evil in his followers. He has not relinquished his hold on these special days. In fact, according to some observers of satanic holidays, the three major holidays in importance are one's own birthday, Walpurgisnacht (May 1), and Halloween.

Ignore or Recognize?

The early Puritan settlers rejected Halloween as a pagan holiday because it was literally associated with death and the supernatural. Around 1900, Halloween began to be acceptable as a modern holiday and is only symbolically associated with death. This symbolism is represented by costumes of ghosts, skeletons, witches, devils, werewolves, and vampires. Yes, we do have Cinderellas, Supermen, and George

Washingtons, but it is not the costume that makes the day a celebration of devils; rather, it is the day itself, a blatant celebration of Satan, which even innocent costumes cannot change.

Is it not blatant and obtrusive to foist upon us beginning in September store aisles covered with artificial cobwebs, cardboard witches sitting on shelves, and imitation graveyards surrounded by scary or cute ghosts? It is simply another of Satan's snares to misguide humankind into believing death is our friend.

In view of the disreputable past of October 31, today's Bible-believing parent may be in a quandary. They mentally and spiritually wrestle within themselves. Do we forbid our children from participating in Halloween festivities? Do we let them participate and use the opportunity as a teaching tool? Do we let them participate but costume them only as biblical or patriotic characters? Is it only harmless fun?

According to Colossians 2:16, no one is to judge us in respect to a holyday. For that matter, can we truthfully say that it ever was a holy day in spite of good intentions and an honorable name for it? Obviously, God didn't institute it as such.

God's commandment is, "Thou shalt have no other gods before me" (Exodus 20:3). Our worship of Him should acknowledge, "Now unto God and our Father be glory, for ever and ever. Amen" (Philippians 4:20). Anything that detracts from His glory should be avoided. We must "abstain from all appearance of evil" as 1 Thessalonians 5:22 enjoins us. Make no mistake. Death is our enemy—the last one to be destroyed—and not to be glorified literally or symbolically. This is one "holiday" that must be shunned.

CHAPTER 23

Election Day

Election Day in the United States is not a federal holiday. However, it is a legal holiday in Delaware, Hawaii, Kentucky, Maryland, Montana, New Jersey, New York, Ohio, and West Virginia.

Elections for national office are always held on the Tuesday following the first Monday in November of every even-numbered year. In the early days, it often took many days to get the totals in from all areas of a state. Therefore, it has been speculated that Tuesday was chosen as Election Day to avoid vote counting on Sunday.

All members of the House of Representatives are elected for two-year terms, and a third of all senators are elected for six-year terms. Electors for president and vice president are chosen in years evenly divisible by four.

Background of Federal Election Day

The first Wednesday of December was the date set aside by federal law in 1792 for the meeting of the Electoral College in their respective states.[74] The same law gave permission to the states to hold their presidential elections anytime in a period thirty-four days prior to that date. Obviously, in the 1700s, communications were slow, and the various state elections didn't influence each other very much. With the coming of the railroad and telegraph lines, swifter communications began to influence the outcome of elections. States that voted later could be influenced by a candidate's victory in a state that had voted earlier. Thus, states that voted at a later date could determine the election results.

To make the elections more uniform, in 1845, after much debate, Congress chose the first Tuesday after the first Monday in November. This ensured that the thirty-four-day period mandated by existing Electoral College law would be met.

State and Local Elections

Some states choose different voting patterns for state offices, although most states choose governors in even-numbered years when there is no presidential election. Odd-numbered years are chosen for some offices.

Municipalities, counties, or others holding independent local elections such as school boards are subject to the rules of each state. For example, in Massachusetts, fifty cities are required to hold elections on Election Day, but at least 300 towns are free to choose their own dates for local officials.

Roman Republic in Contrast to the United States of America's Republic

Our system of government took its pattern from the ancient Roman Republic with some significant differences. There, only adult male citizens were allowed to take part in political life. In the early days of our republic, only males voted, but due to the nature of our Constitution, in due course, women won the right to vote.

Rome's citizens could exercise their voting rights only in assemblies. Further, these assemblies were divided into tribes or centuries depending upon the nature of the assemblies. An individual's vote helped determine the outcome of his group. The votes of the majority of the groups determined the decision of the assembly. There was no such thing as liberty and justice for all. The rich or more powerful voted first, the poor last. As soon as a majority was reached, the election was over. Most times, the poor didn't get to vote at all. Also, all voting took place in Rome. Consequently, those in remote areas usually just didn't vote.

Assemblies couldn't debate policy; they could only approve or reject decisions made in the Roman Senate, which determined all domestic and foreign policy. Magistrates and tribunes could call special meetings for purposes of debate, but ordinary citizens had to have the magistrates' permission to speak. Historians indicate some assemblies expressed unofficial opinions. That is, they expressed their political displeasure by yelling, which of course led only to more frustration.

Should Election Day Be a Federal Holiday?

Today, the legal voting age is eighteen, and millions are eligible to vote. However, one lament is the pathetic voter turnout across the nation. People rush to work and rush home, not wishing to stand in long voter lines, so they forgo the precious right to vote. Having a national election holiday might remedy that situation. In the past, such legislation was introduced in Congress but was not voted upon. For now, those cherishing the right to vote must be dedicated to the task of getting to the polls. That is, except in Oregon and Washington. In Oregon, all elections are vote-by-mail; ballots there must be received by a specific time on Election Day. Most counties in Washington are vote-by-mail; ballots must be postmarked by Election Day. That seems simple enough, but it also appears to open the election process to an avalanche of unqualified ballots.

No simple solution is offered. To remain in a free society, we must be constantly vigilant regarding current issues. We must also be willing to take advantage of the priceless voting privilege whether it's convenient or not. As Bible-believing citizens, we can try to stay informed of current fiscal and moral issues and vote accordingly. Specifically, we should "Continue in prayer, and watch in the same with thanksgiving" (Colossians 4:2).

> Wicked rulers are a curse of God on a wicked nation. Now as religion [Christian] tends to prevent such rulers, or at least prevent their choice, there is an obvious connection between politics and religion. Church and State may and ought to be separated; politics and religion ought not, for thus, the State becomes exposed to the curse of God, and political evil follows in the train of moral evil. (This was written in 1856, long before our current "Church-State" discussions.)[75]

CHAPTER 24

Veterans Day

Prelude to World War I

Causes leading to World War I were complex, interrelated factors too detailed to present in this short overview. These factors included imperialism, secret alliances, militarism, and the press. The press often misrepresented situations and didn't publish factors that could have promoted peace. Of these factors, I will focus on known facts regarding the military aspect.

For centuries, European and Asian countries waged continual aggression against one another. Empires or countries invaded, attacked, consolidated, conquered, retreated, and reconquered in seeming endless wars.

As the Byzantine Empire gasped its dying breath around AD 1358, the Ottoman Empire began its expansion westward. Areas whose names frequent our nightly news— Albania, Serbia, Kosovo, Bosnia, and Herzegovina—were scenes of epic battles in the 1400s through the 1700s. The Ottomans (Turks) conquered the vast Hungarian Kingdom and occupied parts of it for one hundred and fifty years, until 1718.

At the height of its greatness, the Ottoman Empire controlled parts of three continents: southeastern Europe, western Asia, and northern Africa. At that time, it ruled over Turkey, Syria, Mesopotamia,

Palestine, Arabia, Egypt, Barbary States, Balkans, and parts of Russia and Hungary.

Ongoing wars included six Russo-Turkish Wars during the 1700s through 1806. A seventh, 1828–1829, helped Greece achieve independence. The Treaty of Adrianople marked the end of that war. In the eighth Russo-Turkish War, 1853–1856, the United Kingdom and France joined in and sided with the Ottoman Empire. The eighth war ended with the Treaty of Paris in 1856. The ninth, final Russo-Turkish War, 1877–1878, officially ended with the Treaty of Berlin.

By 1878, many changes resulted in reconfiguration of territorial maps. Conquered countries repeatedly and unwillingly signed humiliating treaties, setting the stage for retaliation. Some countries that had been independent became assimilated by or joined others. Some, once part of other nations, obtained autonomy. Gradually, the Ottoman Empire disintegrated. However, its final dissolution occurred with the Balkan Wars of 1912–1913 and World War I.

Bulgaria, Serbia, and Greece formed the Balkan League; they declared war on Turkey and conquered Macedonia and Thrace. The Second Balkan War occurred over the spoils of the first war (Bulgaria vs. Serbia and Greece). This enabled Turkey and Romania to enter the war vs. Bulgaria. At that time, Turkey's landmass shrank to its present eastern Thrace boundary.

World War I, 1914–1918

The immediate, ostensible cause for World War I was the assassination of Archduke Francis Ferdinand and his wife in Sarajevo on June 28, 1914. The archduke was heir to the throne of Austria-Hungary. The following month, Emperor Franz Joseph of Austria-Hungary declared war on Serbia. Actual causes, no doubt, were the political and economic policies prevailing prior to that date, policies rooted in over two hundred years of previously mentioned wars.

What began as clashes of the Allied powers (Belgium, United Kingdom, France, Montenegro, Serbia, and Russian Empire) and the

257

Central Powers (Germany and Austria-Hungary) eventually involved thirty-two participating or supportive countries.

On November 7, 1916, President Woodrow Wilson won his second term in office with the slogan, "He kept us out of the war." But by April 6, 1917, at President Wilson's behest, Congress declared war on Germany, and on May 18, the Selective Service Act passed, allowing men to be drafted into the armed forces.

Reasons given for our country's willingness to go to war on foreign soil included repulsion toward Germany's inhumane conduct of war (for example, they introduced poison gas), our cultural inheritance from and natural affinity with England, Allied propaganda, and the press.

Perhaps more exigent were economic factors. In any war effort, who profits most? Certainly not the military men in muddy trenches or dusty deserts. Generally speaking, banking cartels, munitions makers, and opportunistic profit seekers gain while common people lose.

However, the spark that ignited the powder keg of anti-German public opinion was the interception of a secret telegram sent from Arthur Zimmerman, the German foreign secretary, to the German minister in Mexico on January 19, 1917. The telegram suggested a possible German-Mexican alliance in which Mexico would declare war against the United States. The intercepted and decoded message was forwarded to President Wilson.

Meantime, illogical as it was, commercial ocean liners booked passengers on ships traveling through declared war zones. Some of these passenger ships and merchant vessels also carried munitions. Passengers were kept ignorant of the fact, but the wary enemy knew.

In March, a German submarine sank three U.S. merchant ships. The time had come for President Wilson to reveal Zimmerman's message to Mexico, and Congress declared war in April.

This total war into which the United States became ensnared resulted in ten million killed and more than twenty million wounded. It was known as the Great War or the World War until the outbreak of World War II. At that time, the first Great War began to be referred to as World War I.

The Proposed Peace

Before the United States entered the war, President Wilson had urged warring countries to conclude "peace without victory" with freedom and democracy for all concerned. Nearly a year after our entrance, on January 18, 1918, Wilson set forth his Fourteen Points for world peace. From January through October, the Allied and Central powers discussed and negotiated the fourteen terms for a proposed armistice.

The proposed armistice dealt with the war on all its fronts: central powers would surrender all types of weapons, battleships, and warplanes. Under those terms, Germany stood to lose most: 2,000 aircraft, 5,000 trains, 30,000 machine guns, its submarine fleet, plus much more. The German army would also assist in retrieval and destruction of all land mines in evacuated territory. Germany would be subjugated. All Allied and American prisoners of war would be immediately repatriated. Railroads, bridges, telegraphs, and all means of communications would be maintained by the Central Powers without destruction. The Central Powers would pay reparations for all damages.

A few countries, exhausted from war, bowed out before the grand armistice finale of November 11, 1918. Bulgaria ceased fighting on September 30, Turkey concluded an armistice on October 30, and Austria-Hungary did so on November 3.

At 5:00 on the morning of November 11, Germany agreed to the terms of the armistice. The signing took place in the railway carriage of Allied supreme commander Ferdinand Foch and became effective six hours after signing, at 11:00. Hence, the cessation of war officially came at the "eleventh hour of the eleventh day of the eleventh month," although fighting didn't cease in the former Russian Empire and in parts of the Ottoman Empire.

The original armistice was good for thirty days but was renewed regularly until participating countries signed the formal peace treaty at Versailles. However, terms of the original Versailles treaty were rejected by our Congress. Congress revised the treaty, but it was defeated when President Wilson refused to accept the revised version. Under President

259

Warren Harding, Congress officially declared an end to the war that had cost 120,000 American lives.

Armistice Day

"To every thing there is a season, and a time to every purpose under the heaven" (Ecclesiastes 3:1). "A time to love, and a time to hate; a time of war, and a time of peace" (Ecclesiastes 3:8). People the world over rejoiced at the news of war's end; they were ready for their time of peace. Businesses closed, bells rang, and extemporaneous parties demonstrated people's eagerness for a return to normalcy.

On the anniversary of the armistice, in November 1919, President Wilson issued an Armistice Day proclamation eulogizing Allied soldiers and recognizing the heroism of those who had died in the service of their country. Canada, France, and Great Britain also proclaimed the holiday.

In 1927, Congress requested President Calvin Coolidge to issue a proclamation requiring the flag to be displayed on all public buildings on November 11.

In 1938, Congress passed a bill that dedicated November 11 to the cause of world peace, naming the day Armistice Day. Across the nation, veterans groups, most prominently the American Legion, organized parades and religious services.

For sixteen years, the United States formally observed the day of truce. The president or his representative placed a wreath on the Tomb of the Unknown Soldier. Traffic stopped at 11:00 a.m. for two minutes of silence in honor of the war dead. Rites concluded with volleys fired and taps sounded.

World War II and Name Change

Two decades later, World War II erupted, it was even more horrific than the war that was to have ended all war. Historians of varied biases consider the Versailles Treaty's punitive nature in regard to Germany as the major contributing factor.

Adolph Hitler appealed to the patriotism of Germans, who chafed at the hated treaty. German citizens welcomed him to power in 1933 with renewed hope for their beloved country. He rearmed Germany, overturned most provisions imposed by the Versailles Treaty, and led Germany to war again. Unfortunately, the citizenry conformed blindly to his leadership and followed him en masse to their eventual downfall.

Germany invaded Poland on September 1, 1939. Country after country chose sides with either the Axis powers or the Allied powers until at war's end on September 2, 1945, 25 million troops and 30 million civilians worldwide had been killed. Sixty-one countries involving three-fourths of the world's population had been affected.

Armistice Day Changed to Veterans Day

Armistice Day and the word *armistice* meant little to veterans returning from World War II twenty-seven years after the fact. Patriotic veterans' organizations proposed that all American veterans from all American wars be honored on November 11.

Emporia, Kansas, gets credit for giving the impetus to rename the holiday. Instead of observing Armistice Day on November 11, 1954, they held a Veterans Day observance whereby they also recognized veterans of World War II and veterans of the in-progress Korean War. Emporia native Alvin J. King requested Senator Ed Rees, also a native of Emporia, to introduce legislation to officially change the name from Armistice Day to Veterans Day. President Dwight D. Eisenhower, born in Texas but raised in Kansas, signed the legislation into law.

In 2003, the Senate passed a resolution declaring Emporia to be the founding city of Veterans Day. In that resolution, Alvin J. King and Representative Ed Rees were recognized for their contributions to its creation.

Coincidence of Einherjar

Einherjar were spirits of warriors who had died heroically in battle in the old Norse religion. The word *einherjar* is thought to mean something akin to "those who are now in the army of the dead." Modern pagans celebrate Einherjar on November 11 to honor those who have fallen in battle and have gone to join Odin's warriors. (Odin is considered the master of magic, poetry, chaos, and death. We get our name Wednesday from him.)

According to legend, Odin and Freyja, the fertility goddess of love and beauty, divided the dead between them. Half went to Odin's great hall of honor, glory, and happiness, Valhalla. The others were escorted to Freyja's hall, *sessrumnir*, the hall of pleasure.

Knowledgeable sources state that the einherjar are prominent in some of today's violent video games and music. In the video games, the einherjar have great power and are almost undefeatable. A Norwegian Viking heavy metal band calls itself Einherjar. Other Nordic music groups regularly call upon traditional Norse goddesses and gods, including Odin.

These creative entities have without doubt been influenced by the revival of Nordic religion. Commencing in the 1960s and '70s, the Asatrú was established. The Asatrú, a polytheistic movement, focuses on reviving the Norse pagan system that was common prior to the introduction of Christianity over a thousand years ago. Asatrú's proponents make no secret of their goal to dechristianize Scandinavia.

At least one Asatrú group lists our American Memorial Day as Einherjar, but most celebrate it on Veterans Day. They leave an offering of a small, decorated drinking horn at the Vietnam Veterans Memorial on November 11. This honors those who have died in war and have gone to join Odin's warriors in Valhalla.

Do Heroes Go to Heaven?

Most of us honor and respect our military personnel for sacrifices they made and make and what they do. Whether our country is right or wrong, our warriors obey the call. Of my three brothers, one joined the navy, one the air force, and one the army. They are three of my military heroes. Fortunately, none died in battle. Had they died in defense of our country, would they have gone to a warrior's heaven? To the Bible believer and specifically to the student of right division, this is patently a rhetorical question. "Jesus said unto him, I am the Way, the Truth, and the Life: no man cometh unto the Father, but by me" (John 14:6). Clearly, there is no such thing as a warrior's heaven in the biblical sense.

Those of us who are blessed to have been "chosen in Him before the foundation of the world" (Ephesians 1:4) and to have acknowledged Him as the Head of the body (Colossians 1:18) face another kind of warfare, a spiritual one. We are told specifically how we are to fight the battles constantly encircling us and that often threaten to engulf us.

> Put on the whole armor of God that you may be able to stand against the wiles of the devil. For we wrestle not against flesh and blood, but against principalities, against powers, against the rulers of the darkness of this world, against spiritual wickedness in high places. Wherefore take unto you the whole armor of God, that ye may be able to withstand in the evil day, and having done all, to stand (Ephesians 6:11-13).

Ephesians 6:14–16 specifies God's armor that we must use with no option to exchange them for weapons of our own choosing. God's weapons of engagement are the most effective, much better than any we could devise.

Next Veterans Day, when we honor our beloved who have fought and died to keep our nation free, let us give thanks for them and thank Christ for our freedom, but let us not be deceived into wishful thinking or getting our patriotism swirled in with someone else's mixed-up theology.

CHAPTER 25

Thanksgiving

God has placed within each heart the capacity for gratitude, but when God has been willfully rejected and ejected from knowledge as explained in Romans 1, something else will fill the void. If in our hearts we have the space for and the spirit of gratitude but acknowledge not God, to whom will we give thanks? Gratitude must have a recipient.

Throughout time, ancient and modern men have designated harvest time as a special time of thanksgiving. Many festivals were times of rejoicing for good harvests, but the knowledge of God had ceased and gratitude became mingled with pagan religious rites. However, two historic celebrations notable for their God-honoring themes are the ancient Hebrew Sukkoth and the modern American Thanksgiving.

Hebrew Thanksgiving

Sukkoth (also spelled Sukkot, Succoth, Sukkos, Succot, and Succos) or the Feast of Tabernacles, is the name given in the Old Testament to the harvest festival; this festival is also known as the Feast of Ingathering and is mentioned in Exodus 23:16, Exodus 34:22, and Leviticus 23:34. The festival is characterized by building huts of branches to commemorate the days when the Israelites lived in huts (*sukkoth*) while wandering in the wilderness for forty years.

In today's Jewish celebration, booths or huts are built in the five days between Yom Kippur and the festival. It begins on the fifteenth of Tishri, corresponding to our September or October. Many pious Jews eat and sleep in these huts. On the seventh day, willow, citron, myrtle, and palm branches are waved as the people make a circle seven times around the synagogue, an imitation of the ritual performed in the ancient temple as related in Leviticus 23:40. This seventh day is called Hoshana Rabba, "Great Hosanna."

On the eighth day of the festival, Shemini Atzeret, "Eighth Day of the Solemn Assembly," singing and dancing accompany the completion of the annual cycle of reading from the Torah.

American Thanksgiving

Various Indian tribes claim to have celebrated the first Thanksgiving predating our better-known pilgrim one. Other groups claim to have been the first on American soil to have a formal Thanksgiving Day. For example, Spaniards searching for gold in 1541 were starving when they found food and prepared a feast of thanksgiving, according to a road sign along Arizona State Route 27.

The French Huguenots in 1564 held special days of thanksgiving in what is now Jacksonville, Florida. Other claims for the first Thanksgiving are confirmed along the Kennebec River, Maine 1607, and in Virginia's Jamestown settlement in 1610. In Charleston, Massachusetts, a long-overdue shipment of supplies reached the settlers in 1630; they were so thankful that they held the first Thanksgiving. However, we will trace our custom of Thanksgiving from the pilgrims through the first national Thanksgiving proclamation by Abraham Lincoln to the present.

Pilgrims

On November 21, 1620, the *Mayflower* dropped anchor in the harbor off present-day Provincetown, Massachusetts. On December

21, the oldcomers, later called forefathers or founders, landed on the site of Plymouth Colony and established a government based on the Mayflower Compact, the first constitution written in America.

Only approximately half of the original hundred and two settlers survived the cruel winter. After the first harvest of 1621, Governor William Bradford proclaimed a day of feasting and prayer that included all the colonists and neighboring Indians. Indeed, in spite of the loss of loved ones, our forefathers felt they had much to be thankful for. The Indians had given them enough seed corn to plant twenty acres, and it had done well. Barley and other vegetable seeds they had brought with them also flourished in this new land. Meat roamed freely for the taking. When Governor Bradford sent men to hunt for fowl, they returned with enough wild turkey and waterfowl to last for a week. Fishermen added cod and bass to the table. Indian hunters contributed five deer. Along with ninety Indian guests and their chief, Massasoit, the colonists feasted for three days.

The exact date of this feast is not known, though it probably happened before December 11, 1621. On that date, Edward Winslow wrote a letter to a friend in England describing in detail the food and recreation of the day. However, there is no record of this feast having been called Thanksgiving.

The founders often appointed special days for giving thanks or for prayer, whatever the times demanded. In 1623, a terrible drought occurred. As was their custom, they fasted and prayed for rain. When the rains came during their prayers, they immediately set apart a day of thanksgiving.

This New England custom gradually turned into an annual celebration following harvest. However, the first actual proclamation of thanksgiving appears to have been on June 20, 1676. The governing council of Charlestown, Massachusetts, instructed Edward Rawson, the clerk, to proclaim June 29 as a day of thanksgiving. One paragraph of that proclamation is here quoted.

> The Council has thought meet to appoint and set apart
> the 29th day of this instant June, as a day of Solemn

Thanksgiving and praise to God for such His Goodness and Favour, many particulars of which mercy might be instanced, but we doubt not those who are sensible of God's Afflictions, have been as diligent to espy him returning to us; and that the Lord may behold us as a People offering Praise and thereby glorifying Him; the Council doth commend it to the Respective Ministers, Elders and people of this Jurisdiction; Solemnly and seriously to keep the same Beseeching that being persuaded by the mercies of God we may all, even this whole people offer up our bodies and souls as a living and acceptable Service unto God by Jesus Christ.[76]

Other Colonists

The middle and southern colonies also gave thanks for good harvests as well as for victories over the Indians. President George Washington issued the first presidential thanksgiving proclamation in 1789 in celebration of the new constitution. New York State adopted an official Thanksgiving Day in 1817. As new states were added to the Union, they held their own Thanksgiving Days.

It was not until 1820 that the oldcomers or founders became known as pilgrims. A manuscript written by Governor William Bradford had been recovered. In it, Bradford referred to the saints who had left Holland as "pilgrimes." Orator Daniel Webster used the phrase *pilgrim fathers* in a bicentennial celebration that year. The colorful, descriptive name swelled his listeners' hearts with pride and thus the term came into common usage.

Official Holiday

In 1846, Sarah Josepha Hale, editor of *Godey's Lady's Book*, a popular women's magazine, began her campaign to make Thanksgiving a national patriotic holiday. She sent letters to the state governors, the president, and many other influential people. She proposed the name Union Thanksgiving in hopes that the states would form a closer union since at the time the question of slavery was tearing the Union apart.

It was not until October 3, 1863, that she saw her dream materialize. President Lincoln believed the Union had been saved and proclaimed a national day of thanksgiving to be celebrated on Thursday, November 26, as well as every year thereafter on the fourth Thursday of November.

Every president following Lincoln has proclaimed this holiday each year. President Franklin Roosevelt in 1939 felt that Thanksgiving came too close to Christmas and declared it to be the third Thursday of November, but in 1941, Congress changed the date to the fourth Thursday, where it remains.

There are 138 references in Scripture containing the root word *thank*. Only two are here quoted: "In every thing give thanks, for this is the will of God in Christ Jesus concerning you" (1 Thessalonians 5:18). "Sing unto the Lord with thanksgiving; sing praise upon the harp to our God" (Psalm 147:7).

As we know from right division of the Word, God doesn't command us to have a special day of Thanksgiving, but He does admonish us to always have thankful hearts.

Our Thanksgiving Day must be a glory to Christ! It has been secularized and somewhat commercialized, but it is nevertheless still a Christ-honoring holiday. Why else would Satan be attacking it? Is there any other reason that certain groups are specifically urging us to have Thanksgiving Day replaced with a National Diversity Day?

CHAPTER 26

Biblical Account of the Birth of Jesus Christ

Christmas is the time of the year we as children were all taught to love. How could a child not love the ornately decorated trees, the delightful aroma of cookies baking, and Santa Clauses in stores and on street corners? A favorite song would be on our lips or running through our minds. And what child ever refused to tell what he or she wanted for gifts? Family gatherings topped off the perfect season.

Perhaps this is ancient history to some readers, but there was a time in our land when children in government schools participated in recreating the nativity scene. You older readers know the routine. Timid children were given nonspeaking parts, wore bathrobes, and tried to look Oriental while others sang carols and read or recited from the Bible. Of course, good came from it all because people actually heard a portion of God's Word. Doesn't the Scripture say God uses even the wrath of men to praise Him? "Surely, the wrath of men shall praise thee: the remainder of wrath thou shall restrain" (Psalm 76:10).

Perhaps more significantly in regard to superficial listeners (those lacking a high degree of interest but attending Christmas programs to see Suzie or Johnnie perform), "For the word of God is quick, and powerful, and sharper than any two-edged sword, piercing even to the dividing asunder of soul and spirit, and of the joints and marrow, and is a discerner of the thoughts and intents of the heart" (Hebrews 4:12).

God promises that His Word will reach its target. "So shall my word be that goes forth out of my mouth: it shall not return unto me void, but it shall accomplish that which I please, and it shall prosper in the thing whereto I sent it" (Isaiah 55:11). Thus we know that anytime Scriptures are read in a sacred or secular assembly, something unexplainably powerful happens. Satan realizes this fact much more than we do. Why else would he be so determined to expunge all references to God's Word from public venue?

Fifty years ago, God's Word offended only the vilest sinner; today, it appears to be chic to be offended by it. To the mid-1960s, schoolchildren and their parents were blessed to hear the biblical account of Jesus' birth read each December.

> And it came to pass in those days, that there went out a decree from Caesar Augustus, that all the world should be taxed. (And this taxing was first made when Cyrenius was governor of Syria.) And all went to be taxed, every one into his own city. And Joseph also went up from Galilee, out of the city of Nazareth, into Judaea, unto the city of David, which is called Bethlehem; (because he was of the house and lineage of David:) To be taxed with Mary his espoused wife, being great with child. And so it was, that, while they were there, the days were accomplished that she should be delivered. And she brought forth her firstborn son, and wrapped him in swaddling clothes, and laid him in a manger; because there was no room for them in the inn.

> And there were in the same country shepherds abiding in the field, keeping watch over their flock by night. And, lo, the angel of the Lord came upon them, and the glory of the Lord shone round about them: and they were sore afraid. And the angel said unto them,

Fear not: for, behold, I bring you good tidings of great joy, which shall be to all people. For unto you is born this day in the city of David a Saviour, which is Christ the Lord.

And this shall be a sign unto you; Ye shall find the babe wrapped in swaddling clothes, lying in a manger. And suddenly there was with the angel a multitude of the heavenly host praising God, and saying, Glory to God in the highest, and on earth peace, good will toward men.

And it came to pass, as the angels were gone away from them into heaven, the shepherds said one to another, Let us now go even unto Bethlehem, and see this thing which is come to pass, which the Lord hath made known unto us. And they came with haste, and found Mary, Joseph, and the Babe lying in a manger. And when they had seen it, they made known abroad the saying which was told them concerning this child. And all they that heard it wondered at those things which were told them by the shepherds. But Mary kept all these things, and pondered them in her heart. And the shepherds returned, glorifying and praising God for all the things that they had heard and seen, as it was told unto them.

And when eight days were accomplished for the circumcising of the child, his name was called JESUS, which was so named of the angel before he was conceived in the womb.

And when the days of her purification according to the law of Moses were accomplished, they brought him to Jerusalem, to present him to the Lord (Luke 2:1-22).

Melda Eberle

Prophecy Fulfilled

The Hebrew Scriptures presented a great, ongoing, prophetic picture of the coming Messiah with over 456 messianic references. But all that Israel really hoped for was national restoration and renewal of its glory. It was not particularly concerned with the salvation of the world, of being, "A light to lighten the Gentiles, and the glory of thy people Israel" (Luke 2:32), and by the time of the Messiah's birth, certain fundamental doctrines had ceased to be held by the rabbis. At the top of the list were the doctrines of Original Sin and the natural, sinful state of man.

Keep in mind that the Jews had been dispersed to the east and west. The Jewish dispersion in the west, that is, the Hellenists, was influenced by Greek language and culture. Jewish religion became a mixture of Old Testament truths and the Greek philosophies of Plato and Homer.

Hebraized Greek and Latin words intermingled with and became part of the Hebrew language. In addition, the Hebrew Scriptures had been translated into Greek, the Septuagint, commonly referred to as the LXX, Roman numerals for seventy. On the one hand, Hebrew Scripture manuscripts were expensive, out of reach of the common Hebrew. On the other hand, hundreds of slaves copied manuscripts in Greek and Latin, undoubtedly with errors due to their prodigious output. But these Greek manuscripts were affordable and obtainable as well as readable by the Hellenist Jews, who by that time actually knew little Hebrew.

Much as the King James Version is considered the common people's Bible among English readers, so the LXX was considered the people's Bible among the Hellenists. There were probably at least three LXX versions. However, the original was completed in Egypt during the reign of Ptolemy III (247–221 BC). Although only a translation, it was considered inspired. The availability of translations, even with copyists' errors, should have prepared the Hebrews, particularly those of the western dispersion, for the coming Messiah. Unfortunately, what they were expecting the Messiah to be was not what should have been in light of the prophetic knowledge available.

Who Has the Whole World in His Hand?

The Roman Republic had degenerated into the Roman Empire with Caesar Augustus as its first emperor, though he was not necessarily known then by that title. He did take his position quite seriously and thought he was in charge of the world. His special decree to register the entire Roman world, including its subjugated Hebrews, seems arbitrary. Unknowingly, he became an agent in the fulfillment of God's Word. "But thou, Bethlehem Ephratah, though thou be little among the thousands of Judah, yet out of thee shall He come forth unto me that is to be ruler in Israel; Whose goings forth have been from of old, from everlasting" (Micah 5:2).

It has been suggested by many researchers that the purpose of the enrollment required by Quirinius was probably twofold. They suggest it may have been for future taxation purposes as well as for a census numbering eligible young men for military recruitment into the Roman army. In these assumptions, one very important point is forgotten: while Herod lived, taxes were paid directly to him. We know this is true because when Herod died, the Jews implored Archelaus, Herod's son and successor, to relieve them of their burden of excess taxation.

This registration cited by Luke near the birth of Christ was interrupted by the death of Herod and accomplished over a period of years. That special enrollment was made for the first time when Quirinius was governing (not necessarily with the title "governor") in Syria. Cyrenius is the English transliteration of the Greek. His full Latin name was Publius Sulpicius Quirinius.

In these enrollments, people would go to the town from which they originated. Families of Jewish descent would be registered according to their tribe, family, or fathers' "houses." Mary and Joseph naturally went to Bethlehem, for both were descendants of the house of David.

In a tax census, tax collectors would check the records for inheritances and then demand taxes based on their value. Like modern countries, Rome taxed anything taxable. They had land taxes, customs taxes, capitation taxes, which were similar to our personal or income tax, and inheritance taxes. Our experience with taxes makes it easy to believe that the whole purpose was for taxation. However, the word *apagrapho* translated "taxes" in the KJV is translated "registered" in the New King James.

"Registered" meant to record the names of men, their property, and income. Roman citizens' registration lists were updated every five years and kept securely in specific cities or centers throughout the Roman Empire. It was done routinely—nothing special about it—which brings us to a more probable explanation for the meaning of the registration required in Luke 2.

Preparations for the 750th anniversary of the founding of Rome were in the making. The grand year of celebration would be in 2 BC our calendar time. It would also be the silver jubilee of Emperor Caesar Trajanus Hadrian Augustus's rule.

Twenty-five years earlier, the senate and the people of the empire had given Augustus their complete allegiance. What better time to renew loyalty requirements than on his silver anniversary soon to come? The title *Pater Patriae,* "father of the country," would be conferred on Augustus in February 2 BC, but of course it was not a secret; he knew about this far ahead. Therefore, all in his realm were required to swear allegiance long before February so proper documents could be prepared for the grand presentation. Jewish historian Josephus states that around six thousand Pharisees refused to swear allegiance and were put to death by Herod.[77]

Neither Roman nor Jewish custom required women to personally appear to be enrolled. Husbands or fathers could ordinarily enroll them. It has been said that Mary hadn't been obligated to travel to Bethlehem with her husband. In like manner, no edict forbad her accompanying Joseph. Some assume that Mary simply didn't wish to be alone in Galilee waiting for her baby while Joseph traveled to Judaea. However, what woman in her right mind would set off on an uncomfortable, bumpy ride on an animal or in a cart a few days before her delivery date? Mary had no choice in the matter. Her presence was obligatory.

Mary and Joseph, although poor, were descendants of royalty. According to prevailing Jewish law, Mary, a descendant of David, could have claimed kingship for her offspring. As a claimant to the throne, she had to go to sign any official documents regarding inheritances or those professing loyalty to Augustus. While most people went to their local neighborhood, Mary and any others of royal Judaic lineage were required to register in Bethlehem.

This registration allowed King Herod or any others who might be concerned about their throne occupancy to know exactly who all the people were who claimed royal lineage. It has also been suggested that Herod's stratagem to keep a political eye on his subjects was accomplished as a game of cat and mouse. Many "mice" enjoyed the prestige of traveling to Bethlehem as royal claimants while the "cat" awaited an opportune time to pounce.

From Nazareth to Bethlehem required a careful and unhurried three days' travel for one whose pregnancy was nearing full-term. As they neared Bethlehem, they no doubt chatted with other travelers concerning Herod's resplendent castle known as Herodium.[78] The castle was secured within strong fortress walls and enclosed in a natural hill that had been encompassed and elevated with fill so that it rose over a hundred meters above the surrounding area. The upper portion Herod kept for his family's personal use; the lower portion housed his guests. Below ground level, a network of four cisterns ensured a good water supply. This union of natural and man-made mountain, the highest in southwestern Bethlehem, was clearly visible to many journeying for enrollment. Travelers no doubt gawked and longed for such a dwelling.

In stark contrast to Herod's magnificent dwelling, we find Mary and Joseph in utmost humility. After what must have been an exhausting trip, Mary and Joseph suffered the indignity of having no clean, comfortable place to rest. No one stepped forward to donate sleeping quarters to one so obviously with child. Possibly a gloomy, malodorous cave or grotto ordinarily inhabited by animals gave them shelter.[79] There is also a school of thought that believes Christ's birth occurred during the Feast of Tabernacles, and thus He could have been born in a temporary tabernacle.

Even though dramatization of the Christmas story usually depicts the innkeeper turning away the couple, the Bible makes no mention of an innkeeper, a barn, or a cave. It uses the word *kataluma,* which can be translated "room," "guestroom," or "house."

Houses of this period there consisted of two stories. The ground floor rooms might store tools and garden produce as well as provide a place for food preparation and eating. Animals also shared this space at night for several reasons: wild animals roamed the countryside and could easily have taken or killed domestic animals. And if not somehow fenced in, the animals could have wandered off. If they were inside the house, the owner knew the animals were safe from thieves as well. Milk from the animals provided food for the family, another good reason to have them under the same roof. In addition, warmth from the animals provided a degree of comfort to those sleeping on the second floor.

Of course, animals brought flies, fleas, and manure. Dried manure was used as heating fuel, a handy source in these circumstances. However, as we know, the hygienic properties of the house were less than desirable. Nevertheless, animals and humans dwelled together commonly far into the eighteenth century in Europe and Asia, and in primitive societies, they continue to do so today.

The same word translated "inn" in Luke 2:7 is translated as "guest-chamber" in Mark 14:14 and Luke 22:11. Luke 10:34–35 actually had an "inn" (different word, *pandocheion)* complete with an "innkeeper," *pandocheus.*

If Mary and Joseph arrived at Joseph's family home later than they had hoped, they may have found it full of older members of the family, who would have had superiority in guest privileges. Gossip regarding Mary and Joseph probably traveled to Bethlehem faster than the couple had. Being well grounded in the law, those well-intended elders may have shunned the couple with the "unusual" pregnancy. Perhaps they whispered behind their hands that the stable downstairs was good enough for *that* young lady!

The Scriptures are silent regarding Mary's labor, only that she "brought forth." Picturing the unclean surroundings, we are prone to imagine Mary having a horrible time, alone, and without the comfort of another woman. We assume she was alone at the time, for she is the one who laid Jesus in the manger. Can we also assume Mary had a perfect, painless delivery of the perfect Son of God? We only know that she wrapped him with narrow strips of cloth used to restrict the infant's movement and placed Him in a manger.

Where did Mary get these cloths? Would a woman about to deliver her baby leave home without making provision for her infant? Possibly—depending on her financial situation. If such were the case, the swaddling cloths might have been provided by the shepherds who watched over the sacrificial flocks from their position in a tower a moderate distance away. These cloths protected the young lambs from injury, for they must be without blemish in order to be used in the sacrificial ritual. How appropriate then, that our perfect sacrifice be wrapped in cloths intended for sacrificial lambs! (The Tower of the Flock referenced in Genesis 35:21 and Micah 5:2 is "David's city," Bethlehem. Some researchers declare Christ was born in the actual tower where sacrificial lambs were born.)

The word *phatnē*, translated "manger," was a ledge in the end of the room where animal keepers deposited hay or grain. So whether in cave, barn, grotto, tabernacle, or lower animal room of a house, Christ was placed in a manger and "the Word was made flesh, and dwelt among us (and we beheld His glory, the glory as of the only begotten of the Father,) full of grace and truth" (John 1:14).

A few miles away in Jerusalem, priests placed a sacrificial lamb on the altar. As was their custom, the priests blew three trumpet blasts proclaiming "the kingdom of God, the providence of God, and the final judgment."[80]

Outside Mary and Joseph's foul-smelling dwelling, a herald angel interrupted the night's calm by announcing the fulfillment of Jerusalem's prophetic trumpet. Night blazed in glorious brilliancy, brighter than any noon sun, as the glory of the Lord surrounded the terrified, unpretentious shepherds. They had cause to fear, for God had consigned His most important messenger to announce this majestic birth of their awaited Messiah. After the angel's unprecedented announcement, a multitude of other heavenly beings joined him in praise to God.

Christ had come not as a fully grown King in splendor but as a humble infant to mature, to ultimately present himself as perfect Ruler of His kingdom, to bear the burden of sin for the world. Intended to ridicule and scorn, evil, ignorant sinners announced that very truth later at his crucifixion, "a superscription also was written over Him in letters of Greek, and Latin, and Hebrew, THIS IS THE KING OF THE JEWS" (Luke 23:38).

The angel soothed the terrified shepherds and directed them to the manger. We are not told how they found the baby. Others have speculated that an angel led them, or that a special light did, or that they knocked on many doors before they found the right place.

These were undoubtedly devout men who were anticipating the coming Messiah, like Simeon and the prophetess Anna. Unlike many other Hellenistic Jews, these shepherds' minds and hearts were prepared and eager; prepared hearts follow the Lord's leading more easily. The world would call it intuition, knowledge gained without thoughts directed by others, but many Bible believers can attest to the Lord's leading in ways that are unexplainable to the worldly minded.

"I will instruct thee and teach thee in the way which thou shall go: I will guide thee with Mine eye" (Psalm 32:8). Many think this verse is for spiritual and moral guidance only. Sometimes, people use the word *literalist* derisively to describe those who adhere too closely to a verbatim translation of God's Word. But speaking nonderisively of our Lord, it is safe to say that God is a literalist as well as omnipotent. He certainly had the power to literally direct these humble shepherds to the place where their Messiah lay.

After they beheld the infant Jesus, they spread this astonishing news—news impossible to keep to themselves. The shepherds' names are not known to us, obviously with good reason. How many monuments would have been built in their honor or how many towns named for them would there have been? God intended the message of the Messiah to point specifically to Him.

The Magi

Now when Jesus was born in Bethlehem of Judea in the days of Herod the king, behold, there came wise men (magi) from the east to Jerusalem, Saying, "Where is he that is born King of the Jews? For we have seen his star in the east and are come to worship him." When Herod the king had heard these things, he was troubled, and all Jerusalem with him. And when he had gathered all the chief priests and scribes of the people together, he demanded of them where Christ should be born.

And they said unto him, "In Bethlehem of Judaea: for thus it is written by the prophet, 'And thou Bethlehem, in the land of Juda, art not the least among the princes of Juda: for out of thee shall come a Governor, that shall rule my people Israel.'"

Then Herod, when he had privily called the wise men, inquired of them diligently what time the star appeared. And he sent them to Bethlehem, and said, "Go and search diligently for the young child; and when ye have found him, bring me word again, that I may come and worship him also."

When they had heard the king, they departed; and lo, the star, which they saw in the east, went before them, till it came and stood over where the young child was. When they saw the star, they rejoiced with exceeding great joy. And when they were come into the house, they saw the young child with Mary his mother, and fell down and worshipped him: and when they had opened their treasures, they presented unto him gifts; gold, and frankincense, and myrrh. And being warned of God in a dream that they should not return to Herod,

they departed into their own country another way.
(Matthew 2:1-12).

The Greek New Testament uses three different words translated as "wise men": *sophos* (1 Corinthians 1:26, "not many wise men ... are called"), *phronimos* (1 Corinthians 10:15, "I speak as to wise men"), and *magos*. Magi is the plural form of the Greek *magos* used in Matthew 2 in reference to the men who were looking for the newborn King of the Jews.

The historian Herodotus wrote that the magi were originally one of the six tribes of the Medes. Other early accounts of the magi indicate they were Chaldean contemporaries of the Hebrew prophets. The prophets considered them wise men but scorned them as sorcerers and conjurers. The names Chaldean and magi became interchangeable because of their close connections. Magianism was found also among the Medes and Persians. In fact, Cyrus is credited with bringing magianism to Persia; thereafter, Persian priests were known as magi. They were reputed to have profound religious knowledge but looked down upon Babylonian magi as imposters.

After Babylonia defeated Judah, it was in turn defeated by the Medes-Persians. It is speculated that the libraries of Judah went to Babylonia and ended up in Persia. Also, with the scattering of the Jews, seeds of knowledge of a future king of Israel were undoubtedly planted among the magi.

The magi were a higher caste among Persians, Medes, and Babylonians who formed the kings' private council and performed the kings' coronation ceremonies. Besides being religiously oriented, they were skilled in medicine, the occult, dream interpretation, and astrology. In fact, part of their job description was to supply the kings with divine insight concerning daily affairs.

Daniel had to contend with dream interpreters in Babylon. His faithfulness and giving glory to God for his own ability to interpret dreams rewarded him with what we might call the presidency of the magi there: "Then the king made Daniel a great man, and gave him great gifts, and made him ruler over the whole province of Babylon, and chief of the governors over all the wise men in Babylon" (Daniel 2:48). Some have referred to Daniel as master of the magi, a "wise man" in the truest sense of the word.

Magi customarily visited kings and others they considered important. A group of magi visited Plato at his birth, and Josephus recorded a visit of magi to Herod around 10 BC. Tiridates, king of Armenia, led a group of magi in AD 66 to pay homage to Nero. Magi were associated with the birth of Mithridates, Caesar, and Augustus. Therefore, early readers of Matthew's account would find nothing extraordinary about magi visiting the newborn King of the Jews.

No country of origin has been proven for the magi who visited Christ. Arabia, Babylonia, Persia, Parthia, even Egypt and Ethiopia have been offered as possibilities. Chinese astronomers claim one of the magi to be Chinese. However, early Christian painters portrayed the magi wearing Persian clothing.

No means of transportation is mentioned in Matthew. We just assume they traveled by camel, perhaps because of a Hebrew prophecy, "The multitude of camels, shall cover thee, the dromedaries of Midian and Ephah; all they from Sheba shall come: they shall bring gold and incense; they shall show forth the praises of the Lord" (Isaiah 60:6).

The Bible states three gifts brought by the magi: gold, frankincense, and myrrh. We know these costly gifts helped finance Mary and Joseph's hasty exit to Egypt. Two thousand years later, these three commodities continue to be symbols of wealth and honor.

Consider gold. We know that gold makes beautiful jewelry because of its lustrous yellow color. Due to its malleability, one ounce can be flattened into a thin sheet covering three hundred square feet or made into wire fifty miles long. It is noncorrosive, and because of its reflective properties, it is used on satellites and astronaut visors. Of course, gold coins have been coveted for centuries and are truly gifts befitting kings.

Frankincense has been used throughout history in perfumes, for embalming, and in religious rites. Its aromatic, whitish resin is tapped from boswellia trees found in Somalia in Africa, and Oman and Yemen (formerly Sheba) on the Arabian Peninsula. It is a scarce commodity and still much sought after and very costly.

The word *myrrh* comes from the Hebrew *murr* or *maror* and means "bitter." It too comes from plants native to Somalia and Ethiopia, the *Commiphora*. Its reddish-brown sap prevents insects from damaging it by gumming up the mouth of its attacker. Myrrh has antibiotic properties and was used to reduce decay in Egyptian mummies. It is highly aromatic and was considered more valuable than gold or frankincense.

Today's health researchers have found a dietary supplement from the myrrh bush, guggul lipid. Guggul lipid is suggested as an alternative to pharmaceutical drugs for maintaining cholesterol and triglyceride levels within the normal range as well as maintaining the blood's normal viscosity.

The Bible doesn't state that there were three givers, nor are any names mentioned; the traditional names Gaspar, Melchior, and Balthazar were devised later. Syrian tradition names them Gushmasaph, Hormisdas, and Larvandad, and other countries have different names. Also, it was not until the fifth century that they were depicted as kings.

The magi who visited Christ were portrayed as honest, sincere seekers, the antithesis of Simon in Acts 8:9 or Barjesus as described in Acts 13:6–12. These magi focused their energies on the study of the stars. There is no hint of sorcery or magical powers practiced by them, so they probably considered themselves astronomers more than astrologers. They brought expensive gifts with no expectation of material gain or getting anything in return. Being of the higher caste, they were probably persons of wealth and social status, able to put together a caravan easily. In all probability, there were twelve to fifteen traveling with an entourage.

Picture a fairly large caravan of Gentiles—we assume they were Gentiles, but the Bible doesn't say—seeking a Jewish newborn king. Imagine the sensational rumors spreading through the city. The populace knew Herod was considered a commoner, a mixture of Idumaean and Arab. He had replaced Hyrcanus, a Hasmonean, who was permitted to occupy the Jewish throne until such time as someone else could prove he was of David's royal line. Herod had married Mariamme I, a Hasmonean descendant, to make his reign legitimate. No wonder Herod and all Jerusalem were "troubled"!

Before we discuss the star of Bethlehem and Herod's reaction to the wise men, we need to mention briefly time and calendar difficulties.

God's Perfect Timing

Millions accept Jesus was born on December 25. After all, the date has been traditionally celebrated since at least the middle of the fourth century! Even so, through the centuries, many have considered that date problematic.

At one time in the East, Christians celebrated January 6 as Christ's birthday. Clement of Alexandria, in the third century, wrote that some celebrated it on April 20, while others observed May 20. In fact, every month of the year at one time or another has been postulated to have been our Lord's birth month! For example, of the eighteenth and nineteenth century commentators,

> Lightfoot assigns the Nativity to September, Lardner and Newcome to October, Wieseler to February, Paulus to March, Greswell and Alford to the 5th of April, just after the spring rains, where there is an abundance of pasture, Lichtenstein places it in July or December, Strong in August, Robinson in autumn, Clinton in spring, Andrews between the middle of December 749, to the middle of January 750 A.U.[81]

Not only is the day and month of Christ's birth disputed, but also the year. Years from 10 BC to AD 10 have been postulated to have been the year.

Sifting through the possibilities is a difficult task. Since there is such disparity of opinions and speculations, should we just throw our hands up and abandon the search as too obscure to ever ascertain?

A modern aphorism states, "If all else fails, read the directions." But an aphorism applicable to our study could be, "If all the church fathers, chronologists, and erudite commentators have made you bewildered and confused, search the Scriptures." In reality, a verse of inspired Scripture serves as better commentary for another verse than several pages of speculation.

Before we search for the month and day of Christ's birth, it would be in order to try to ascertain the year. The year of Christ's birth has been speculated, estimated, calculated, and meditated upon for centuries. Due to the various calendars and ways of reckoning of time by Babylonians, Hebrews, and Romans, it is nearly impossible to know. Many well-meaning academicians and chronologists have ascertained with supposed certainty that their specific date is correct. All are based on historical, astronomical, and biblical occurrences, yet there is wide disparity among the searchers.

Time Out for Time Considerations

Old Testament Hebrews needed understanding of the phases of the moon to ascertain the months. The Sanhedrin in Jerusalem held exclusive authority to proclaim the date of the new moon, the beginning of a new month. Its reasoning was that if the date was not proclaimed by that ruling body, different Jewish communities would be celebrating holy festivals on different days. Furthermore, the calendar was changed to make sure that the Day of Atonement didn't fall on a Friday or a Sunday; restrictive difficulties would have arisen from the intervening Sabbath. In addition, the seventh day of Tabernacles couldn't fall on a Sabbath.

The Sanhedrin also added extra months to the year when necessary. Additionally, knowledge of astronomy was necessary to correctly fix the dates of festivals, and knowing the position of the sun allowed this. Therefore, in essence, they had a lunisolar calendar. Herein lay the problem.

Their religious calendar began on Nisan 1. If only the lunar cycle was followed, the year would have 354 days. In a solar calendar of 365 days, Nisan would "shift" backward over the years. To keep the shift to a minimum and to reconcile it with the Julian calendar, a nineteen-year cycle was determined. Hebrews give credit for this discovery to Hillel II (358 BC), and others give credit to Meton (432 BC), a Greek astronomer. Generally known as Meton's cycle, the premise is that there are seven leap years in every nineteen-year cycle with seven extra months spread over the nineteen years. After a nineteen-year cycle, the sun and moon are not totally synchronized again but have an approximate equivalence. According to this Metonic cycle and the day and time of the new year lunation, the Jewish year has possible lengths of 353, 354, 355, 383, 384, and 385 days in it. To confuse matters more, in the centuries before the Gregorian calendar, the Romans intercalated their calendar without consistency or uniformity.

Alan D. Corré, professor emeritus of Hebrew studies at the University of Wisconsin in Milwaukee and others have created computer programs harmonizing the solar and lunar yearly cycle using the nineteen-year Metonic cycle. Today's Jewish calendar is based on mathematical formulas, but as Corré states, the ancient Jews didn't consistently calculate either.

This means that when the New Moon appeared, a new month was declared, and if the spring month was approaching, but there were no signs of spring, they would insert an additional month prior to the month immediately preceding the spring month, so there would be two months designated Adar, of which the second was the 'real' Adar. This means that they could, if necessary, decide not to intercalate a month, even if it seemed necessary to do so, for economic reasons, because intercalating would delay the time when they could utilize the new crop according to Biblical law.[82]

Corré cautions that even with a calculated date—easier with computerization—we can't be certain that a specific date was actually observed as such in a particular year. So even with all the wonderful modern tools at our disposal, we are back to where we started. After all, even though a computer may calculate faster than we can comprehend, if incorrect data is the input, incorrect data will be the output.

We will use our knowledge of the Scriptures to determine as closely as possible the date of our Lord's birth. We will continue to utilize secular historians to affirm or deny our best speculations.

Year of Christ's Birth

King Herod died painfully at his winter palace in Jericho, probably of syphilis. Secular historians have for centuries assumed he died shortly before Passover near the end of March 4 BC, after a lunar eclipse, which would put the year of Christ's birth at 6 or 7 BC. This assumption is also assuming that Josephus, who wrote after the fact, was specific enough. In this case, what is questionable is not that Herod died after an eclipse of the moon and before Passover, but which eclipse did Josephus mean?

To determine Herod's year of death, let's examine possible lunar eclipses occurring around that time. A lunar eclipse can happen three times in a year but only when there is a full moon. In 4 BC, there were two: one on Adar 14–15 (March 13) and one on Tishri 14–15 (September 5). Both were partial and wouldn't have been particularly noticeable in Jerusalem. In 3 BC, there were no eclipses. In 2 BC, there were two partial eclipses. In 1 BC, on Tebbeth 14–15 (January 10), a total eclipse lasted for fifty-one minutes near midnight centered at 15 degrees east longitude. This one would have been obvious in Jerusalem and is probably the one viewed before Herod died.

That would put Christ's birth in 3 or 2 BC. (Detailed calculations for lunar eclipses can be found at the National Aeronautics and Space Administration.[83]) Also, perhaps with the recent discovery of Herod's sarcophagus and continued work by archaeologists, this fact will be confirmed or denied in the near future.

Beautiful Star of Bethlehem: Was It Planet, Angel, or Star?

The Bible has much to say regarding stars. "When I consider Thy heavens, the work of Thy fingers, the moon and the stars which Thou hast ordained" (Psalm 8:3). They serve a purpose.

> And God said, "Let there be lights in the firmament of the heaven to divide the day from the night, and let them be for signs and for seasons, and for days and years, And let them be for lights in the firmament of the heaven to give light upon the earth; and it was so" (Genesis 1:14-15).

God not only knows how many stars He created, He named them all: "He tells the number of the stars; He calls them all by name" (Psalm 147:4). He divided them into constellations.

> For the stars of heaven and the constellations thereof shall not give their light: the sun shall be darkened in his going forth, and the moon shall not cause her light to shine (Isaiah 13:10).

The names of some are revealed to us.

> Canst thou bind the sweet influences of Pleiades, or loose the bands of Orion? Canst thou bring forth Mazzaroth in his season? or canst thou guide Arcturus with his sons (Job 38:32)?

God displays His majesty and glory by His starry universe. He tells the message of redemption every night through the witness of the constellations, from Virgo the Virgin through Leo, the Lion of the tribe of Judah. From the most suave sinner to the most unsophisticated sinner, we are all without excuse.

The heavens declare the glory of God; and the firmament shows his handywork. Day unto day utters speech, and night unto night shows knowledge. There is no speech nor language, where their voice is not heard (Psalm 19:1-3).

Is it so surprising, then, that the magi were led by a star? Astronomers and Bible teachers have for centuries felt the need to "explain" the star. Novas, supernovas, planetary conjunctions, and comets have been identified as "the" star. In all, there are about eight different theories. Let's look very briefly at a few.

The Comet Theory

Origen, in the third century, was the first to propose an identification of the star. The object of his explanation was a comet, definitely an attention getter. Comets brilliantly stretch across the sky, appearing to have a front and back and giving the impression of pointing at something. What we now know as Halley's comet has been reasoned to have been the star. Halley's comet comes around every seventy-six years. It appeared in late summer of 12 BC, too early for the birth of Christ. The Hale-Bopp comet appeared in 1997. Before that, it appeared 4,000 years ago, and it will not appear for another 2,000 years, so that's out of the running.

Comets were generally associated with bad news such as impending war or the death of a prominent person such as a king. Thus, the comet theory didn't gain much popularity. However, in 1991, the theory gained favor again with the work of astronomer Dr. Colin Humphreys. He cited Chinese records of a comet appearing sometime between March 9 and April 6, 5 BC. The Chinese observed it for seventy days.

Based on further research, Humphreys calculated the birth of Christ to have occurred between March 9 and May 4, 5 BC. An April birth would be consistent with shepherds in the fields, but the Roman registrations generally took place from August through October. Those two facts are incongruent, and April can probably be ruled out.

The Saturn/Jupiter /Mars Triple-Conjunction Theory

Another early attempt to define the star dates to the eighth century. Astronomer and astrologer Masha'allah thought the massing of the planets of Jupiter, Saturn, and Mars, which occurred three times over a two-year period, signaled the magi to begin their journey. In February 8 BC, Jupiter and Saturn disappeared behind the setting sun. In March 8 BC, they reappeared close together, which they do every twenty years. They appeared to pull away from each other but then pulled toward each other and had another massing on September 29, 7 BC.

Normal movement of Earth caused the planets to appear to reverse direction for the second meeting. On February 26, 6 BC, Mars joined Saturn and Jupiter for their third conjunction. The first conjunction would have happened rising in the eastern sky. The other two would have fallen in line for a journey from Jerusalem to Bethlehem. But double conjunctions of Saturn and Jupiter are normal. How would the magi have known that Mars would join Jupiter and Saturn? The time lines do not fall into place for this to have been the star the magi followed.

The Nova/Supernova Theory

Another popular theory was proposed by astronomer Johannes Kepler in 1614, when he observed a supernova. Scientists inform us that when a star explodes, it may reach luminosity one billion times that of the sun. As the light reaches us, a new star appears in the sky visible even during the daytime. Ancient Chinese astronomers recorded a supernova appearing on July 5, 1054, in the constellation of Taurus that was visible for twenty-three days. They also recorded one in March-April 5 BC in Capricorn that was visible for seventy days.

A supernova wouldn't move through the sky, nor would it stand still. Furthermore, supernovas were never associated with the birth of a king.

The Spica Theory

Spica, the brightest star in the Virgo constellation, in ancient Arabic was known as Al Zimach, "the branch." Its Latin name, Spica, means "ear of corn." The constellation Virgo is important in that it was her seed who was prophesied. Egyptian zodiacs call her Aspolia, "ears of corn," or "the seed." In Egyptian religion, she represented Isis. Greek mythology represented the virgin as Ceres, who also held grain in her hand. We can immediately recognize these corruptions of God's prophetic Word. "Behold I will bring forth my SERVANT the BRANCH" (Zechariah 3:8), and "In that day shall the BRANCH of the Lord be beautiful and glorious, and the fruit of the earth shall be excellent and comely for them that are escaped of Israel" (Isaiah 4:2).

According to astronomers using precise computer calculations, Spica rose exactly 90 degrees in 2 BC. But stars don't rise and set in precisely the same position every night. Over the years, these positions change. Hipparchus knew this and calculated well. Nevertheless, modern astronomers tell us that Hipparchus's star charts were in error. He didn't have computer technology at his disposal. Consequently, if the magi used his charts in anticipation of the Jewish Messiah and the rising of Spica in the east, they would have been expecting Spica in a 90 degree location but in 20 BC rather than around 2 BC.

Herod asked the wise men exactly when the star had appeared, when they had observed it, not when did they calculated it should have appeared. Herod knew the magi followed a physical light.

Discovery of Uranus by Magi

It is theorized that a magos discovered Uranus, that due to its faint light it was lost to view but later sighted again as they neared Bethlehem.

Five planets have been known from man's earliest ages. Consequently, the discovery of a new planet brings jubilation among astronomers, as it did when Sir William Hershel discovered and named Uranus in 1781.

Uranus is faint and generally visible only in a clear sky and when one is observing another planet, such as Saturn. Uranus and Saturn may have been observed in conjunction in 9 BC, and Uranus may have been observed in conjunction with Venus in April AD 6. The question arises, how did a faint planet, Uranus, notify the magi of its importance in the birth of Messiah? Very unlikely.

Meteors

One has to be grasping at straws to imagine a meteor as the star of Bethlehem; nevertheless, one of the theories states that this is possible. Pieces of rock and iron floating in space fell into Earth's atmosphere and were heated by friction. They appeared as streaks of light, which the magi saw close to home and again as they neared Bethlehem about two years after. But meteors could not be said to rise; nor would they stand over a specific location.

Planetary Conjunctions

After having delved into eight possible naturalistic explanations of the star of Bethlehem, including the five previously mentioned, the most believable natural phenomena are the planetary conjunctions that were visible between 3 and 2 BC were researched by astronomer Dr. Ernest L. Martin.[84] But let's return to the Bible for our clues and some backdating to arrive at our destination to see if his research is believable or acceptable.

According to Luke 3:1, John the Baptist began preaching in the wilderness in the fifteenth year of the reign of Tiberius Caesar. We know from historians and coin dating that Caesar Augustus died AD 14 and Tiberius began his reign on August 19, AD 14. Add fifteen years to that, and we have the year covering August 19, AD 28 to August 18, AD 29. However, Luke probably thought in terms of Tishri 1 of the Jewish calendar. Thus, Tiberius's fifteenth year would have been from Tishri 1, AD 27, to Tishri 1, AD 28. Priests had to be thirty years of age, so John would have been around thirty in AD 28. Therefore, John's birth would have been around 3 BC. We know John was approximately six months older than Christ. Thus, Christ would also have to have been born around 3 BC.

What were the unusual planetary configurations that got the magi's attention? The first of six planetary events occurred in the predawn hours on August 12, 3 BC; Jupiter and Venus, two of the brightest planets, came within 0.23 degrees of one another. (To clarify, astronomical facts along with possible astrological interpretations will be given. It is assumed that readers understand the astrological names of the zodiac are corruptions of the Jewish mazzaroth.)

Jupiter was known as the father of the gods, Venus or Ishtar, the goddess of fertility. With the two in apparent "marriage union," did this signify the birth of a king? At the same time the Sun (father), the Moon (mother), and Mercury (messenger of the gods) were all in Leo. The Bible speaks of the association between Leo and the tribe of Judah.

The union of Jupiter and Venus was followed on September 1 by Venus and Mercury coming within 0.36 degrees of one another. At that time, they were in Leo, but the Sun was entering the constellation of Virgo, the virgin.

The date given to Herod by the magi might have been September 14, 3 BC, after Jupiter had moved on. That was the date Jupiter had the first of three conjunctions with Regulus, the brightest star in the Leo constellation, often called the king star because of its association with the conception or birth of kings. It is between the feet of the lion in the constellation. "Weep not; behold, the Lion of the tribe of Judah, the Root of David, has prevailed to open the book, and to loose the seven seals thereof" (Revelation 5:5).

The second of the three conjunctions took place February 17, and the last conjunction was on May 9, 3 BC. At that time, Jupiter and

Regulus were 1.06 degrees apart. This conjunction wouldn't have been seen in Jerusalem, but it undoubtedly further alerted the magi.

On June 17, 3 BC, Jupiter and Venus appeared to merge, again in the sign of Judah (Leo) and during a full moon. To the human eye, they would have seemed to have been one object; astronomers say they were 0.05 degrees apart.

The final scene of this planetary drama occurred on August 27, 2 BC. At this point in the two-year celestial drama, Mars and Jupiter passed within 0.14 degrees of one another. Except for Saturn, all the major planets were massed in Leo. Not only that, Jupiter, the king planet, united with Regulus, the king star, on three occasions that year. Jupiter and Regulus would have appeared as one extremely bright star. In summary, Jupiter would have had three conjunctions with other planets and three conjunctions with Regulus.

But Jupiter's job wasn't quite finished. The magi observed that Jupiter appeared to head westward each morning when they made their predawn observations. They followed it until they reached Jerusalem, the city of the king. At Jerusalem, their instructions were to go to Bethlehem. The star stood over Bethlehem, not the specific house but the town.

Astronomers inform us planets do seem to stop at times in their courses when it is time for their retrogression or progression. Jupiter evidently became stationary when it reached its zenith over Bethlehem, where it stayed for six days. The time? December 25, 2 BC. The constellation? Jupiter stopped in Virgo. This was not the time of Christ's birth, but the magi could have presented their gifts to the holy family then.

Herod was called "great" because of his political might and his outstanding building projects, which archaeologists and historians confirm yet today. However, he could have been called Herod the Murderer, Herod the Adulterer, or many other uncomplimentary appellations. Besides the uncooperative Pharisees mentioned earlier, over his lifetime, he put to death two of his own sons by his wife Mariamme I, Aristobulus and Alexander. He later killed Mariamme I and Antipater, a son by wife Doris, another of his eight wives. He also caused to be slain the brother and mother of Mariamme I as well as her grandfather, John Hyrcanus. Jerusalem well knew Herod's rivalries, jealousies, and fits of uncontrollable rage toward anyone he considered even a slight threat to his kingship. When the magi's entourage enquired of the newborn King, inhabitants of Jerusalem may have tiptoed gingerly and avoided all appearances of collusion, fearing what might have happened. They were soon to once again observe Herod's furor.

At the time of the magi's visit to Mary and Joseph's dwelling, Christ was no longer referred to as a *brephos* (infant) as in Luke 2:12, but as a *paidion* (toddler) in Matthew 2:11. Christ may have been a year and a half to nearly two years old. When Herod inquired exactly when the star first appeared, he had no way of knowing if it signaled conception or birth. He took no chance of any of the male toddlers being a possible threat to his kingdom.

Herod had slain all Bethlehem's two-year-olds and under. Due to the small population of Bethlehem and its environs, the number slain may have been only twenty children, according to Edersheim; not a large number in the eyes of the world, and not large enough for Josephus to mention. But Matthew informed us that Herod's despicable act fulfilled the prophecy of Jeremiah 31:15: "Rachel weeping for her children."

Rebuttal of the Planetary Conjunction Hypothesis

Reading about planetary conjunctions in this light excites our imaginations, and we are inclined to believe what we read. It is certainly consistent with our human reasoning. Unfortunately for that theory, a good argument is given against the planetary conjunction concept on the grounds of the usage of the Greek words. Matthew's account states that there was one star, *astros*. It is reasoned that if Matthew had meant a conjunction of planets, he could have said so. The Greeks had the word, *planētēs,* from which we get our word *planet.*

Obviously, planetary and star configurations held great significance for the magi; otherwise, they wouldn't have started on such a remarkable journey whatever the year. We cannot sell the stars short in importance. The starry heavens continue to reveal the redemption story.

Another alternative is the miracle of an angel leading, guiding, and stopping. Angels are messengers who appeared in dreams or in person to warn or instruct. We know angels are sometimes referred to as stars. "The seven stars are the angels of the seven churches" (Revelation 1:20). God had created countless stars and innumerable angels. He would have had no need to create a new angel or a new star for the task of guiding the magi. Had He so desired, and perhaps He did, He could have plucked a star from the far reaches of the universe and brought it forward for this miraculous job, or He could have commissioned one of his holy messengers as he did Gabriel.

Nevertheless, all the descriptions of the star relate to physically observable attributes of stars, not angels. This particular star was seen "at its rising" in the east, appeared at a specific time, went before them, and stood over. If it had been an angel, neither the wise men nor Matthew knew it! God is omniscient; He created all languages and can express Himself. We must give Him credit for knowing what He means. He said "star"; we must not presume otherwise. "Keep back thy servant also from presumptuous sins" (Psalm 19:13).

Did the magi realize that the Creator directed them at every turn and fork in the dusty thoroughfare, around every obstacle, and past Herod's evil intentions? Whatever method the Creator employed to get them there (new star, old star), the journey of the magi can be viewed only as truly phenomenal and nothing short of awesome. Alleluia!

John's Conception and Birth

From extrabiblical evidence, it is quite plausible the year of Christ's birth could well have been in 3 BC, but what of the month? Most biblical commentaries begin with the conception of John the Baptist to pinpoint the natal day of John and Christ. Let's assume 3 BC is correct and return to Luke to ascertain those months. A reading of most of Luke 1 is necessary to glean the information we need. Verses 5–28 follow.

> There was in the days of Herod, the king of Judaea, a certain priest named Zacharias, of the course of Abia: and his wife was of the daughters of Aaron, and her name was Elisabeth. And they were both righteous before God, walking in all the commandments and ordinances of the Lord blameless. And they had no child, because that Elisabeth was barren, and they both were now well stricken in years. And it came to pass, that while he executed the priest's office before God in the order of his course,
>
> According to the custom of the priest's office, his lot was to burn incense when he went into the temple of the Lord. And the whole multitude of the people were praying without at the time of incense. And there appeared unto him an angel of the Lord standing on the right side of the altar of incense. And when Zacharias saw him, he was troubled, and fear fell upon him. But the angel said unto him, Fear not, Zacharias: for thy prayer is heard; and thy wife Elisabeth shall bear thee a son, and thou shall call his name John. And thou shall have joy and gladness; and many shall rejoice at his birth. For he shall be great in the sight of the Lord, and shall drink neither wine nor strong drink; and he shall be filled with the Holy Ghost, even from his mother's womb. And many of the children of Israel shall he turn to the Lord their God. And he shall go before Him in the spirit and power of Elias, to turn the hearts of the fathers to the children, and the disobedient to the wisdom of the just; to make ready a people prepared for the Lord. And Zacharias said unto the angel, Whereby

shall I know this? for I am an old man, and my wife well stricken in years.

And the angel answering said unto him, I am Gabriel, that stand in the presence of God; and am sent to speak unto thee, and to shew thee these glad tidings.

And it came to pass, that, as soon as the days of his ministration were accomplished, he departed to his own house. And after those days his wife Elisabeth conceived, and hid herself five months, saying, Thus hath the Lord dealt with me in the days wherein he looked on me, to take away my reproach among men.

And in the sixth month the angel Gabriel was sent from God unto a city of Galilee, named Nazareth, To a virgin espoused to a man whose name was Joseph, of the house of David; and the virgin's name was Mary. And the angel came in unto her, and said, Hail, thou that art highly favored, the Lord is with thee: blessed art thou among women.

The Twenty-Four Courses and the Course of Abia (Abijah)

To gain understanding concerning the priestly courses, we must study several Hebrew Scriptures. A good place to start is with 1 Chronicles 24, in which the twenty-four courses or shifts are specified. These had been established by Samuel and David in 1 Chronicles 9:22 because of the large number of descendants in the line of Aaron.

The Aaronic priesthood had become so large that its members couldn't all officiate at one time in the temple. Consequently, it became necessary to divide the priests into twenty-four groups to maintain an orderly progression to fulfill the obligations of worship. Of the original twenty-four courses, only four returned from captivity. Ezra authorized the four to be divided into twenty-four. Even though twenty of these family courses were different from the original twenty-four, the original family names were kept to reflect the courses as they had been in David's time.

Two times each year, the twenty-four groups served for one week in the temple. The first course served the first week beginning at noon on the Sabbath, the second course the second week beginning at noon on the next Sabbath, and so on. At the end of six months, the twenty-four courses would have accomplished their administrations. Then the order or series started over.

The lunisolar calendar of the Jews contained about fifty-one weeks. As stated before, at times, the Jewish authorities added an extra month of thirty days. Twenty-four courses times two weeks per year leaves three weeks unaccounted for. During those three weeks, the regular rotation of service didn't prevail. Those were times of three major Jewish holy weeks: Passover, Pentecost, and Tabernacles. During those weeks, all Jewish men were required to travel to Jerusalem. All courses of priests served together to accommodate the crowds.

In 1 Chronicles 24, we get in detail the names of the twenty-four priestly courses from the first, Jehoirib's, to the twenty-fourth, Mazzaiah's. Zechariah was of the course of Abia (Abijah), the eighth course, thus his term of service would have been the eighth week of each term. The first term began Nisan 1, the second on Tishri 1, seven months later.

Zechariah was probably around sixty at the time of his service, and the lot fell to him to offer incense, a once-in-a lifetime privilege; therefore, knowing he would be allowed to offer incense this one time only, he probably looked forward to it with grave reverence. In the prescribed ritual, the priests prayed in silence as the cloud of fragrant incense rose to the Holy Place from the golden altar. Zechariah prepared to bow in worship, but Gabriel, standing between the altar and the candlestick, interrupted his worship. The angel informed Zechariah his prayer had been heard and he would indeed have a son as he had longed and often prayed for. The shock overwhelmed Zechariah; he questioned the angel how that could possibly be. As a sign that it would definitely be, Zechariah was struck dumb from that point on until after the birth of his son, John.

We don't know in which of the two ecclesiastical shifts the angel came to Zechariah and granted his prayer for a son. If it were the Nisan (March) administration, the beginning of the ecclesiastical year, Zechariah would have been serving from May 19 to May 26. Some feel that due to Zechariah's impairment of dumbness, he would have been disqualified from serving as per Leviticus 21:16 and would have left for home immediately. Allowing time for Zechariah to travel home and possibly rest a little, John would have been conceived somewhere near the end of May or beginning of June. The human gestation period is 280 days, ten lunar months; hence, John's birth would have been in March 3 BC.

We know from Scripture that Mary conceived sometime during the sixth month of Elizabeth's pregnancy. If John were born in March, Christ would have been born in September.

On the other hand, if Luke is referring to the second six months of service or the autumn administrations, then of course John would have been born in September and Christ the following March/April by our general subjective reasoning.

An opposing viewpoint is stated in the *Catholic Encyclopedia*. According to rabbinical tradition, the first class of service, Jehoiarib, was serving in the temple when Jerusalem was destroyed in AD 70. Counting backward to AUC 748 (4 BC), they calculate Zechariah served October 2–9 with John's conception in October and Christ's in March. Thus Christ, presumably, could have been born in December.

According to Dr. Corré's perpetual Jewish/civil calendar, October 2–9 of 4 BC would have been on Friday, and we know each priestly course began duty at noon on the Sabbath.

Once again, we rely on human reasoning to fill in the gaps. Roman censuses were taken generally from August to October, not in the spring rainy season or wintry cold months, when it would have been harder to travel. In addition, it is unlikely that Christ was born in one of the three holy weeks of Passover, Pentecost, or Tabernacles because Jewish males were required to be in Jerusalem during those times (Deuteronomy 16:6, 11, 16) and not each "into his own city" as was the case of Mary and Joseph going to Bethlehem.

Let's return to Dr. Martin's research. He takes us a step further in his recalculation. Using the information contained symbolically in Revelation 12 and his knowledge of astronomy, he concludes Christ was born just after sundown on September 11, 3 BC in the sign of Virgo. September 11 in 3 BC was Tishri 1 on the Jewish calendar. Today, it is known as Rosh Hashanah, or as the Bible calls it in Leviticus 23:23–27, the Day of Trumpets, the Jewish new year!

Calculations of Dr. E. W. Bullinger

James Ussher and E. W. Bullinger agree Christ was born 4,000 Anno Mundi (in the year of the world). Ussher interprets the Gregorian year as 5 BC, whereas Bullinger thinks it's 4 BC. Those familiar with Bullinger's works appreciate his scholarly and holy dedication toward arriving at truth. Based on his knowledge of the twenty-four Jewish courses and his knowledge of secular history, he has concluded that John was conceived on Sivan 23, our June 23–24, and that he was born on Nisan 7, our March 28–29.

Bullinger calculates the miraculous conception of Mary as occurring on Tebeth 1, our December 25, with birth the following Tisri 15, our September 29.

Even though Bullinger had written *The Witness of the Stars*, detailing meanings of the twelve signs of the mazzaroth, he refrained from stating that Christ was born in any specific sign, such as Virgo. Bullinger's chosen date of September 29 would not be the sign of Virgo, but would be in the mazzaroth sign, Mozanaim, the "scales"; in Latin, it would be Libra, still meaning "the scales."

It is intriguing to observe how a noted Bible scholar and an accomplished astronomer working approximately one hundred years apart arrived at similar natal dates based on similar basic information.

Other than their difference on the date of King Herod's death, another difference in their calculations centers around the dates of the beginning of the ministry of John and Christ, who were both "around thirty" in the "fifteenth year of the reign of Tiberius" (Luke 3:1). Martin doesn't antedate or count the two-year coregency of Tiberius and Augustus as part of the fifteen-year reign of Tiberius, though Bullinger does. Thus, a difference exists in their conclusions.

We can safely conclude Christ was born from 5 to 2 BC and most likely in the autumn. Anything more dogmatic than this would make us vulnerable to spiritual attack. "Be sober, be vigilant; because your adversary the devil, as a roaring lion, walketh about, seeking whom he may devour" (1 Peter 5:8).

Why Celebrate Christ's Nativity on December 25?

There were several pagan celebrations occurring around December 25 that get credit, probably unjustly, for celebrating on that date. We will look briefly at the better-known ones.

Attis

We mentioned Attis and Cybele in the chapters on pagan spring celebrations. Attis worship began around 200 BC, and many versions of the Attis myth abound. Most of them are carnally explicit and could not in good conscience be told in these pages. However, we will briefly summarize. Attis was a Phrygian god of fertility and vegetation, or pine tree spirit, who in a fit of intense love and madness for Cybele, castrated himself under a pine tree and died on March 25. On the same date, he reentered his virgin mother, Nana—other versions have other names—to beget his reincarnation with his birth following on December 25.

Another version of the Attis myth that Bible detractors like to repeat is similar to Christ's birth. Attis, son of a virgin, Nana, was born December 25, was crucified on a tree, spent three days in the underworld, and arose on Sunday as the solar deity. Followers symbolically ate his body in the form of bread.

Dionysus

Another pagan deity worshipped throughout much of the Middle East including Jerusalem was Dionysus (also known as Bacchus or Liber). Greek mythology identifies him as the son of Zeus, the chief god, and Semele, a mortal. Zeus had disguised himself as a mortal and visited Semele as mortal, impregnating her with Dionysus. As the myth goes, Zeus appeared to his wife Hera and his lover, Semele, in blazing thunderbolts. Semele, being mortal, couldn't withstand the divine fire and burned to death. Zeus rescued Dionysus from the womb, sewed him into his thigh, and carried him to fetal maturity. Dionysus, for this reason, was sometimes called "twice-born."

As the only god born of a mortal parent, Dionysus had powers from both worlds. He was the god of wine, fertility, and pleasure, but his specialty was wine. Winter months were months of suffering for him, and orgiastic celebrations by women were held to comfort him. These celebrations were held in December, January, and February. As a god of the earth, people considered winter as his death and spring as his rebirth. Dionysus is also connected with the savage rite of *omophagia* (eating raw flesh). His followers symbolically ate his flesh and blood in the form of bread and wine. Some say one of his festivals was held December 25.

Osiris

The etymology and pronunciation of the Egyptian Osiris's name is uncertain since it is derived from hieroglyphic form and with no vowels. Osiris worship occurred as early as 2400 BC. Considered a merciful judge in the underworld, Osiris also granted life and all vegetation along the Nile.

Osiris was the brother and husband of Isis and the son of the sky goddess, Nut, and the Earth god, Geb. His is another rather gory tale. Killed by his brother and placed in a wooden chest, Osiris was thrown into the Nile. The chest floated to Byblos on the Syrian coast, where Isis found it and returned it to Egypt. His brother discovered the chest, tore the body into fourteen pieces, and scattered it over the land. Isis searched until she had found all fourteen pieces and brought Osiris back to life. He remained in the underworld, some say, as the judge of the dead.

Somewhere along the line, Osiris became identified as the sun god. J. G. Frazier in *The Golden Bough*, published in 1922, believes this is dubious and based on vague information. Frazier maintained Osiris to be a god of vegetation rather than a god of the dead or a sun god.

Egyptians associated three stars of the constellation Orion (Orion's belt) with Osiris. The Giza pyramid complex consisting of the three pyramids Giza, Khafre, and Menkaure is said by astronomers to be a sky map of the belt of Orion, or Osiris.

Mithra

The Persian cult of Mithra dates to around 1400 BC. This exclusively male cult worshipped the sun and was heavily involved in astrology. In this myth, Mithra sprang from a rock, fully grown and armed with a torch and a knife. Shepherds tending their flocks witnessed this miracle and ran to offer him the firstfruits of their harvests and flocks. Seven levels of initiation represented by seven ladder rungs led to immortality. Initiates into the cult killed a bull and baptized other candidates in the bull's blood; this reenacted Mithras's killing of the bull of creation as well as symbolizing victory over death. Emblems of the zodiac surrounding Mithras alluded to his status as a god of the complete year. He too, supposedly, was born December 25.

Saturnalia

From December 17 to December 21, Romans celebrated the Saturnalia festival, named after Saturn, the god often depicted as a gloomy old man with a sickle in his hand, like Old Father Time. And well he should have been gloomy. One version of the myth states that he ate his own children rather than let them become greater than he. On the other hand, he is often depicted as a beneficent, kindly king. His female counterpart, Lua, a goddess of death and destruction, accompanied him.

For the sun to rise again from such a gloomy time of year, the old man had to be banished. Feasting and drinking were necessary to bring on the rebirth of the sun and the renewal of optimism. Rome's streets filled with licentious revelers chanting the season's greetings, "Io Saturnalia." Celebrants lit fires representing the sun and no doubt to keep warm.

Worshippers laid sacrifices in front of Saturn's temple. Saturn's statue, generally tied at the feet with bands of wool, was untied. Exuberant carousers invited him to join the fun. During this eight-day period, schools recessed and gifts were exchanged. Social order was reversed in that slaves could be disrespectful to their masters and gambling flourished with official permission. This custom symbolically revived the golden age of Italy when it was governed by a benevolent monarch named Saturn and all men held all things in common, no masters or slaves. Masters made sure, however, that slaves didn't subvert the existing social order, for in a few days, the old way of life returned.

Some authors identified Saturn with Baal. Moreover, it's relatively certain the deity with two goat legs, Satur in Greek mythology, is also identified with Saturn, who in turn older Jewish writings identified as Satan. The planet took its name from the god, and the seventh day of the week became his day, Saturn's day, now Saturday.

Sol Invictus

As we have seen by naming just a few gods, the Romans worshipped a bevy of gods and sun gods around the time of the winter solstice. Roman emperor Aurelian was hostile to all things Christian; he chose Sol, the sun god, as his preferred god. Aurelian instituted a college of pontifices and dedicated a temple on December 25, 274, to Sol Invictus.

The Roman Empire was collapsing under the weight of its moral decay and internal rebellions in outlying territories. Aurelian's dedication to Sol Invictus unified the various pagan cults, a move he hoped would rejuvenate the empire and simultaneously make a political statement against Christianity.

By AD 354, the festival Dies Natalis Solis Invicti, "birthday of the unconquered sun," emphasized the fact that several gods could be worshipped collectively. The apparent intended message was this: in spite of shortened daylight hours and the apparent death of the sun, with lighting of fires representing the sun and festivities to honor the sun, the sun would ultimately prevail and rule the heavens again.

Some political posturing thrown in might also have convinced the people that their sun worship would keep Rome in its dominant, worldwide role.

Pagan rites and celebrations get credit for establishing December 25 as Christ's birthday, but there are other considerations.

The Jewish fest of Hanukkah (Chanukkah) is held near the beginning of winter. The New Testament refers to is as the Feast of Dedication. "And it was at Jerusalem the Feast of Dedication, and it was winter" (John 10:22). God didn't authorize this feast as He had the other three weekly festivals; nevertheless, Hanukkah was a happy time of feasting and gift giving. It commemorated the time the temple had been cleansed of Gentile idols and temple services restored in 164 BC. Lamps and torches lit the inside and outside of houses, synagogue, and temple for the entire eight days. Josephus referred to the celebration as the Feast of Lamps and indicated that an elevated mood prevailed in the Jewish community at that joyous time.

Because of variance of the Jewish months, this feast could be early (November 28), or late (December 27). In 3 BC, the eight-day festival of Hanukkah began on December 23. What if the magi had indeed presented their gifts to Christ on December 25 as Martin reasons? What if not in that particular year but in another year, the magi had presented their gifts coincidentally with Hanukkah? Would this not be vindication for maintaining the gift-giving custom on December 25?

In our chapter concerning Christ's resurrection, we concluded that Christ rose on Nisan 17 according to the Jewish calendar. We won't go into calendar difficulties again, but we will just remember that for the most part, early Christians separated themselves from Judaism and entered their own calendar world.

Although not found in Scriptures, Judaism at one time believed that the prophets died on the same date as their conception or birth. This idea carried over into the early speculations of Christ's death and birth. Second-century Christians first thought March 25 or April 6 was the date of Christ's birth. They changed their reasoning and assigned

March 25 as the date of Christ's conception with birth following nine months later on December 25. Nine months from April 6 is January 6, now celebrated by Roman Catholics and others as the Epiphany, the commemoration of the magi's visit to Christ. The Armenian Apostolic Church continues to observe January 6–7 as His birthday.

From the current Roman Catholic standpoint, arriving at the December 25 date had nothing to do with a Roman pagan feast. Roman Catholics realize, along with the rest of us, that Christ was probably not born on December 25, but they maintain the date arose from those early efforts at determining the date of His death.

Contemporary Roman Catholic apologists also protest that when Emperor Aurelian dedicated December 25 to Sol Invictus in AD 274, he did so to divert attention from Christian celebrations already prevalent in the empire. They assert that Christians later reappropriated the day from the Birth of the Unconquered Sun to the Sun of Righteousness. The title comes from a messianic prophecy: "But unto you that fear My name shall the Sun of Righteousness arise with healing in His wings, and ye shall go forth and grow up as calves in the stall" (Malachi 4:2).

Bullinger affirmed that Christ was conceived on December 25 and born on September 29, a date long celebrated as Michaelmas, or Festival of Michael and All Angels, though no one could remember why. To Bullinger, the answer was obvious. The birth of the King of Israel, the only begotten Son of God, surpassed in relevance or importance anything the world had witnessed up to that point. Although unnamed in Matthew or Luke, who better to announce such a transcendent event than the prince of the children of Israel, the head of the heavenly host, Archangel Michael? (See Daniel 10:21 and Daniel 12:1.)

Natal Day or Christ's Mass?

There is evidence from debates around AD 200 of early church fathers commemorating Christ's birth, though as seen before, dates observed varied widely, and gaudy decorations and elaborate feasting didn't appear to be involved. Around AD 245, Origen protested the idea stating that only sinners celebrated their birthdays.

Various authorities assume none of the early believers observed any day as Christ's birthday until around AD 336. Maybe we have jumped to conclusions. An analogy might be made to the doctrine of the Trinity. Should we assume the Trinity was not taught until it was set forth in the statements of Tertullian, Hippolytus, and Novatian in the years preceding the Council of Nicea? That assumption would be wrong. Those ante-Nicene fathers were battling the forces of Gnosticism, Monarchianism, and modalism. Attacks and misinterpretations against Greek Scriptures forced them to define exactly what it was they believed. Likewise, we know earlier believers battled immorality and paganism on all sides. It is entirely possible—whether right or wrong—they felt impelled to define a date for Christ's birth. Subsequently, in imitation of Jewish festivals, Christians developed the Feast of the Nativity. As of AD 354, December 25 became the recognized date.

In spite of that, it was not until AD 435 that Pope Sixtus III performed an official Christ Mass. Our English word *Christmas* is a contraction of the two words whose derivation are from Middle English *Christemasse* and Old English *Cristes maesse*, first recorded in 1038.

During the Middle Ages, feasting, gift giving, dancing, and caroling were routine. With the arrival of the Reformation and into the 1800s, Protestants criticized the celebration as trappings of popery; they were referring to the Mass and its teaching of transubstantiation. In short, transubstantiation is the belief that the bread and wine of the Eucharist literally become the actual body and blood of Christ. Hence, Christ would be sacrificing His body anew and constantly suffering. What happened on Calvary happened once. "For Christ also hath once suffered for sins, the just for the unjust, that He might bring us to God, being put to death in the flesh, but quickened by the Spirit" (1 Peter 3:18).

England's Puritan rulers banned Christmas in 1647 after Puritan sympathizer King Charles's victory in Parliament. Rioting followed for several weeks in many cities. The ban ended in 1660, following the election of a different Parliament, but reformers and Puritans didn't cease their disapproval.

In the American colonies, emulating Puritan examples and objections, Christmas was outlawed from 1659 to 1681 in Boston, punishable by a five-shilling fine. Although banned in Boston, New York and Virginia celebrated the holiday, and gradually, other colonies did also.

Clement Moore's poem *A Visit from Saint Nicholas* and several short stories of the 1880s revived interest in Christmas. Alabama became the first to declare Christmas a legal holiday in 1836; Oklahoma was the last in 1907.

Protestantism, most of whose members no longer protest much, accepts the generic term *Christmas* and doesn't stop to consider the origin of the word. People in general, even those untrained in religious matters, have a vague understanding of the significance of the birthday of Jesus. The secular world wants to keep all the fun trimmings and dispense with nativity scenes and all things biblical. In contrast, the religious world battles to keep Christ in Christmas.

At this point in our history, Christmas is recognized as a federal holiday. The U.S. Supreme Court's decision on December 19, 2000, upheld the decision of *Ganulin v. United States* (1999), "the establishment of Christmas Day as a legal public holiday does not violate the Establishment Clause because it has a valid secular purpose."

Current Customs in the United States

From scriptural and sublime realities of the birth of Messiah, we now turn to current culture. Several subtopics could be presented at this point, but three will suffice. Sincere Bible believers with whom we speak seem to be concerned with what to teach children about mistletoe and other greenery customs, Santa Claus, and Christmas trees.

Mistletoe

Mistletoe's common name may have come from the old German word *Mist,* meaning "dung," and *Tang,* "branch." Originally, mistletoe referred to *Viscum album,* a plant native to Europe and northern Asia that is related to *Phoradendron serotinum* of North America.

Mistletoe is a semiparasitic plant in that it is able to produce some photosynthesis on its own, but it relies mainly on the host tree for mineral nutrients and water. It may cause complete destruction of its host, or it may only stunt its growth. Modern naturalists recognize its better characteristic of providing food and habitat for forest and woodland animals. Mistletoe produces white berries near the time of the winter solstice and is popular throughout the Christmas season because of an old recognized English custom: men and women meeting under the mistletoe are required to kiss.

Of course, today's Bible believers are not so much concerned with physical characteristics but with pagan practices of bygone eras in northern Europe. The mistletoe fruit's content is suggestive of human semen, undoubtedly influencing druid priests to prescribe herbal mistletoe remedies for sterility and related reproductive maladies. As might be expected with any herbal healing, superstitions surrounded its use.

Mistletoe was abundant on apple and other trees, but when found on the oak, the spirit tree of the druids, it was more highly venerated. In fact, nothing was more sacred than the mistletoe and the oak on which it grew. Mistletoe remains green in winter after the oak has lost all its leaves, which may have led to belief that the life of the oak was in the mistletoe. Evidence suggests some tribes used the mistletoe as their symbol. Not surprisingly, tribal names also indicated some tribal beliefs that they were descended from sacred tree spirits. It is worth noting one particular tribal name, Vivisci, translates to "Mistletoe men."

Superstitious rituals accompanied gathering of mistletoe. Tradition mandated it had to be culled on the sixth day of the new moon. All preparations for feasting and sacrifices had to have been accomplished under the oak where the mistletoe had grown. A druid dressed in a white robe climbed the tree and cut the mistletoe with a golden sickle.

Someone below caught the leaves and berries with a white cloth, for if it touched the ground, its healing properties would be gone. After that, two white bulls were sacrificed and prayer to the god of the tree, the tree-spirit followed.

Another superstition connected mistletoe and Allhallowmas Eve (Halloween). A sprig of mistletoe must be cut with a new dagger. The cutter must circle the oak tree three times toward the sun while chanting a specific spell. This ritual guarded against any witches who might be bent on evil that night. The same observance guaranteed victory in battle.

To give another example, babies received protection with mistletoe gathered in the required manner. Placed in infants' cribs, it defended them from being exchanged for elf babies by the fairies.

Today in Europe, leaves and twigs of mistletoe are legitimately valued for their medicinal properties, and European herbalists recommend them for treating respiratory and circulatory ailments and cancer. However, because of mistletoe's past associations with druid oak-tree worship, many Christians refuse to associate with it in any form or use it in church building decorations at Christmas time.

In the same category of anathematized greenery are holly and ivy. Dionysus, or Bacchus, the god of intoxication, was depicted wearing a wreath of ivy because ivy was thought to counterbalance the effects of wine. Leaves of common ivy (*Hedera helix*), not poison ivy, were boiled in wine and drunk for this reason. At one time, the Church forbad decorating with holly and ivy because of pagan associations.

Santa Claus

Santa Claus sports several names and even comes dressed in different colors in various countries. Some better known names include Kris Kringle, Father Christmas, and Saint Nicholas. His most common attire is a red suit with white cuffs and collar and a black belt around his ample middle.

Kris Kringle is the German and Pennsylvania Dutch name for Santa Claus. It comes from the word Christkindl, "Christ Child." His original image, a young child with a gold crown, over the years evolved into the

Saint Nicholas image. Kris Kringle carries a Christmas tree and enters the house via an open window. After he has delivered his presents, he rings a bell to let the family know he is leaving.

St. Nicholas, a fourth-century bishop of Myra in Lycia (now Turkey), devoted his life to giving gifts to the poor. Persecuted by the government and troubled by the Church, he refused to compromise. He spent time in prison for his strong faith. (In 1087, the Roman Catholic Church built a basilica to house his relics.)

In folklore, Saint Nicholas rode flying white horses and was said to have freed an Ethiopian slave boy. In gratitude, the boy devoted his life to helping Saint Nicholas in his philanthropic gift giving. Modern versions depict the boy as a servant whose face is black from his trips down the chimney. That particular Saint Nicholas has helpers, Zwarte Pieten, equivalent to the American Santa's elves.

Some early Germanic folktales involved a monster coming down the chimney, slaughtering children, and keeping them in a sack to eat later. Saint Nicholas trapped the monster and ordered him to pay for his sins by going to every house and delivering gifts to children every year at Christmas.

Norway and Denmark blended Saint Nicholas with local folklore producing a rather strange figure riding their pagan Yule goat who brought presents on Christmas Eve.

Father Christmas, native to Britain, was dressed in a green, fur-lined robe. He too was a jolly, bearded, well-fed man. The identities of Father Christmas and Saint Nicholas became blended with other folklore to become a new identity, Santa Claus, a contracted form of the Dutch, *Sint Nicolaas*.

Who doesn't know that Santa lives at the north pole with a plump, jolly Mrs. Claus, originally had eight reindeer, and has countless elves working year-round to manufacture presents for children on Christmas Eve?

These of course are short summations; it is assumed all know the current culture of cartoon-character stories shown on television every year, the addition of the drummer boy added to the nativity scene, and the addition of Rudolf to Santa's fictional reindeer team.

Santa is such a nice guy; how could we not like him? Here are a few reasons to help put Santa to the test.

Does he point to the Lord Jesus Christ? When little children sit on his lap, does he tell anything biblical at all, or does he assume divine characteristics for himself?

Children's songs tell them that Santa knows all things. He knows when they are sleeping, when awake, when they have been good, bad, and so on. If he did, that would make him omniscient, wouldn't it? How much better to teach them that the Lord knows all things.

Santa comes down every chimney precisely at midnight. That's quite a feat, one that would make him omnipresent if true. Adults have corrected their erroneous teachings somewhat; they now tell children Santa actually can't do quite all that. He hires many sleighs and fake Santa drivers to make all the rounds at the appointed time.

Santa flies over rooftops in his sturdy sleigh pulled by his delightful nine reindeer and slides effortlessly down chimneys. For those children with no chimney, he slides under doors to place presents under the tree. Is that a bit scary? If Santa can do that, what monsters might also slide under doors, an imaginative child might ask. Such an amazing ability would make Santa omnipotent, a description of God alone. "And ye are complete in him, which is the head of all principality and power" (Colossians 2:10).

The Santa issue has been discussed more of late by several denominations. Some accept the custom unreservedly as innocent fun for the children, while others denounce it vociferously. To many modern minds, worse than the Grinch are fuddy-duddies who teach their children the truth about Santa and who deny their children the pleasure of believing a lie for seven or eight years, the age most children begin to see though the Santa myth. Parents perhaps should be judiciously concerned how the child views their credibility at that point.

Possibly, some readers have endured the hostility of the myth-pushers. What are we to do? Perhaps we can take a cue from apostolic times, when the apostles were forbidden to teach in the name of Jesus. "But Peter and John answered and said unto them, Whether it be right in the sight of God to hearken unto you more than unto God, judge ye" (Acts 4:19).

Christmas Trees

There are many customs and items relevant to discussions of Christmas, but due to space considerations, the Christmas tree will be our final item.

Most of us probably grew up in homes decorated with Christmas trees. It didn't stunt our growth or turn us into worshipping tree-spirits. Then we heard about the verses in Jeremiah and became quite concerned. We read,

> For the customs of the people are vain: for one cutteth a tree out of the forest, the work of the hands of the workman, with the axe. They deck it with silver and with gold. They fasten it with nails and with hammers, that it move not (Jeremiah 10:3-4).

Our first reaction is one of dismay. That certainly describes the Christmas tree decked with silver and gold, though not real precious metals. We don't want to be associated with that. We read further,

> They are upright as the palm tree, but speak not: they needs be borne because they cannot go. Be not afraid of them, for they cannot do evil, neither also is it in them to do good (Jeremiah 10:5).

At that point, we begin to scratch our heads. Yes, people nail or fasten the tree down so it stays in place, but how many have ever been afraid of it? Something doesn't quite jell here. Because of misleading interpretation by well-meaning preachers, the passage is declared to be condemning the Christmas tree as a pagan custom. Let us look at another translation.

For the customs and ordinances of the peoples are false, empty and futile. It is but a tree which one cuts out of the forest [to make for him a god], the work of the hands of the craftsman with the axe or other tool. They deck the idol with silver and with gold; they fasten it with nails and with hammers, so it will not fall apart or move. Their idols are like pillars of turned work— upright [and stationary] as a palm tree—like scarecrows in a cucumber field; they cannot speak; they have to be carried, for they cannot walk. Do not be afraid of them, for they cannot do evil, neither is it possible for them to do good—it is not in them (Jeremiah 10:3–5 Amplified Bible).

Another translation reads,

For the customs of the people are worthless; they cut a tree out of the forest, and a craftsman shapes it with his chisel. They adorn it with silver and gold; they fasten it with hammer and nails so it will not totter. Like a scarecrow in a melon patch, their idols cannot speak; they must be carried because they cannot walk. Do not fear them; they can do no harm, nor can they do any good (Jeremiah 10:3-4 NIV).

What God condemns here is idolatry. The tree was cut down, chiseled into an idol, and overlaid with gold and silver. Worshippers had to carry it wherever they wanted it. That itself should have shown the idolaters the worthlessness of their creative handiwork, but hardheaded and hardhearted attitudes usually accompany rebellious ones who seek to not keep God in their remembrance and who seek new gods. Sometimes, it takes an earthquake to get their undivided attention.

But the Lord is the true God, He is the living God and the everlasting King; at His wrath the earth shall tremble, and the nations shall not be able to abide his indignation (Jeremiah 10:10).

This is not a defense or vindication of the Christmas tree; it is intended to show that those who have trees are not tree worshippers who fear the tree spirit inhabiting the tree. Mainly, the Christmas tree is a behemoth distraction diverting attention from Christ.

The Big Question: Celebrate or Not Celebrate Christmas?

Let's begin with some simple things first. If holly, mistletoe, ivy, or poinsettias are in abundance and on sale in December, should we refrain from buying them because pagan worshippers did in the past and continue today to use them in their worship? If so, we might miss the enjoyment of some of God's beautiful creations available to us in the short, dreary days of winter.

Celebrating Christ's nativity is not commanded nor condemned by the New Testament; for that reason, it will always be a gray area for some. Most Roman Catholics and others who partake of Mass will definitely continue to partake. Evangelicals and fundamentalists will see the season as a time to bring glory to Christ through reenactments of the events in Matthew and Luke. Other Bible believers including those who consider themselves right dividers may choose to avoid it, believing it to be pagan.

Rather than keeping Christ in Christmas, how about removing the "mass" and keeping Christ's nativity? Until God gives us further enlightenment, perchance we can do as Bullinger suggests.

> Believe that "the Word became flesh" (Christ's conception occurred) on December 25, and "... many who have hitherto been troubled with scruples concerning the day, being, as they have been taught, the anniversary of a Pagan festival, will be enabled to

worship on that Day, without alloy of doubt as the time, when the stupendous miracle which is the foundation stone of the Christian faith, came to pass."[85]

And whatsoever ye do in word or deed, do all in the name of the Lord Jesus, giving thanks to God and the Father by Him (Colossians 3:17).

CHAPTER 27

Summary and Conclusion

In our brief study of the officially recognized holidays in the United States, we have traced the development of some purely man-made holidays and the development of two of our most important religious holidays, which some aggressively declare are also man-made. As stated, a few seem to be a mix of traditional paganism and Christianity. In tracing their histories, it was not always so easy to discern who took whose day and turned it into one of their own doing. In other instances, it was quite obvious how pagan practices became purposefully adapted into Christian worship activities. We must understand for ourselves and reiterate to others the persisting conflict between Satan and God's children. Of course, Satan wants to confuse us all; the more mixed up we become, the greater his glee.

We need to reemphasize to any who will heed that the Son is eternal with the Father and didn't come into existence in Bethlehem. Also, Christianity is not a man-made religion in competition with other man-made religions. We need to clarify that before paganism or polytheistic mythological gods, the Creator was worshipped. That is, before men and women chose to veer away from pure worship to serve man-made idols—which sometimes were indwelt with demonic spirits—every day was recognized as belonging to the Lord.

When one stops to consider each of the two major religious days in the Western world, Resurrection Day (Ishtar's Day, Easter) and

Christ's nativity (Christmas), each day is equivalent to two distinct days. Believers in God will honor Him while unbelievers will use the day as an excuse to do whatever they want to do. The two types of celebrants don't travel in the same circles or follow the same practices. Even the vocabulary of the two is vastly different. An alien from outer space—if there were such a one—would never recognize the two as celebrating the same holiday if an earthling tour guide didn't tell him.

In regard to days, suppose we wait for the perfect day to honor the Lord? On Sunday, we say, "I can't get out of bed today. This day is dedicated to the sun, and I don't want anything to do with it. I'll get up tomorrow."

Monday comes along, and we realize Monday has been dedicated to the moon. All the week through Saturday, we simply cannot get out of bed and run the risk of honoring a pagan god, for all days have been renamed for one or another. We definitely don't want to honor them by writing their names on our business stationery! Wait a minute. Are we painting ourselves into a corner? What are we to do about holidays? Should we acquiesce, maintain the status quo, hold the fort, or should we take advantage of the opportunity of specific days to advance and reclaim the day for Christ? David sought to renew the right precept as he penned, "This is the day which the Lord hath made" (Psalm 118:24).

The body of Christ is not obligated to observe ordinances or Jewish feast days (see Colossians 2:14 and 2:20). Nor is the body obligated to observe any feast days voluntarily observed by many Christians. "Let no man therefore judge you in meat, or in drink, or in respect of an holyday, or of the new moon, or of the Sabbath days" (Colossians 2:16).

We wish no one to judge us when we refuse to glorify witches and goblins on Halloween. Likewise, we must not be too judgmental of those who don't esteem the Word as we do and honor Christ on days we might not wish to magnify.

As stated at the beginning of this book, my purpose is not to condemn or reprove those who observe specific days. I hope I have informed with some facts not generally known about holidays and that the reader's passage through this book was as enjoyable and rewarding as the research was to me. May each experience the peace only God dispenses.

> Grace be to you, and peace, from God our Father, and from the Lord Jesus Christ (Ephesians 1:2).

NOTES

Chapter 1: A Brief Review of Organized Religions

[1] John Walton, "Is there archaeological evidence of the tower of Babel?" from Associates for Biblical Research, www.christianasnwers.net; accessed 3 November 2005.

[2] See *The Gospel in the Stars* by Joseph A. Seiss or *The Witness in the Stars* by E. W. Bullinger.

Chapter 3: New Year's Day

[3] Alexander Hislop, *The Two Babylons*. Second ed. (Neptune, New Jersey: Loizeaux, 1959).

[4] Traditional Catholics may continue to celebrate the Feast of the Circumcision if they wish.

[5] Joseph L. Gardner, ed., *Mysteries of the Ancient Americas: The New World before Columbus* (Pleasantville: Reader's Digest, 1986).

Chapter 4: Martin Luther King Day

[6] C. H. Welch, *The Just and the Justifier*, (Surrey: Leonard A. Canning, 1948), 164.

[7] John F. McManus. "Honoring the King Myth". The New American. January 4, 1999.

[8] www.inaugural.senate.gov/days-events/days-events/presidents-swearing-in-ceremony.com

[9] Clinton's 1997 speech was the first broadcast live on the Internet.

[10] President Obama's inaugural address was the first to include closed captioning in the live webcast.

[11] www.chuckbaldwinlive.comc2005/cbarchive.200506.html; accessed August 10, 2009.

Chapter 6: Valentine's Day

[12] *The New Schaff-Herzog Encyclopedia*, 1882.

[13] *Hamlet*, act 4, scene 5.

[14] We know from Genesis 10:10 that Nimrod founded the cities of Nineveh and Babel. The historians Josephus and Apollodorus believed Nimrod and Ninus to be identical, and from this information (perhaps disinformation) was pieced together the legend of Nimrod and Semiramis. James Ussher in the *Annals of the World* stated that Nimrod founded the Assyrian Empire in 1267 BC. Ninus, the younger, later became king of the empire and is known in the Bible as Tilgath Pileser in 1 Chronicles 5:6 and Tiglathpileser in 2 Kings 15:29. It would be impossible for Ninus and Nimrod to be identical. The Tower of Babel was destroyed in 2348 BC, approximately 106 years after the flood. The founding of the Assyrian Empire would have been 975 years after the destruction of Babel. Would Nimrod have been living? After the flood, longevity was immediately half what it had been before the flood.

> H. R. Hall in *The Ancient History of the Near East* identifies Semiramis as the wife of Shamshi-Adad V (822–811 BC). "Adad-nirari's mother, the queen of Shamshi-Adad, was named Sammuramat, and this is obviously, as has always been recognized, the original of the name Semiramis given to a legendary Assyrian queen in Herodotus (i. 183) and Ktesias. She was especially remembered because she was regent after Shamshi-Adad's death, and was celebrated later for her devotion to the god Nabu, whose priests told Herodotus about her (?)."

Chapter 7: Presidents' Day

[15] G. W. Parke Custis, *Recollections and Private Memoirs of Washington*. (Bridgewater: American Foundation Publications, 1999)

[16] Ibid. 134

[17] Ibid. 134

[18] Ibid. 134

[19] Ibid. 507

[20] Ibid. 275

[21] Ibid. 304

[22] Ibid. 304

[23] Ibid. 364

[24] C. H. Welch, *An Alphabetical Analysis, Part 4: R to S*. (London: Berean, 1961).

322

Chapter 8: St. Patrick's Day

25 F. F. Bruce, *Light in the West* (Grand Rapids, MI: Eerdmans, 1953).

26 See Chapter 12 Traditions of Past Easters

27 Maire B. DePaor, *Patrick: The Pilgrim Apostle of Ireland* (Dublin: Veritas, 1998).

28 H. A. Ironside, *The Real St. Patrick* (New York: Loizeaux Brothers, pamphlet; no date).

29 Oscar M. Baker, "Faith," Radio Class, Tuesday 7:15 p.m. WRSW FM 107.1, *Truth for Today*, January 1949.

Chapter 9: Spring Celebrations: Precursors to Confusion

30 J. Ussher. *Annals of the World.* (revised by Larry and Marion Pierce, 2003). Green Forest: Master Books.

31 Frederick Brininger, C.H. Welch. *The Berean Expositor,* vol. 16. 1925, London: Berean Publishing Trust. 1980.

32 Brian Branston, *The Lost Gods of England.* (Oxford University Press: Oxford, 1976).

Chapter 10: Pagan Goddesses Honored on or around Passover

33 Corn is a generic term meaning grain in general. It would have referred to wheat or barley, the two grains of that particular location. What we call corn was not in existence in the Old World before Columbus brought it back from America after November 1492.

34 Georges Dumézil, *Archaic Roman Religion.* Trans. Phillip Krapp. (Baltimore: Johns Hopkins University Press, 1996).

35 Robin Lane Fox, *Pagans and Christians.* New York: (Alfred A. Knoff, Inc. 1989).

36 Alexander Hislop, *The Two Babylons.* 1916. Neptune: (Loizeaux Brothers. 1959).

37 F. F. Bruce, *The Dawn of Christianity.* (Grand Rapids: William B. Erdman Publishing Co. 1953).

38 Ibid. 146

39 Coneybeare and Howson, *The Life and Epistles of St. Paul.* (Grand Rapids: William B. Erdman Publishing Co. 1957).

40 Ibid. 423

41 How ludicrous to dishonor God's magnificent creation! Orion will be discussed in detail in Chapter 26 Biblical Account of the Birth of Jesus Christ.

42 Coneybeare and Howson, *The Life and Epistles of St. Paul.* (Grand Rapids: William B. Erdman Publishing Co. 1957).

Chapter 11: Pagan Goddesses and Customs Honored in the British Isles

43 John Davies, *A History of Wales.* (London: Penguin Press. 1993).

44 *Babylonian Liver Omens.* Copenhagen: Museum Tusculanum Press. 2000

45 Robin Lane Fox, *Pagans and Christians*. (New York: Alfred A. Knoph, Inc. 1989).
46 E. W. Bullinger. *The Companion Bible*. Appendix 42. (Grand Rapids: Zondervan. 1974).
47 Bede, *Ecclesiastical History of the English People*. Questia.com/online_library.
48 www.tuathaedebrighid.org
49 Nerthus. *Encyclopedia Britannica* N, 232. 1965.
50 Prostitution. *Encyclopedia Britannica*, vol. 18. 1965.

Chapter 12: Traditions of Past Easters

51 *Catholic Encyclopedia*, vol. 1. 22 June 2006. http://newadvent.org.
52 Alexander Hislop, *The Two Babylons*. 1916. Neptune: (Louzeaux Brothers. 1959).
53 *The Catholic Encylcopedia*, vol. 1. 22 June 2006. http://newadvent.org
54 E. W. Bullinger, *Number in Scripture*. (Grand Rapids: Kregel Publishing. 1967).
55 Merrill Unger. *Unger's Bible Handbook*. (Chicago: Moody Press. 1966).
56 Scholars differ regarding the meaning. Tammuz may mean "possessing mighty power, or a ruler," or it may mean "disappearance" or "dying."
57 A. T. Mann and Jane Lyle, *Sacred Sexuality*. (London: Verga. 2002).

Chapter 13: Should We Celebrate Easter, Passover, or Resurrection Day?

58 John Peter Lang. *Commentary on the Holy Scriptures, Acts*, trans. by Phillip Schaff. (Grand Rapids: Zondervan 1871).
59 Ibid. 230
60 Ibid. 231
61 Eusebius, *Ecclesiastical History*. Ch. IX. http://www.biblehistory.ca/history/fathers. Oct. 2006
62 C. H. Welch, *Dispensational Truth or the Place of Israel and the Church*. (Surrey: Berean Publishing Trust. 1912).

Chapter 17: Father's Day

63 Rev. Jesse Lee Peterson. *Scam*. (Nashville: WND Books. 2003).
64 www.census.gov/archives; accessed November 19, 2006.

Chapter 18: Flag Day

65 Verna Hall. *Christian History of the Constitution*, vol. 1. (Los Angeles: American Christian Constitution Press. 1960). 371.

Chapter 19: Independence Day

66 The United States has ceded sovereignty over Independence Hall to the UN through the UN's Heritage Convention (1972). The UN is cosovereign over

designated World Heritage Sites including the Grand Canyon and the Statue of Liberty.

Chapter 20: Labor Day

67 U.S. Department of Labor, www.dol.gov/ora/aboutdol/laborday.htm.
68 The term "white collar" worker for office workers and "blue collar" for industrial laborers stemmed from this period and the popularity of the detachable collar.
69 The shoemakers named their union for Crispin Crispian, shoemaker in Shakespeare's *Henry V,* act 4, scene 3, for his speech before St. Crispin's Day.
70 In 1985, in preparation for a possible centennial commemoration, Chicago researchers could find no documentation concerning the Haymarket Square riots. All documentation had allegedly been transported to Communist East Berlin.
71 www.umwa.org/history; accessed January 29, 2007.

Chapter 21: Columbus Day

72 www.rense.com/general.htm. Accessed 3-2-07
73 Samuel Elliot Morrison. *Admiral of the Sea: A Life of Christopher Columbus.* (Boston: Little, Brown and Co. 1942). 195–96.
74 Top Treasures Gallery, American Treasures of the Library of Congress. www. loc.gov/exhibits/treasures; accessed April 16, 2007.

Chapter 23: Election Day

75 The founding fathers feared mob rule, or direct selection of the president. The electors created a sort of buffer as well as giving more power to less-populated states. Under this system, each state has the same number of electors as they have representatives in Congress. The Constitution refers to "electors." The word *college* refers to a group of people who act as one unit. The group of distinguished citizens chosen as electors became known as the Electoral College, and the term was written into federal law in 1845. A simple majority of 50.1 percent gives the winner all the electoral votes for that state. It is not a perfect system, but to change it would require a constitutional amendment; smaller states would not likely go along with that. The founding fathers were exceedingly wise.
76 T. V. Moore, *Post Exile Prophets,* as quoted in Lange's *Commentary on Zechariah.* Trans. Phillip Schaff. (Grand Rapids: Zondervan 1871).

Chapter 25: Thanksgiving

77 Prepared by Gerald Murphy (the Cleveland Free-Net aa300).

Chapter 26: Biblical Account of the Birth of Jesus Christ

[78]   Flavius Josephus. *Antiquities, Book XVII* chapters 2–3. Trans. William Whiston. (Philadelphia: John C. Winston Co.).

[79]   On Monday, May 7, 2007, Ehud Netzer, archaeology professor of the Hebrew University in Jerusalem, announced the discovery of the tomb of Herod the Great after thirty-five years of searching.

[80]   The present Church of the Nativity in Bethlehem stands over the reputed birthplace of Christ. The first such structure was built in the fourth century AD with the support and influence of Helena, Constantine's mother. That structure was destroyed. Byzantine Emperor Justinian in the sixth century built a more complex structure that has been fought over by a succession of armies. Today, its various parts are controlled jointly by the Armenian Church, the Roman Catholic Church, and the Greek Orthodox Church.

[81]   Alfred Edersheim, *Life and Times of Jesus the Messiah*, 2 vols. (Grand Rapids: Wm. B. Erdmans Publishing Co. 1965). 188.

[82]   John Peter Lange *Commentary on the Gospel of Luke*. Trans. Phillip Schaff. (Grand Rapids: Zondervan). 36.

[83]   The Jewish/Civil Calendar Program, UniversityWisconsinMadison.

[84]   sunearth.gsfc.nasa.gov/eclipse/phase/phasecat.html.

[85]   Ernest L. Martin. *The Birth of Christ Recalculated*. (Pasadena: FBR Publication. 1980).

[86]   E. W. Bullinger. *The Companion Bible*. Appendix 179. (Grand Rapids: Zondervan. 1974).

WORKS CONSULTED

Chapter 1: A Brief Review of Organized Religions

Seiss, J., *The Gospel in the Stars*, second printing. Grand Rapids, MI: Kregel, 1975.

Walton, J. "Is There Archaeological Evidence of the Tower of Babel?" *Associates or Biblical Research* 5. Available from Christiananswers. net.html; accessed October 27, 2005.

Chapter 3: New Year's Day

Bullinger, E. *The Companion Bible*. Grand Rapids, MI: Zondervan, 1964.

Eberle, J. *The Workman's Interlinear*. Lafayette: Truth for Today, 2009.

Edwards, J. *The Resolutions of Jonathan Edwards*. Available at www. JonathanEdwards/com/text.htm; accessed November 11, 2005.

Heyerdahl, T., D. Sandweiss, and A. Navaraez, A. *Pyramids of Tucume*. New York: Thames and Hudson, 1995.

Hislop, A. *The Two Babylons*. Neptune: Loizeaux Brothers, 1916.

Reader's Digest. *Mysteries of the Ancient Americas: The New World before Columbus*. Pleasantville, 1986.

Schaff-Herzog Encyclopedia of Religious Knowledge, 1882, "New Year's Celebration," vol. 1, 1642.

Ussher, J., *Annals of the World*. Revised by Larry and Marion Pierce. Green Forest: Master Books, 2003.

Chapter 4: Martin Luther King Day

Genovese, Eugene. Essay from *The Southern Front: History and Politics in the Cultural War.* University of Missouri Press, 1995.

"King, Martin Luther, Jr.," Microsoft Encarta 98 Encyclopedia, 1993–1997.

McManus, John F. "Honoring the King Myth." *The New American,* January 4, 1999.

Mecham, J. "Pillar of Fire: America in the King Years, 1963–65." Book review, *Newsweek* (January 19, 1998), 62.

Meier, August. "On the Role of Martin Luther King." *New Politics,* vol. 4, 1 (1965): 174–18

Pappas, Theodore. *Plagiarism and the Culture War: The Writings of Martin Luther King Jr., and Other Prominent Americans.* Hallberg: 1994.

Welch, C. H. *Just and the Justifier.* Surrey: 1948, 164.

Chapter 6: Valentine's Day

Bullinger, E. W. *The Companion Bible.* London: Samuel Bagster and Sons, 1974.

"Lupercalia." *Encyclopedia Britannica.* 1965, vol. 14, 244.

Hall, H. R. *The Ancient History of the Near East.* London: Methuen, 1913.

Hislop, A. *The Two Babylons.* Neptune: Loizeaux Brothers, 1916.

Schaff-Herzog Encyclopedia of Religious Knowledge. 1882. "St. Valentine," vol. 3, 2445.

Shakespeare, *Hamlet.*

The Continental Encyclopedia. "St. Valentine's Day," vol. 7. New York: Orastmus Turner Harris, 1905.

World Book. "Lupercalia," "Valentine's Day." Chicago: World Book, 1995.

Ussher, J. *Annals of the World.* Revised by Larry and Marion Pierce. Green Forest: Master Books, 2003.

Chapter 7: Presidents' Day

Custis, G. W. Parke. *Recollections and Private Memoirs of Washington.* Reprint. Bridgewater: American Foundations, 1999.

Freeman, Douglas. *Washington.* New York: Charles Scribner's Sons, 1968.

"George Washington." www.sc94ameslab.gov/TOUR/gwash.html.

Schleier, Curt. "President George Washington Founding Father: His Sense of Duty, Honor Set the Standard for Our Nation." *Investors Business Daily.* Los Angeles, February 21, 2006, A3.

Welch, Charles. *An Alphabetical Analysis: Part 4, R to S,* 3. London: Berean Publishing, 1961.

Chapter 8: St. Patrick's Day

Baker, Oscar. "Faith." Radio class, Tuesday 7:15 p.m. WRSW FM 107.1 *Truth for Today.* Warsaw, January 1949.

Bruce, F., *Light in the West.* Grand Rapids, MI: Eerdmans, 1953.

De Paor, Maire. *Patrick: The Pilgrim Apostle of Ireland.* Dublin: Veritas, 1998.

Ironside, H. A. *The Real St. Patrick.* New York: Loizeaux Brothers, pamphlet; no date.

St. Patrick: His Confession. Translated from the Latin by Ludwig Bieler; accessed January 10, 2001; www.netcom.com~rsbo/Patrick/htm.

Chapter 9: Spring Celebrations: Precursors to Confusion

Branston, Brian. *The Lost Gods of England.* London: Thames and Hudson, 1957.

Brininger, Frederick and C. H. Welch. *The Berean Expositor,* vol. 16. London: Berean Publishing, 1980.

Ussher, J. *Annals of the World.* Revised by Larry and Marion Pierce. Green Forest: Master Books, 2003.

Chapter 10: Pagan Goddesses Honored on or around Passover

Bruce, F. F. *The Dawn of Christianity.* Grand Rapids: Eerdmans, 1953.

Coneybeare, W. J. and J. S. Howson. *The Life and Epistles of Paul.* Grand Rapids, MI: Eerdmans, 1957.

Dumézil, Georges. *Archaic Roman Religion*. Translated by Phillip Krapp. Baltimore: John Hopkins University Press, 1996.

Fox, Robin Lane. *Pagans and Christians*. New York: Knopf, 1989.

Hislop, Alexander. *The Two Babylons*. Neptune: Loizeaux Brothers, 1959.

Chapter 11: Pagan Goddesses and Customs Honored in the British Isles

Bruce, F. F. *The Dawn of Christianity*. Grand Rapids MI: Eerdmans, 1953.

Bulfinch, Thomas. *Age of Fable*, vol. 1. New York: Thomas Y. Crowell, 1913.

Coneybeare, W. J. and J. S. Howson. *The Life and Epistles of Paul*. Grand Rapids, MI: Eerdmans, 1957.

Davies, John. *A History of Wales*. London: Penguin, 1993.

Dumézil, Georges. *Archaic Roman Religion*. Translated by Phillip Krapp. Baltimore: Johns Hopkins University Press. 1996.

Fox, Robin Lane. *Pagans and Christians*. New York: Knopf, 1989.

Hislop, Alexander. *The Two Babylons*. Neptune: Loizeaux Brothers, 1959.

Koch-Westenholtz, Ulla. *Babylonian Liver Omens. The Chapters Manzoza, Padān, and Pān Takulti of the Extispicy Series, mainly from Assurbanipal's Library*. Copenhagen: Museum Tusculanum Press, 2000.

"Nerthus." *Encyclopaedia Britannica*, vol. 16. Chicago: University of Chicago Press, 1965.

"Prostitution." *Encyclopaedia Britannica*, vol. 18. Chicago: University of Chicago Press, 1965.

Chapter 12: Traditions of Past Easters

Bullinger, E. W. *Number in Scripture*. Grand Rapids, MI: Kregel, 1967.

Hislop, Alexander. *The Two Babylons*. Neptune: Loizeaux Brothers, 1959.

Lange, John Peter. *Commentary on the Holy Scriptures; Acts*. Translated by Phillip Schaff. Grand Rapids Publishing, 1871.

Lange, John Peter. *Commentary on the Holy Scriptures: Ezekiel, Daniel.* Translated by Phillip Schaff. Grand Rapids Publishing, 1871.
Mann, A. T. and Jane Lyle. *Sacred Sexuality.* London: Vega, 2002.
Unger, Merrill. *Unger's Bible Handbook.* Chicago: Moody Press, 1966.
Catholic Encyclopedia vol. 1. newadvent.org; accessed June 22, 2006.

Chapter 13: Should We Celebrate Easter, Passover, or Resurrection Day?

Ecclesiastical History of Eusebius Pamphilus. Philadelphia: Lippincott, 1879; reprint, Grand Rapids, MI: Baker Book House, 1966.
Ecclesiastical History of Theodoret. Chapter 9: "The Epistles of the Emperor Constantine, Concerning Matters Transacted at the Council, Addressed to the Bishops Who Were Not Present." www.biblehistory.ca/history/fathers; accessed October 2006.
Lange, John Peter. *Commentary on the Holy Scriptures: Acts.* Translated by Phillip Schaff. Grand Rapids Publishing House, 1871.
The Diary of Samuel Pepys. www.pepysdiary.com; accessed October 2006.
Welch. C. H. *Dispensational Truth or the Place of Israel and the Church in the Purpose of the Ages.* Surrey: Berean, 1912.

Chapter 14: May Day

The Companion Bible. Grand Rapids, MI: Zondervan, 1974.
The Continental Encyclopedia. New York: Orasmus Turner Harris, 1901.
Douglas, George William. *The American Book of Days.* New York: H. W. Wilson, 1948.
Encyclopaedia Britannica. "Belenus," "Beltane," "May Day." Britannica.com and Encyclopaedia Britannica, 1999–2000.
Microsoft Encarta 90 Encyclopedia. "Bel," "Baal," "Dagon," "FireWorship," "Flora," "May Day," "Kremlin and Red Square." Redman, WA: Microsoft, 1993–1997.
Schaff-Herzog Encyclopedia of Religious Knowledge, 1882. "Bridget, St.," vol. 1, 325.

Chapter 17: Father's Day

Barth, Kelley. www.wvculture.org/History/miscellaneous/fathersday. Dominion Post. Morgantown, WV, June 21, 1987; accessed November 7, 2006.

Peterson, Jessee Lee. *Scam: How the Black Leadership Exploits Black America*. Nashville: WND Books, 2003.

www.census.gov/archives; accessed November 19, 2006.

Chapter 18: Flag Day

"Flag." *Encyclopedia Britannica*, vol. 9. Chicago: University of Chicago Press. 1965.

Hall, Verna. *Christian History of the Constitution*, vol. 1. Los Angeles: American Christian Constitution Press. 1960.

Making Music Your Own—6. Morristown: Silver Burdette, 1968.

Chapter 19: Independence Day

Carson, Clarence. *The Colonial Experience 1607—1774*. Wadley: American Textbook Committee, 1983.

Carson, Clarence. *The Beginning of the Republic 1775—1825*. Wadley: American Textbook Committee, 1983.

Hall, Verna. *Self-Government with Union*. San Francisco: American Constitution Press, 1962.

Chapter 21: Columbus Day

Catholic Encyclopedia. newadvent.org; accessed February 16, 2007.

Dyson, John. *Columbus: for Gold, God, and Glory*. New York: Simon and Schuster, 1991.

Internet Medieval Source Book. www.fordham.edu; accessed February 16, 2007.

Kent, Zachery. *Christopher Columbus*. Chicago: Children's Press, 1991.

Morrison, Samuel Elliot. *Admiral of the Ocean Sea—A Life of Christopher Columbus*. Boston: Little, Brown, 1942.

Chapter 22: Halloween

Ashe, Geoffrey. *The Discovery of King Arthur.* London: Guild Publishing, 1985.

The Companion Bible. Grand Rapids, MI: Zondervan, 1974.

Douglas, George William. *The American Book of Days.* New York: H. W. Wilson, 1948.

Encyclopedia Britannica. "Druidism," "Halloween," "Witchcraft." 1965.

Microsoft Encarta 98 Encyclopedia. "All Saints' Day," "Festivals and Feasts," "Halloween," "Medicine Man," "Native American Religions," "Ordeal," "Shaman," "Superstition," "Witchcraft." Redman, WA: Microsoft, 1993–1997.

The Satanic Bible. New York: Avon, 1969.

Schaff-Herzog Encyclopedia of Religious Knowledge, 1882, "Druidism," vol. 1, 667.

Chapter 23: Election Day

Lance, John Peter. *Commentary on the Holy Scriptures: Zechariah.* Translated by Phillip Schaff. Grand Rapids, MI: ChaPublishing House, 1871.

Chapter 25: Thanksgiving

Britannica.com. 1999–2000. "Pilgrim Fathers," "Sukkoth."

The Companion Bible. Grand Rapids, MI: Zondervan, 1974.

Douglas, George William. *The American Book of Days.* New York: H. W. Wilson, 1948.

Microsoft Encarta Encyclopedia. "Sukkot—Feast of Tabernacles." 1993–1997.

"NEA Running U.S. Education." *Middle American News.* Raleigh, NC, March 2000.

Model, Eric. "In Search of the First Thanksgiving." *USA Today,* November 3, 1995.

Murphy, Gerald. Cybercasting Services Division of the National Public Telecomputing Network. "The First Thanksgiving Proclamation—20 June, 1676."

Strong, James. *The New Strong's Exhaustive Concordance of the Bible.* Nashville: Thomas Nelson, 1990.

Chapter 26: Biblical Account of the Birth of Jesus Christ

The Amplified Bible. Grand Rapids, MI: Zondervan, 1965.

Broadus, John A. *Commentary on the Gospel of Matthew.* Philadelphia: American Baptist Publication Society.

Bullinger, E. W. *The Companion Bible.* Grand Rapids, MI: Zondervan, 1974.

Bullinger, E. W. *The Witness of the Stars.* Grand Rapids, MI: Kregel, 1972.

Deissmann, Adolf. *Light from the Ancient East.* Grand Rapids, MI: Baker Book House, 1978.

Edersheim, Alfred. *The Life and Times of Jesus the Messiah.* Grand Rapids, MI: Eerdmans, 1965.

Holy Bible, New International Version. Grand Rapids, MI: Zondervan, 1978.

Josephus, Flavius. *The Life and Works of Flavius Josephus.* Translated by William Whiston. Philadelphia: John C. Winston, no date.

Lange, John Peter. *Commentary on the Holy Scriptures: Chronicles, Esther.* Translated by Phillip Schaff. Grand Rapids, MI: Zondervan, 1871.

Lange, John Peter. *Commentary on the Holy Scriptures: Luke.* Translated by Phillip Schaff. Grand Rapids, MI: Zondervan, 1871.

Lange, John Peter. *Commentary on the Holy Scriptures: Matthew.* Translated by Phillip Schaff. Grand Rapids, MI: Zondervan, 1871.

Martin, Ernest L. *The Birth of Christ Recalculated.* Pasadena, CA: Foundation for Biblical Research, 1980.

Rolleston, Frances. *Mazzaroth.* London: Gilbert and Livingston. Republished by Kessinger.

Schaff-Herzog. *Encyclopaedia of Religious Knowledge.* 1882. "Christmas," vol. 1, 450–51.

Ussher, J. *Annals of the World.* Revised by Larry and Marion Pierce. Green Forest: Master Books, 2003.

Printed in the United States
By Bookmasters